MANAGEMENT AND MORALITY

MANAGEMENT AND MORALITY

A Developmental Perspective

Patrick Maclagan

SAGE Publications
London • Thousand Oaks • New Delhi

SAGE Publications Ltd
6 Bonhill Street
London EC2A 4PU

SAGE Publications Inc.
2455 Teller Road
Thousand Oaks, California 91320

SAGE Publications India Pvt Ltd
32, M-Block Market
Greater Kailash – I
New Delhi 110 048

British Library Cataloguing in Publication data

A catalogue record for this book is
available from the British Library

ISBN 0 8039 7679 8
ISBN 0 8039 7680 1 (pbk)

Library of Congress catalog card number 97-062444

Typeset by M Rules
Printed in Great Britain by Biddles Ltd, Guildford, Surrey

Contents

Acknowledgements

In reflecting on the origins, preparation and completion of this book I have come to appreciate the debt I owe to many people. By covering for me in my absence, a number of colleagues at the University of Hull made it possible for me to have a period of leave in 1996 during which most of my writing was done. I am particularly indebted to Pippa Carter, who has also provided welcome advice and encouragement. Others, both in Hull and elsewhere, whose contributions have been greatly appreciated include John Donaldson, Norman Jackson, Norma Romm and Robin Snell. Finally, I must mention the editorial and other staff at Sage Publications, with whom it has been a pleasure to work.

PART ONE   ETHICAL THINKING AND MANAGEMENT PRACTICE

1   Introduction

Concern for morality in organizations, not only in business, is a growing but much misunderstood area of academic enquiry and professional practice. In those contexts it arouses curiosity, puzzlement, scepticism and even hostility. Common misconceptions relate to the aims of those who pursue the subject, and to its relevance for managers. In this introduction I intend to clarify these issues with particular reference to the overall perspective which I adopt, to expand on some of the points raised, and to outline the chapter content and rationale of the book as a whole.

The institutionalization of business and management ethics

Except in the increased scale of the movement, this interest in ethics and morality – which I treat as synonymous – is not a new phenomenon. Philosophers and theologians have for centuries commented on the ethics of institutional governance, and on the morality of business practices such as usury. In nineteenth-century Britain, industrialists such as Robert Owen and Joseph Rowntree brought their moral concern to bear on the improvement of working conditions for their employees. In the USA, a number of business schools have, for many decades, included a concern for corporate social responsibility and ethics in their programmes. And well before the middle of the twentieth century, writers on management such as Mary Parker Follett ([1925] 1973) and Chester Barnard (1938) had addressed the moral implications of management in business and other organizational settings.

Now, however, there is a much more focused and publicized interest. In the USA this has been evident since the early 1970s. In Europe it took about ten years longer to appear. There is also significant active concern in the Japanese, South East Asian and Australasian regions, both in teaching and research. In the 1980s the *Journal of Business Ethics*, and *Business and Professional Ethics Journal* were launched from North America; *Business*

Ethics: A European Review followed about a decade later. Various bodies have been formed to promote the subject area, such as the Society for Business Ethics in America, the European Business Ethics Network, the International Society of Business, Economics and Ethics, and Ethics in the Public Service: an International Network. All of these bodies organize meetings or conferences which are usually aimed at practitioners as well as academics, while in the UK during the 1990s there has been a spate of workshops and conferences on ethics, many specifically for practitioners in business and the public sector.

A developmental perspective

Such activity reflects increased public concern regarding corporate and managerial behaviour. This concern contains an element of cynicism which is the source of much misunderstanding. Assuming that the focus is on the conduct of unethical individuals, sceptics assert that the whole exercise is futile, since, they argue, one cannot reform such people anyway. But most of those involved in providing programmes or consultancy in managerial ethics would agree with that. Their aim is not to convert 'unethical' individuals, but rather to help the majority of essentially well-meaning people in organizations appreciate and understand the moral significance of events around them, and to respond appropriately.

To some extent the cynical, pessimistic, view rests on a failure to reflect on the difference between what *is* and what *could be*. Quite often the events which provoke moral indignation may be explained in terms of systemic factors in and around organizations, rather than as the conscious decisions or deliberate malpractice of individuals. Of course it is true that individuals may be negligent, concerned to look after their own interests, instead of attending to matters which may not seem pressing at the time, or may not be their official responsibility. But it is necessary to consider factors that may encourage this: particular types of incentive and control system, staffing shortages, deficient information channels, or organizational culture. Then one can look for ways of improving the situation.

Moral development

As noted already, and in line with accepted practice (for example Singer, [1979] 1993: 1; and many others) I use the words morality and ethics interchangeably (see also Donaldson, 1989: 63). As a foundation for much that I have to say in this book I shall also emphasize a significant, if simplified, distinction between social, and personal or individual, conceptions of morality. As Neil Cooper has said:

> Those who suppose that morality is or ought to be wholly or mainly a social concept may recommend submission to a tradition. Those, on the other hand, who

suppose morality to be primarily an individual or independent concept will recommend independent decisions. (1970b: 72–3)

Where the latter is concerned, we may assume that individuals' moral beliefs and principles represent something of importance to them (Cooper, 1970a; Midgley, 1972). Clearly, however, not everyone in a particular situation will necessarily agree on what is most important, on what is the morally right thing to do. While on many issues there will be a prevailing consensus, reflecting the values of the social system in question, at other times such conventional norms may be in conflict, so that people have to make their own judgments on how to proceed, on how to conduct themselves. And there will also be occasions when some individuals choose to adopt a dissenting moral position, opposing a dominant view.

The concept of moral development which underpins much that I shall say in this book assumes that individual or personal morality, *in so far as it is the product of critical thought*, is an advance on unthinking conformity with social norms. Furthermore, the developmental perspective which is associated with this includes a concern for the improvement of organizational systems so that such personal morality can find expression.

Thus my emphasis is on structures and processes associated with such moral development – for example the encouragement of critical modes of thought by people in organizations – rather than on the substance of specific business or management dilemmas (although I shall of course use examples of that sort). This goes some way to answering critics who suggest that one should not prescribe moral values, or that one cannot 'teach ethics' because people acquire their morality in childhood. Nevertheless it is unavoidable that particular values are supported by my argument; most obviously, that of personal moral judgment and responsibility.

I start from the assumption that most people in most organizations are essentially well-intentioned. I am less concerned with where they get their moral values from, than with the fact that they have them. (However where organizations, especially as employers or in the educational context, play a part in inculcating such values, then that would be more directly relevant to the theme of this book.) Our task is, then, to help people articulate and act upon their moral values where appropriate. And in that context it is important to stress the difference between knowing (or thinking one knows) what is the morally right thing to do, and being able to carry this out in practice, something which seems to be overlooked by many writers.

Management and morality

This book is about morality and *management*. Although the term 'business ethics' is widely used (and I concede that I shall use it where expedient) it can be misleading. The ethics of management, where management is construed as a generic activity or process, differs from business ethics in the same way that an interest in such management action itself differs from a detailed focus on functional areas of commercial organizations like finance, marketing or purchasing. That latter distinction was clearly stated by Henri Fayol ([1916] 1949) and was underlined by Gulick in his famous acronym for the executive process, POSDCORB: Planning, Organizing, Staffing, Directing, Co-ordinating, Reporting and Budgeting, which he derived from Fayol's earlier work (Gulick, 1937). Both Fayol and Gulick were adamant that this was the foundation for a universally applicable prescriptive theory (or science) of management and administration, which allows us to think in terms of all types of organization, public sector and voluntary as well as commercial enterprises. As such, it has stood the test of time, especially if one discards the assumption that management is necessarily a distinct function performed by those who control the activities of other people (Hales, 1993: 3).

Thus on the one hand the term 'business ethics' is misleading and need-lessly restrictive if it fosters the idea that its subject matter has little relevance to non-profit organizations. On the other hand, it is dangerously inappropri-ate in so far as such use of language (as with indiscriminate reference to 'business studies' in educational contexts) reinforces the uncritical and incau-tious acceptance of a commercial ethos in public service and voluntary settings. The words 'management' and 'organization' are relatively value-neutral by comparison. The concept of management as an activity is also perhaps more compatible with the idea of ethics as human conduct, to be contrasted with some sort of purely intellectual enquiry into particular issues and dilemmas faced by people in organizations. Thus the ethics of manage-ment can be viewed as a dimension of organizational behaviour.

The classical model offered by Fayol, Gulick and others, has its uses as a prescriptive idealization, but it can never be more than an elliptical represen-tation of the managerial task – essentially comprising broad classifications and sets of principles. Even so, it has a reassuring tone, which encourages some to believe, naively, in the possibilities suggested; possibilities for what Simon ([1947] 1957) called 'organizationally' (as opposed to 'personally') rational action, perhaps informed by textbook theory. This view, which Anthony (1986: Chapter 7) termed the 'official theory' of management, appears to have been countered by empirical research showing managerial work to be fragmented, time-pressured, and fraught with persons' conflicting values and opinions; and managerial activity to be *ad hoc*, intuitive, judg-mental, but also quite political (Mintzberg, 1973, 1985; Stewart, 1967). To say that such research, which Anthony called 'real theory', refutes the classical position would be mistaken, however; that would be to confuse the func-tions of prescriptive and descriptive writing.

In the field of business ethics one finds a parallel distinction between those writers who present a prescriptive decision-model, which assumes the rational application of ethical principles (for example, Vallance, 1995), and those like Jackall (1988) who describe the fate of morality in actual organizational sit-uations: a fate understood in terms of power, conflict, expediency, bureaucratic pressures, communications breakdowns, self-interest and negligence. And then there are some, such as Green (1994) and Snell (1993), who synthesize these two positions. While their primary concern is with the practice of ethical decision-making in organizations, they recognize and allow for personal and institutional constraints on the straightforward application of moral theory in the work situation.

The reality of managers' moral concerns

On the question of relevance, there is both theoretical argument and empirical evidence to support the assertion that managers (and others) in organizations do face moral issues and dilemmas. *Issues* can be understood in terms of specific moral values, principles and concerns. The right to a decent standard of living, and the threat to that ideal when workers are faced with unemployment, indicates an issue. But when the handling of that issue brings it into conflict with other moral values and principles (such as public safety, requiring the closure of the factory in question) or when it means that one has to make difficult choices from within the same broadly defined value position (such as the more widespread redundancies which are expected to follow if a small number of job losses are not accepted in the short term) then one faces a *dilemma* (Toffler, 1986).

Child (1972) has explained how managers can exercise choice regarding matters such as the market in which an organization operates and the level of performance sought. He subsequently interpreted this in terms of the social implications of organizational design; if there is choice, then one can avoid forms of organization which might have a harmful impact on people (Child, 1973). Anthony also observes that it is reasonable to assume that people in organizations have 'considerable leeway in the decisions they take and in the way they behave before they reach the ultimate influence of economic necessity' (1986: 193). And Treviño, in a widely cited paper, states that 'managers engage in discretionary decision-making behavior affecting the lives and well-being of others. Thus, they are involved in ethical decision making' (1986: 601).

What such writers are saying, if only implicitly, is that the conventionally understood goals and values of organizations, such as profit-maximization, or particular measures of effectiveness, are not absolute. Moral choices are possible, and in any case such ethical concern is frequently quite compatible with high organizational performance in the traditional sense. Now while most employees, including managers, are quite capable of demonstrating moral awareness outside the workplace, empirically based research monographs in the field of organizational and managerial behaviour, at least until recently, have seldom made explicit reference to any such expressed ethical concern. Of course, it may be that people in organizations are often blissfully unaware or unappreciative of the moral significance of situations. Events are not defined as a question of, for example, dishonesty or lack of respect for human wellbeing. People may act according to 'scripts' generated from the established culture and practice, set in a particular institutional milieu, and which 'typically include no ethical component in their cognitive content' (Gioia, 1992: 388). Or, more obviously, they may simply be denied access to information about the moral implications of the activity in question. But equally probable is that they suffer from 'moral muteness' (Bird and Waters, 1989). They may be unused to, or unwilling to entertain, the idea of speaking in moral terms in the workplace, even when ethical issues do trouble them. The organizational culture may inhibit the articulation of such concerns.

Whatever the reasons, this clearly affects researchers' ability to pick up the ethical component in organizational discourse. Yet the developmental perspective which I am adopting, and emphasize in later chapters, demands that one should be concerned with what could be, not simply with what is. This means that ethics has to be put onto the agenda for research, education and practice in management. It is interesting that while at least one recent empirical study has accentuated managers' moral concerns (Watson, 1994) many earlier and in some respects comparable sources do not make such explicit mention of the ethical side to managerial behaviour. Yet a careful reading of such earlier works can yield examples of dialogue or reported episodes from which one can *infer* both moral issues and persons' awareness of these as such (for example, Crozier, 1964: 23, 136–7; Pettigrew, 1973: Chapter 8; 1985: Chapter 4). This draws attention to the significance of the perspective adopted, questions asked and language used in organizational research: whether or not individuals' moral concerns are articulated depends very much on these things.

If, as I suggested earlier, people disagree on the relative importance of issues, then by the same token they may not always agree that something is of moral concern in the first place. This indicates a further reason why sometimes the language of ethics does not feature when one might have expected it to. Questions concerning the scope of ethics arise here; for example, to what extent are animal rights, or our treatment of the natural environment, moral issues? The distinction between the more dramatic cases which make the media headlines (such as the Bhopal disaster in 1984, or the collapse of Barings Bank in 1995) and everyday moral issues in organizations, is also significant (Waters et al., 1986). Waters et al., Toffler (1986) and Snell (1993) have all shown that managers quite often face relatively minor ethical issues in their dealings with colleagues and staff, and with their various stakeholders: the public, customers, clients, suppliers and others. Of course, there is a continuum in terms of degree of seriousness, but even minor situations, sometimes simply matters of conduct, of demeanour, appropriateness, timing, language used and so on, remain a proper subject for management ethics research, and for development programmes at individual and organizational levels.

The structure of this book

The overall perspective I am adopting is one which emphasizes the moral development of individuals in organizations. This concept of development is defined in terms of persons' capacity for critical, independent, thought, rather than mere conformity with institutional norms, codes and rules. In the next chapter, following a discussion on the role of personal values in action, I introduce Lawrence Kohlberg's contribution in this area, the significance of which pervades the book. Thus in Chapters 3 and 4, the applicability of moral philosophical theory to this aspect of management practice is critically considered. I conclude that discussion by outlining two broadly defined and complementary approaches to the handling of ethical issues and dilemmas in organizations. One of these focuses on the need for moral judgment in the context of actual situations; the other focuses on the need, as often as not, for dialogue between people who have conflicting views on the issues involved. Each of these approaches is necessary, but is usually insufficient on its own.

In Chapters 5 to 9 I address selected topics and concepts in organizational behaviour: trust, work and its organization, equality and discrimination, responsibility, loyalty and dissent. I examine these in terms of moral issues and dilemmas that can arise for managers and employees generally. This part of the book serves three purposes. First, it provides some examples of situations where the need for judgment and dialogue arises in the handling of moral problems. Second, it points out respects in which improvement can be made in organizational systems and management practice, so that individuals' moral development may be facilitated and their moral viewpoints articulated, for example through enhanced employee participation. Third, it makes a contribution to the conceptualization of these areas in relation to ethics. A particular emphasis, especially in Chapter 6, concerns the idea of work as service, informed by individuals' moral awareness. I connect this with the concept of responsibility, which is explored further in Chapter 8, where I consider whether organizations, as opposed to their members, can be held responsible for events; and in Chapter 9, where individuals' moral dissent, especially whistleblowing, is considered.

These ideas give rise (in Chapters 10 and 11) to a distinction between the idea of organizations which, in terms of the visible outcomes they generate, are ethically 'acceptable', and those whose ethically aware members form a 'moral community'. The latter is seen as a more developed state, consistent with Kohlberg's conceptualization. In that context I consider the question of organizations' responsiveness to their environments through their governmental structures and processes, codes, cultures and leadership. Then, in the final chapter, I comment on the provision of management education and development as a contribution to moral improvement in organizations. An appreciation of this is, I feel, important not just for those who provide such programmes, but for participants also, so that they may share in reflections on the rationale for the learning process in which they are involved.

Conclusion

In this chapter I have addressed a number of points and pursued some key themes which arise when business and management ethics is discussed. In the process, I have introduced my own perspective on the subject, and I have also indicated the direction in which we shall head in the coming chapters. But there are inevitably areas or aspects of the overall subject which I shall not address as distinct topics, and some of these might be regarded as significant omissions. Since one aim in writing this book has been to contribute to a greater appreciation of the overlap between ethics and the field of organizational studies in general, I shall conclude by offering a very brief comment on four themes (not in any order of significance) which I feel require particular mention.

First, adequate treatment of the *cross-cultural* dimension to management ethics would probably require more explicit attention than I have been able to give to it. I would stress that in saying this I am not referring to the application of Western ethical theories to matters of international business, but to the development of a comprehensive framework which could accommodate other philosophical and religious traditions. However, as I observe in Chapter 3, the perspective which I am adopting, emphasizing the form of moral thinking rather than its content, can cater for such different positions (except perhaps in so far as my elevation of persons' capacity for independent reasoning might offend those who give primacy to particular religious value-systems).

Second, the question of *gender* is only dealt with explicitly at two points. I touch upon feminist perspectives on ethics in Chapter 3; and in Chapter 7 I deal with some aspects of discrimination and other matters relating to the 'management of differences'. But we ought, as Marshall says, 'to consider gender as potentially relevant in every area of study, as well as to pay it separate attention as appropriate' (1995: S56). The reader is invited to bear this in mind continually, for it undoubtedly applies to much of the subject matter in this book (see Doyle, 1990; Mahoney, 1993).

Third, I suspect that the potential of contemporary *information technology* (IT) for the ethical improvement of organizations, remains largely untapped. I am not referring to the ethics of IT (although that is important) but to the way in which IT can contribute to organization development in the context of ethics. This could arise with, for example, work design, participation, and ethical audits, topics which I address in later chapters.

Finally there is the question of *postmodernism* and its relationship to ethics in management and organizations. I have not allowed myself to get drawn into that debate, but some connections and suggestions are offered at the end of both Chapters 4 and 10. Those interested could also refer to Rasmussen (1993) and other papers in the same source.

2 Personal Values and Moral Development

In the previous chapter I contrasted a relatively simple impression of the management process, as something 'rational' and therefore technical, with a view depicting the complexity of organizational situations, where people pursue their various interests, articulate their conflicting concerns (or don't, as the case may be) and where the plurality of values involved becomes apparent. Attempts at making sense of individuals' actions frequently fail to reveal their *underlying* concerns. Values may be operating beneath the surface, and this is a reminder that the concepts we employ should be sensitive to the variety of possibilities in such situations. Thus an often overlooked potential for moral action by individuals should be recognized.

Such moral values influence persons' choice of work and employment, their recognition of actual and potential ethical issues in the work context, and guide their conduct accordingly. In this chapter I shall comment on the sources of individuals' values and the way in which these may be influenced in the workplace. I shall also consider the logical relationship between values and action in organizations. The possibility of a moral dimension to such action raises epistemological issues, since we may overlook the existence of ethical values unless we deliberately look out for them. Thus the idea of a 'moral orientation' towards work and employment is introduced, building on the 1960s and 1970s sociological literature on that theme.

Finally, I shall outline the essence of Lawrence Kohlberg's theory of individual moral development – concerning the degree to which people demonstrate a capacity for independent moral reasoning and action – in order to provide a link between the largely social scientific paradigm out of which much of the chapter is written, and the moral philosophical perspective which will be adopted in Chapters 3 and 4.

Personal and managerial values

Values are inescapable. While they are most commonly associated with decision-making (for example, Harrison, 1975) they permeate conduct in general. Organizational researchers talk of managerial beliefs, attitudes, priorities, thinking and orientations, and on closer inspection one finds that much of this is concerned with values. However, most of the literature in this area is concerned with conventionally defined performance considerations, such as motivation and effectiveness. Is financial remuneration or intrinsic job interest more important to this or that category of executive? What is needed to attract and retain good staff? Do managers place a high value on retaining control over decisions, such that organizational performance suffers through their unwillingness to delegate or invite participation? No doubt these matters have indirect ethical significance, but the values in question are not obviously indicative of managers' *moral* thinking.

In one of the more frequently cited definitions of a 'value', Kluckhohn described it as '*a conception, explicit or implicit, distinctive of an individual or characteristic of a group, of the desirable which influences the selection from available modes, means and ends of action*' (1951: 395). Clearly this could be indicative of the two definitions of morality that I introduced in Chapter 1. Values which are characteristic of a group may reflect, in part, a social morality; those to which an individual adheres may be part of her or his set of personal moral beliefs. We may not, of course, agree with them; and we may not agree that they deserve the label *moral*. The value someone places on an attractive landscape, or on passing professional examinations, does not at first sight seem to address ethical concerns. But if, as various philosophers have suggested, whatever is of particular importance to people may be of some moral significance to them, then by the same token, persons' values, whatever they are, may have some bearing on moral issues as they see them.

Sources of individuals' values

Individuals' values are derived initially from upbringing in specific groups such as community and family, and are then subject to the impact of formal education, professional training, and the experience of life and work generally. They are thus liable to continual reaffirmation and reordering, especially following episodes where moral conflicts have been encountered.

The most obvious influences are the family and society. Parental values are frequently mentioned as factors, and help to explain differences between individuals within a particular culture. As one item of evidence here, research by Kraut and Lewis (1975) into the political values of 400 American students suggested that those from left-wing family backgrounds had absorbed not only their parents' ideological beliefs, but also a preparedness to articulate these publicly (although the intense impact of late 1960s radicalism should be borne in mind here). Furthermore, variables associated with membership of particular socio-economic classes, such as the disadvantageous situation experienced by many women and members of minority groups, can affect such individuals' aspirations and hence their values as expressed in action (Fox, 1971: 22–5; Parkin [1971] 1972: Chapter 3).

Research into managerial values

Research into managers' values has tended to deal in broadly defined concepts, seeking correlations between such values and a number of contextual factors (for example, functional role in the organization, national culture, age or education). Such empirical enquiry has been extensive, and has spanned several decades. Much of this has dealt with comparative study across national cultures (for example, England, 1975; Haire et al., 1966; Hofstede, 1980). A number of authors have addressed specific cultural contexts, for example in the USA (England, 1967), Malawi (Jones, 1988) and Malaysia (Zabid and Alsagoff, 1993). Then there are numerous studies which, although they address specific issues such as motivation or career orientations, are essentially about managers' personal values and priorities (for example Scase and Goffee, 1989). In practice, however, the way in which situations are perceived, evaluated and then acted upon by individuals will reflect specific personal and biographical differences which are less susceptible to identification through large-scale survey-based research. Aspects of background and upbringing, reaction to immediate circumstances, and, where ethical issues and dilemmas are involved, the individual's acquired capacity for moral thought and action, are all important here.

This whole field, therefore, is enormously complex. A number of books for managers have stressed the importance of values (notably Peters and Waterman, 1982), with reference to which Watson has said: 'To talk about "managing through values" sounds straightforward in its glibness. But we have to remember that "values" are notions of what is good and bad, right and wrong. These are deep waters indeed' (1994: 15). What is being raised here are questions concerning what managers *ought* to do, as opposed to a purely technical concern with *how* they should do it. So it is doubtless on the specifically ethical dimension that most people might wish to plumb the depths. But, ethics aside, there is great difficulty in combining general applicability with comprehensiveness when it comes to discussing managerial values. The convolution of means and ends, at both the individual and the organizational level, suggests a morass, and I have no intention of getting immersed, for it is doubtful whether it is hugely relevant to my overall argument. A few words are called for nevertheless. In particular, there is the question of global cultural variations, the possibility that uniformities in the management process can override this, and the possibility, also, that even where managers' ethical values are not mentioned explicitly in such research, they may be inferred.

An early inspiration for comparative study in this area was the question of convergence; of whether the industrialization process would lead to an institutional and cultural uniformity throughout societies (Kerr et al., [1960] 1973). In one major study, Haire et al. (1966) found only partial evidence for such a trend at the time of their research, which covered fourteen countries. Some aspects of managerial thought and practice showed signs of convergence, perhaps due to the transnational impact of management education and training, other aspects reflected national cultural differences, and there was also some evidence that the state of economic and industrial development was a factor.

Haddon (1973) observed that one weakness in the argument for cultural uniformity was the presence of political regimes which could both inhibit particular forms of economic development and, in various ways, shape the beliefs, values and behaviour of their citizens. As I have already remarked, individuals' values and aspirations may be shaped by their expectations as to what is possible. The political and cultural environment can vary from the more restrictive and homogeneous to the liberal, pluralist societies characteristic of the Western nations. Fox (1971: 2) noted how managers in the then Soviet Union were exposed to an 'ideology of perpetual national emergency' in the face of the perceived Western capitalist threat. Meanwhile their American counterparts had to operate in, and would to some extent reflect, the conflicting values of a mass-consumption society in which, on the one hand, hard work was valued, and, on the other, there was an anti-materialistic youth culture which rejected the work ethic and associated consumerism (Roszak, 1969). More recent events point towards greater commonality between these two geopolitical blocs, but the general argument retains its force.

Given that cultural variations are important, there is also the question of *ethical* values. There have of course been studies addressed to this matter specifically, or which have at least recognized it explicitly (for example, England, 1967; Zabid and Alsagoff, 1993). But an implicit moral dimension is discernible in more general work too. In what was one of the more influential cross-cultural empirical investigations, Hofstede (1980) identified four key variables concerning societal values: individualism, power distance, uncertainty avoidance, and masculinity. Each of these has significant implications for the management of organizations, and also has implications for management ethics. A central element of Hofstede's work involved mapping different countries on the various dimensions, showing how, at the time of his research, the USA and the UK, for example, differed from, say, Taiwanese or Indian culture. In this brief summary I shall ignore detailed reference to particular societies, as these change over time; what is important for our purposes is the overall idea.

Individualism refers to a cultural tendency for people to emphasize and justify self-interest and concern for immediate family, as opposed to a concern for the wider community. In general, individualism is more typical of Westernized societies. This dimension suggests a parallel with the distinction between personal and social morality, pointed out in the previous chapter, since in a collectivity-oriented society one might expect the culture to be more homogeneous with regard to ethical values and beliefs.

Power distance refers to the way in which people in different societies view inequalities among their citizens. This has obvious significance for ethics in the workplace, corporate social policy, and leadership styles. People in cultures with a large power distance are more likely to accept the normality of hierarchical domination, autocratic leadership and associated power and status differentials.

Uncertainty avoidance relates to the extent to which members of a society avoid risk and seek certainty, as opposed to taking each day as it comes and accepting uncertainty. Hofstede suggests that in uncertainty-avoiding cultures there is less tolerance of marginal values, and more adherence to specific religious doctrines and absolute moral codes. Translated to the organizational context, one would expect greater conformity with moral norms and codes under these conditions (Vitell et al., 1993).

Finally, masculinity is derived from the idea of sex-role differences, but extended metaphorically. 'Masculine' societies have clear sex-role distinctions, and male values (aggressive, competitive, materialistic) dominate. As Vitell et al. (1993) suggest, such cultural environments would not seem to be particularly conducive to ethical business behaviour. By contrast, in 'feminine' cultures there are overlaps between male and female roles, and more emphasis on relationships, quality of life, ecological issues, and the ethical principles which underlie such values.

Sources of values internal to the workplace

Organizational factors shape the processes whereby opportunities arise for people to articulate their personal values, and to share and compare views with colleagues. Significant among these processual norms are the style of leadership adopted by managers (Tannenbaum and Schmidt, 1973), the acceptability of moral language in organizational discourse (Bird and Waters, 1989) and the extent to which people are expected to share in, indeed look for, moral responsibility for activities and outcomes (Maclagan, 1983; Treviño, 1986). But as well as values and norms concerning these *processes* of direction, communication and decision-making, there are *substantive* beliefs and attitudes. For example, what is the prevalent attitude in the organization towards environmental issues? How do we define 'unsafe' products? How seriously are minority rights taken? Do people feel guilty about helping themselves to pens and stationery from the office store for private use?

All of these matters, processual and substantive, are features of the organizational culture. Here an important distinction, to which I return in Chapter 11, is the difference between two views. First, where culture is seen as an internal variable which can be shaped by management as part of a strategy for control; and second, the view that an organization is itself the expression of external cultural values such as efficiency and bureaucratic rationality (Smircich, 1983). From the second standpoint, the boundary between external and internal influences over persons' values is blurred. It also means that separating out culture from other features of organizations, such as formal structure, is more problematic.

There is a literature on deliberate attempts to induce value-changes among managers in organizations (for example Schein, 1968). It has, however, been suggested that internalized values which derive from 'multiple influences in a lifelong process' are the most significant in managerial decision-making (Whitely, 1981: 521). Such multiple influences include past work experience as well as earlier biographical factors. But this process will usually take effect gradually, after reflection on events. Strongly held, internalized, values are unlikely to be affected immediately by deliberate attempts to change them.

This has obvious implications for programmes in management education and development.

The influence of internal organizational factors is, therefore, likely to be less deliberate and controllable than some would wish. The whole area of social cognition and script processing (Gioia, 1986, 1992) is relevant when referring to some of the specific organizational phenomena implicated in this discussion. In his analysis of the Ford Pinto episode Gioia (1992) shows how 'schemas' or 'scripts' structure knowledge so that some features of a situation are emphasized and others ignored. As a link between organizational factors and individuals' actions, schemas and scripts have the effect of sustaining certain practices and values to the exclusion of others. In the Ford case, with regard to the recall of the dangerous vehicles, both the value of individual responsibility and that of safety were overlooked or distorted in the interests of the efficient management of complex and demanding situations. Gioia observes that, as recall coordinator for Ford at the time,

> My cue for labeling a case as a problem either required high frequencies of occurrence or directly-traceable causes. I had little time for speculative contemplation on potential problems that did not fit a pattern that suggested known courses of action leading to possible recall. (1992: 381–2)

Thus while most managers join organizations with a personal adherence to some core values and beliefs, their actual conduct may be guided by factors which are part of the organizational context. As with most people in unfamiliar circumstances, they look for cues as to what is correct behaviour. These, together with formal features of an organization as suggested above, can affect individual values, but the precise process by which this happens is problematic. Visible behaviour does not necessarily mean that values have been internalized, but simply that an individual is conforming to externally defined norms (Kelman, 1961). However, the voluminous body of research and theory on cognitive dissonance would suggest that such change in individuals' behaviour can itself lead to changes in their values. Faced with a need to justify, to others or to themselves, decisions which clearly support particular ethical standpoints, most people avoid the tension threatened by possible inconsistency. So they come round to believing in the moral positions indicated by their own actions (Festinger, 1957; Staw, 1980).

Values and action in organizations

As an aid to structuring this discussion, I shall draw upon Rescher's (1969) contribution on the analysis of values in action. One initial and obvious distinction he made is that between someone's subscription to a value, and the imputation or ascription of a value to another person: 'A person who "subscribes" to a certain value (i.e., has, holds, accepts, is dedicated to, gives his adherence to it, or the like) will be characterized as a *subscriber* to this value' (Rescher, 1969: 7).

This indicates that the individual is committed to that value. By contrast, to impute a value to someone, to say that she attaches great importance to honesty in business affairs, for example, is to make what Rescher regarded as a neutral statement; although that would be questioned by many other philosophers (for example Nagel, 1961: 485–502; and see Hollis, 1994: Chapter 10). Thus research into the values held by members of organizations is concerned with value-ascription. Rescher then pointed to three perspectives from which one may guide, or 'rationalize', action in terms of particular values. In the decision-making context one may ask oneself: 'What am I (are we) to do?' In giving advice or help to another, one is addressing the question: 'What are you to do?' And one may engage in critique or evaluation of action, asking: 'What are the merits (or demerits) of what X is doing (has done)?' (Rescher, 1969: 11–12). This sort of exercise is not unproblematic. As Rescher observed

> whenever something is held to be of value, there is always to be found somewhere on the sidelines a value with respect to which this thing is prized. Thus 'the advancement of his career' is of value to Jones presumably because such items as 'success,' 'financial security,' 'the respect of his peers,' and the like, are among his values. (1969: 8)

What is valued, and why?

Consequently what is needed for the analysis of action is the identification of various elements, which Rescher labelled as follows:

- the *value object* (for example, employment in a particular organization);
- the *locus of value* (the reason why employment is valued; for example, income, or the nature of the service offered by the organization to the public);
- the *underlying values* (for example, the things that money can buy, or the fulfilment of an altruistic need to help others).

This is a useful distinction, whether in clarifying action for an individual or group, or for the observer who is imputing, and possibly engaging in moral judgment of, the motives behind some person's, group's or organization's behaviour. To take a less obvious example which reflects the political side to organizational life, the value object might be a colleague's friendship, the locus of value identifies the context for the individual in which this friendship is valued, such as the pursuit of promotion at work, while the underlying value might be a desire for greater financial rewards and wealth. But of course the very fact that such underlying values and loci of value are usually hidden or disguised, means that moral evaluation of others' action is perhaps hard to justify; do we know *why* someone desires wealth?

Rescher then offered a substantial analysis of the different ways in which values may be classified (1969: 13–19). Among the taxonomies suggested are the sort of benefits associated with their realization (for example, economic, moral, intellectual, aesthetic) and the nature of the relationship between the

value-subscribers and the beneficiaries of their action (for example, sub-
scribers, as the actors themselves, family, profession, nation, mankind). In
each of these there appears to be a distinction to be made, which is of relevance for the present discussion. On the one hand we have moral and
non-moral values; on the other hand self-oriented and other-oriented values.
However, the difference between objects of value, loci of value and underlying values should guard us against any superficial interpretations of action in
such terms. What appears as a (non-moral?) economically motivated action
(for example, as manifest in corporate policy) may have an underlying moral
basis understood in terms of the value of its anticipated consequences (for
example, job security for employees). Using the same example, what looks like
self-interest (or corporate interest) may in fact be motivated by concern for
others.

> Having a certain value is obviously different from having a certain goal or a certain
> preference. But, of course, the goals one adopts or the preferences one has are
> reflections of, and indications for, one's values. The connection between values and
> goals is not straightforward. Usually we can make very plausible presumptive infer-
> ences from values to goals (if someone 'values money,' its acquisition is presumably
> a goal of his). But knowing he has a certain goal, we may be quite uninformed
> about the operative values (e.g. if his goal is 'making money,' we cannot say what his
> values are – he may not, for example, be actuated by any 'selfish' motives at all).
> (Rescher, 1969: 23)

Values and orientations to work

I want now to turn to that cluster of concepts concerned with occupational
and job choice, employee orientations, attitudes, motivation and satisfaction.
As articulated in the literature, especially in the period up until the late 1970s,
such concepts were seldom used in a manner likely to reflect human moral
potential, a point to which I shall return. The truism that people subscribe to
values is, however, necessarily implicit in such work, and is occasionally
explicit; for example in Vroom's expectancy theory of motivation (Vroom,
1964). And by using Rescher's schema it is possible to provoke deeper analysis of actual situations, in a manner not normally invited in the management
literature. To explain this, I intend to focus on the concept of persons' orientation to work. This theoretical construct gained prominence in the UK
during the 1970s in the field of industrial and organizational sociology, and
is particularly associated with research by Goldthorpe et al. (1968).

An orientation to work refers to the 'wants and expectations' which people
have in that context, 'and thus . . . the way in which they *define* their work situation' (Goldthorpe et al., 1968: 8). This research by Goldthorpe and his
colleagues was a landmark in the move away from epistemological positions
which had focused, in their attempts at explanation, on assumed deterministic reactions of employees, in general, to putatively objective organizational
variables such as technology, leadership style or reward-systems. Those
theoretical positions are well documented, and include scientific management

(Taylor, 1911), various forms of human relations theory (for example, Likert, 1961; McGregor, [1960] 1987) and sociological explanations for alienation and dissatisfaction arising out of employees' reactions to particular forms of technological arrangement in the workplace (for example, Blauner, 1964).

However the focus on orientations did not necessarily abandon the assumption that regularities, presumably helpful for predictive purposes, could be identified. Commenting on the 'action' perspective in sociological explanation (Silverman, 1970) Brown wrote that:

> Such orientations, wants, expectations and meanings, are of importance because they are not to be seen as varying randomly from individual to individual but as being socially shared. It is possible therefore to develop 'ideal types' of orientations to work which can then be used to explain different patterns of job choice, job satisfaction, attachment to the employing organization, and so on. (1973: 19–20)

I shall leave aside, for the moment, the more precise nature of these ideal-typical orientations, except to say that in very general terms they categorized people according to whether their wants (implying values) and expectations represented such things as material rewards, career aspirations, social satisfactions or personal development.

Following Goldthorpe and his colleagues' initial studies, the debate on orientations to work broadened out. The concept was applied to professional as well as to manual workers, and there was much argument concerning both the source and the stability of such values and beliefs (Daniel, 1969; Silverman, 1970; and for overviews see Brown, 1973, 1992). As with research into managerial values, it was recognized that individuals' orientations could be affected by work experience, and were not necessarily or solely shaped by culturally defined meanings, acquired prior to joining an organization. Individuals' total situation, work as well as non-work, would have to be taken into account. Even if some core values are stable, significant changes in a person's life, such as starting a family, or redundancy, would normally result in a re-evaluation of priorities. Furthermore, as Fox (1971: 22–3) observed, persons' expectations, in relation to what they assume to be feasible, affect their orientations, and such expectations will also alter over time and depending on circumstances. Indeed, one may question whether many people do have a clear conception of their values and objectives in their work, or even whether, and in what respects, they feel dissatisfied or contented, given that these attitudes can coexist. The differences between choice of work and employment, the subjective experience of that work, and what may be a consequential decision to leave, also emerged as significant. This distinction and its implications had in fact been addressed a decade earlier in the field of organizational psychology, when Katz (1964) had observed that people may be motivated to join an organization by entirely different factors from those which might inspire them to work productively once there.

By the late 1970s 'the "social action frame of reference", which drew especially on the work of [Max] Weber, was no longer very prominent' (Brown, 1992: 163). Nevertheless, it is still employed (Watson, 1994: Chapter 3), and the issues raised in that earlier debate are still pertinent. They amount to a considerable complexity, and this complexity can be related to Rescher's analysis in terms of values. Take the difference between value-subscribers (employees, managers) and ascribers (onlookers, researchers, other managers). To repeat what Rescher said:

> knowing . . . [that someone] has a certain goal, we may be quite uninformed about the operative values (e.g., if his goal is 'making money,' we cannot say what his values are – he may not, for example, be actuated by any 'selfish' motives at all). (Rescher, 1969: 23)

For example, he or she may have a disabled child, and it is important to provide everything possible to enhance that child's life. So ideally, and certainly if we are concerned with a moral evaluation of someone's actions and orientations, we need to understand the full subjective meaning of their situation (although in practice we may well not). Just to talk of someone valuing the material rewards from work, or the intrinsic challenge which it promises, is inadequate. The distinctions between value objects, loci of value, and underlying values, can at least sensitize us to these matters.

Labelling and stereotyping

In Chapter 1, I noted that methodological and epistemological issues arise regarding researchers' ability to discern ethical awareness among people in organizations. I pointed out that if one does not look for something, one is unlikely to find it. This, coupled with the tendency towards 'moral muteness' in organizations (Bird and Waters, 1989) means that researchers (and others) are themselves implicitly adopting a mildly cynical stance when they ignore the possibility of persons' moral values and orientations. Melé comments that most management and social science theory adopts a view in which 'the multidimensional richness of the human being becomes compressed into one or two planes and reduced to a kind of intelligent machine, a being with tendencies or needs, or a mere component of a social or political system' (1990: 99); and he continues by noting the danger that our images of organizations, and of their members, can be influenced by such a view.

Similarly, it has been argued that one of the paradoxes in the 'enterprise culture' of the 1980s and 1990s in the UK has been the manner in which

> The enterprising, personally responsible, free individual, vaunted by the [Conservative] government, stands on the wreckage of the *self*-conscious, self-directing idiosyncratic individual who resists conformity, rejects the social categories that provide the basis of marketing and planning strategy, the individual who assimilates to herself/himself the classifying and homogenising devices of the mass society rather than the other way round. This autonomous individual is the victim of the privilege accorded in Thatcherite practice to economic power: sacrificed to economies of scale; made contemptible not only by economic weakness, but by a refusal to conform to a *regimented*, and therefore, bogus individualism. (Cohen, 1992: 179–80)

Cohen notes the general tendency to label people, losing sight of the way in which individuals see themselves, and the fact that it is such self-perceptions which underlie their motivation. Supporting the view I have already stressed, he then exhorts social scientists to endeavour 'to understand the subtleties, inflections and varieties of individual thought that are concealed by the categorical masks we invent so adeptly' (1992: 192).

I suggested earlier that I would take a closer look at the ideal-typical work-orientations which were offered in the 1970s literature on that subject. These were couched in very general language. Goldthorpe and his colleagues referred to three types: instrumental, where work is a 'means to an end, or ends, external to the work situation'; bureaucratic, where work is seen as 'service to an organisation in return for . . . a career'; and solidaristic, where 'while work, as always, has an economic meaning, it is experienced not simply as a means to an end but also as a group activity' (1968: 38–42). In each of these, but especially the first two, there will be underlying values which could represent an ethical impulse, as with the earlier example of the 'instrumentally' motivated parent with the disabled child. Similarly, Bennett (1974) offered three broadly defined labels: instrumental, relational and personal. Now if we look more closely at one of these, the personal orientation, this referred to 'job interest, use of abilities, *etc.* (i.e. personal growth)' (Bennett, 1974: 154). But is there not a danger that, depending on one's methodology, and the manner in which the label is operationalized, it may fail to capture the richness of individuals' self-perceptions, values and motivations? A 'personal' orientation, and 'personal growth', could, after all, suggest the development of moral awareness.

Yet even where the idea of an explicitly moral orientation *is* offered, caution is needed. Etzioni's category of 'moral involvement', widely used as a root concept by subsequent writers (for example, Fox, 1971: 72; Goldthorpe et al., 1968: 39–41) was in fact subdivided into two: 'social' and 'pure moral'. And even the latter, referring to 'an intensive mode of commitment' is confined to the 'internalization of norms and identification with authority . . . [which] tends to develop in vertical relationships, such as those between teachers and students, priests and parishioners, leaders and followers' (Etzioni, 1961: 10–11). Such a conceptualization reflects the functionalist perspective from which we seem unable to escape. Yet escape we must, if the true potential of managerial or business ethics is to be realized. There must be recognition of a moral potential which goes beyond mere conformity with social and organizational norms, and which could be overlooked if we use standardized conceptualizations and premature labelling.

The possibility of a moral orientation

A survey of British probationer police constables conducted in late 1977 may help to illustrate this. These constables had an average age of 22 and had all been recruited within the previous eighteen months. Two hundred and thirty-one usable questionnaires were returned (Maclagan, 1979). From the information and data collected, I will focus on the responses to two fairly open-ended questions, which were content-analysed.

> 'What was it about the Police which attracted you; was there any special reason?'
> 'What things, if any, give you particularly strong feelings of satisfaction, or of feeling that the work is worthwhile?'

During the process of interpretation, each individual's response to the whole questionnaire was kept in mind and referred to, in an attempt to infer the meaning, for that person, of the actual situation in question. The reasons given for joining the service were varied, and indicated several different orientations, each associated with a particular locus of value (Rescher, 1969). Most common (30–45 per cent of respondents) were the anticipated variety of the work, and job security, while around 12–15 per cent mentioned one or more of: the opportunity to work out of doors, working with people (a social, rather than a service orientation), and the social usefulness of the work (seeing it as a contribution to the community). It was important to distinguish these last two emphases, of which the statements below are typical:

> 'Meeting people from all walks of life. Variety in work.' (A social orientation).
> 'Duties involved, such as keeping law and order, and helping people.' (A service orientation).

As an initial attraction of police work, there was a very slight tendency for the service orientation to be associated with older, more experienced, recruits. But with a year or more of police experience behind them, 40 per cent of the respondents referred to the provision of help to members of the public as a major source of satisfaction, while 38 per cent mentioned the sense of fulfilment in being involved in clearing up crime. This may be contrasted with the 12 per cent who referred to social usefulness as a reason for joining initially. In part, this discrepancy reflects the difference between individuals' value-rankings in the two distinct contexts: the initial occupational choice (where they tended to seek job security and interest) and in the work itself. It could also result from the culture of the occupation. But, alternatively, it could indicate the impact of significant personal experiences in work, as triggers which awaken a moral sensitivity.

Of course such a group is not typical of most organizational employees or managers; it is, after all, a service occupation. And there are doubtless many methodological and other issues that could be raised. Most obviously, given my earlier comments on Etzioni's concept of 'moral involvement', it will be objected that there is no sign here of a *critical* moral position, in opposition to organizational practice; it is just another illustration of the functionalist position. But these objections should not detract from my claim that it is relevant to my overall argument, as I shall endeavour to explain.

Watson suggests that while personal moral values may incline some people to work for charities, 'even within the more pragmatic kinds of work entered by most people there is likely, at the minimum, to be an avoidance of undertaking tasks which clash fundamentally with personal values' (1994: 74). My argument is that methods used in research, the avoidance of premature labelling, recognition of individuals' potential for ethical awareness and sensitivity, and of the possibility that this can be stimulated through experiences at work, are all important. Attention to such things allows us to entertain the possibility of what I shall call the 'moral orientation'.

In one interpretation, this is indicative of someone who seeks out specific 'ethically good' work, as when people consciously join a charity, or a service profession, or choose to avoid working for an organization they perceive as socially or morally contentious. But more generally, it may suggest a sensitivity to moral issues in the workplace. This can predate the experience of particular work, or it can emerge through a reordering of the individual's personal values as a result of significant events after joining. Most people pursue particular occupations for reasons which are not obviously moral, but this need not inhibit the development of their moral awareness. The taxi driver whose experience of street crime convinces him that he wants to work in the police, if we suspend our cynicism, is acting from an acquired moral awareness; the graduate who starts as a management trainee with a large industrial firm, for conventional reasons such as career prospects, may nevertheless become sensitive to the possibility of improper or unethical practice in commercial dealings, employee relations and other aspects of the organization's activities. These examples are indicative of the process of moral development, to which I now turn.

Moral development: an initial statement

The idea of individuals' moral development provides a link between the largely social science perspective from which this chapter has been written so far, and subsequent discussion in later chapters, on ethical theory and management development.

The theory of cognitive moral development is associated principally with the Swiss psychologist Jean Piaget and, more recently, with Lawrence Kohlberg in the USA (Kohlberg, 1969, 1973, 1981, 1986; Piaget, 1932). This work has been primarily associated with childhood and adolescent development, but there has been growing interest in the application of Kohlberg's thinking to adults. His ideas have been employed by a number of writers in the field of management and organization development (for example, Lavoie and Culbert, 1978; Rowan, 1976; Treviño, 1986) and more recently there has been a particular interest in the relevance of Kohlberg to the education and development of individual managers (for example, Maclagan, 1990a; Maclagan and Snell, 1992; Snell, 1993; Weber, 1991).

Kohlberg's theory has provoked intense critical debate and raises a number of philosophical and epistemological questions, some of which will be considered in the next chapter. (One comprehensive source on this is Modgil and Modgil, 1986.) Such is the intellectual uncertainty surrounding Kohlberg's ideas, that for some, not least those engaging with the practice of management development, what may be called for is a 'reinterpretation and adaptation' (Snell, 1993: 13), or indeed a simplification, of his model.

In essence, Kohlberg's proposition is that people can progress, from childhood onwards, through three levels of cognitive moral development, each divided into two stages. Such development refers to persons' capacity to understand the concept of morality, and ultimately to be able to engage in ethical reasoning. In the context of the present discussion, this means a progression from self-interest, through appreciation of, and conformity with, the moral values and norms of society and support for members of one's immediate circle, to greater independence of mind and potential for the questioning, on ethical grounds, of organizational purposes and activity.

At the *preconventional* level individuals defer to social roles and to socially defined conceptions of right and wrong, but only in so far as punishments or rewards are likely to follow as consequences of their action. This indicates a self-interested, amoral, orientation, perhaps involving instrumental reciprocity with particular other people.

At the *conventional* level individuals have learned that their social roles require them to live up to others' expectations. They are aware of the moral force of such norms and expectations, and are thus guided in their actions by what, in Chapter 1, I referred to as a social, or positive, morality, including conformity with the law, and support for the groups and communities of which they are part.

At the *post-conventional* level, individuals have acquired a capacity to engage in independent and impartial moral reasoning, based on principles of justice. Such reasoning enables them to question the norms and values with which, at the conventional level, they would have agreed, and to arrive at their own, sometimes innovative, answers to moral dilemmas.

There has been considerable argument as to whether Kohlberg's post-conventional level denotes a *morally* superior state, or whether it only indicates development in persons' cognitive, reasoning, capacity. I shall not attempt to address this now, although it is clearly an important question, to which I refer again in the next chapter (see Boyd, 1986; Kohlberg, 1986; Siegel, 1986). However, what is true is that when people face conflicting values they often have to fall back on a personal assessment of the situation, thus raising the question of their capacity to do this. They come into organizations at particular levels of moral development, and, as Treviño (1986) notes, this will affect their susceptibility to influences in the workplace: those at the post-conventional level will be more independently minded. Thus, importantly, Kohlberg recognized that cognitive development on its own is insufficient for moral development, in a holistic sense, to take place; other, non-cognitive, qualities (such as control over one's emotional response to situations, and assertiveness) are also needed, if personal moral principles are to be reflected in action (Kohlberg, 1973). With some notable exceptions, such as Treviño (1986) and Snell (1993), this aspect of Kohlberg's work has received insufficient attention in the business ethics literature.

The professionalization of management

While on this theme, it is worth noting the connections between ethics, management education and development, and professionalization. This has been the subject of considerable discussion in the UK recently (Reed and Anthony, 1992; Silver, 1991). Yet explicit attention to ethics seldom featured among the practical concerns of the various governmental and professional agencies involved in that particular debate (Burgoyne, 1989; Maclagan, 1990a), despite the claim that one of the defining characteristics of a profession is a code of ethics (Hall, 1968). Indeed, at various times this century, the possibility of management as a profession, in the sense that its practice would have an ethical basis, has been raised. In the 1920s, Tawney wrote of 'business as a profession', arguing that, compared with teaching and medicine, it 'should be at least equally free from the vulgar subordination of moral standards to financial interests' (Tawney, [1921] 1961: 91–2). A few years later Follett addressed the same issue, emphasizing the need for 'a broader conception of the ethics of human relations [and] . . . the growing idea of business as a public service which carries with it a sense of responsibility for its efficient conduct' (Follett, [1925] 1973: 93). Since then, a number of writers have pursued this theme, such as Schein (1966) and Andrews (1969) in the USA, and Halmos (1970) in the UK. Most of these sources adopt a normative stance, of course, arguing for what *ought* to be. But since, as I suggested earlier, professional membership may influence persons' values, perhaps these authors deserve to be heard.

Conclusion

This chapter holds several implications for the rest of the book, in which a pervasive theme is the tension between conformity and independent moral thought, reflecting personal values. As if to support the latter possibility, most of the ethical theories which, traditionally, have been taught in business and management programmes, demand that people should acquire a capacity for detached moral reasoning. And although there have been recent and justifiable moves away from that approach, in favour of an emphasis on personal character, it can be argued that there will always be a need for some element of critical thought and judgment.

However, as I noted above with reference to Kohlberg's contribution, and as has been explained elsewhere (Maclagan, 1990a; Maclagan and Snell, 1992) this cognitive component, although necessary, is an insufficient condition for individual moral development in a holistic sense, since the actual *enactment* of ethical behaviour calls for personal qualities and interpersonal skills such as courage, strength of will, tolerance and assertiveness. I make this point now so as to indicate caution regarding the place of theoretical knowledge which is derived from books, lectures and seminars. Nevertheless, since it is assumed that such ethical theory is so obviously central to the whole endeavour, its relationship to practice must now be addressed.

3 Ethical Theory and Ethical Thinking

In this and the next chapter, I shall focus on the relationship between ethical theory and the practice of management. This is a problematic subject. First of all, an over-complex philosophical position is normally incompatible with practising managers' day-to-day circumstances; few are trained philosophers and many experience psychological and logistical barriers to the assimilation and use of those theories which tend to feature on business ethics programmes. Second, there is a contemporary view which may be both related to the first point, and be more convincing, which is that much of this rationalistic ethical theory is of limited direct applicability in management situations; although I certainly do not say that it is irrelevant. Additional perspectives and approaches are required. Thus in this chapter I shall also introduce concepts of altruism, emotion, personal character and individual moral judgment. Taken together, these anticipate a number of important themes which emerge later, and which relate to the aims of management education and development programmes as discussed in Chapter 12.

More specifically, the concept of altruism is relevant to discussion in Chapter 6 where I consider the idea of work as 'service', and to the notion of the organization as a 'moral community' (in Chapters 10 and 11). The place of emotion in ethics demands attention because it opposes the idea of a purely rational and impartial moral calculus, and because that has implications for our understanding of Kohlberg's theory of moral development. These topics then lead naturally into consideration of personal character and virtue ethics, and from there to the centrality of moral judgment. Here the theory of prima facie duties is introduced as a way out of the difficulties encountered when trying to apply those rationalistic normative ethical theories to which I alluded in the previous paragraph, and which I shall now outline.

Rationalistic ethics

Most of the ethical theory taught to students of business ethics demands a process of logical, impartial thought by those concerned with matters of moral decision-making or evaluation in organizations. This perspective is compatible with Kohlberg's post-conventional level introduced in the previous chapter. The two main categories of such theory are consequentialism and non-consequentialism. (For a comment on the predominance of these positions, at any rate in 1980s USA texts, see Derry and Green, 1989.) What follows is only an outline and brief comment on the main positions. It is an implicit invitation to those interested, or for whom it is appropriate, to refer to sources on moral philosophy such as Mackie (1977), Raphael ([1981] 1994) or Singer ([1979] 1993).

Consequentialism

The consequentialist position requires us to consider the outcomes of an action, irrespective of the motives behind it. The most widely discussed consequentialist theory is utilitarianism, which is particularly associated with the English philosopher Jeremy Bentham (1748–1832). According to this theory, the morality of an action depends on its impact on the wellbeing or happiness of people affected, perhaps also including other sentient creatures. This is understood in terms of the overall balance of utility resulting from the action in question (the balance of pleasure over pain, or vice versa). A distinction may be drawn between act- and rule-utilitarianism. In the former, reference is to the net utility resulting from a particular decision or action; in the latter, actions are justified according to whether or not they follow rules which it is believed will, in general, produce the greatest good.

The main problems with utilitarianism stem from the attempt to identify and measure happiness and unhappiness, the distribution of such goods and bads, and the delineation of boundaries around the aggregate in question. The utility of an act (or rule) is judged by its contribution to the welfare of all those affected, but consequences are frequently contentious and difficult to predict, which creates considerable ambiguity in the application of this approach. Furthermore, how does one measure the costs (disutility) and benefits (utility) involved? How does one know who is affected? Does one really, in practice, include everyone? Does this include future generations? Is it only the aggregate good which concerns us, or do questions of its distribution concern us also? Depending on the calculations involved, utilitarianism may justify harm to some people if this is outweighed by an apparently greater good: for example a small number of people reaping great benefits from the exploitation of a large number of factory employees; or a manager ensuring the survival of a manufacturing plant, and the employment which this provides, by selling an unsafe product resulting in death for a small number of customers.

Non-consequentialism

Non-consequentialist or deontological ethics refers to those theories which focus on the moral duty to follow courses of action which are believed to be intrinsically right, such as truth-telling, or promise-keeping; and to refrain from wrong actions such as lying, breaking promises or killing people. According to this position, the consequences of an action have no bearing on its rightness or wrongness. In practice, however, this cannot mean that such moral rules are absolutes, for there are many circumstances in which conflicts arise: for example, an employee may have promised to carry out a task which then entails being untruthful to a customer. As I shall explain later, one cannot say *in general* what the right course of action would be in situations of this sort, as it will depend on the circumstances.

Deontology is associated primarily with the German philosopher Immanuel Kant (1724–1804). Kant distinguished between moral injunctions, which are 'categorical' and should be followed as guides to intrinsically right action, and matters of prudence, which are 'hypothetical' and take the form 'if you want to achieve X, do Y'.

Kant's categorical imperative spelled out a fundamental set of deontological principles. Normally, this is understood in terms of three formulations, which, loosely translated, are as follows:

(1) Act as if you were legislating for everyone.
(2) Act so as to treat human beings [including oneself] always as ends and never merely as means.
(3) Act as if you were a member of a realm of ends.
    (Raphael, [1981] 1994: 56)

The first of these formulations concerns the procedure to be followed in order to arrive at an ethical decision. 'Everyone' includes oneself; so if one says that people ought or ought not to act in a particular manner, then this refers to oneself also. In short, for Kant, moral rules should be impartial and capable of being universalized. When assessing the moral worth of an action, or a rule, one must consider how acceptable it would be if everyone was to act in that way, or according to that rule.

The second formulation is usually understood as the principle of respect for persons. Essentially, this concerns recognition of the rights and potential of individuals, and helping them in relation to these. An important aspect of this is the avoidance of manipulative relations with others, in which they cannot even enter into dialogue over the matter in question.

The third formulation highlights the point that other people are moral agents just like oneself, and have an equal right to arrive at their own universalizable moral choices.

Just as with utilitarianism, there are problems with deontological theories in their application. Conflicts arise between different obligations, or duties, as in the earlier example of the employee who cannot reconcile a promise to perform her task, with truthfulness to the customer. In such a case one can only resolve the dilemma in the light of detailed information about the situation: for example, the implications, for everyone involved, of being untruthful. But to ask this is to bring consequences into the picture, thus demonstrating the tendency in practice to take a range of different considerations into account.

The Kantian categorical imperative is of particular relevance to the developmental perspective which I am adopting in this book: I refer especially to the principle of respect for persons, and to the idea of community (the 'realm of ends'). There are also close connections with that cluster of related concepts dealing with rights, justice and discrimination. For example fairness in the allocation of bonuses in the workplace, or in the identification of those who may be made redundant, implies just procedures. However, in practice, the rights and interests of particular individuals in organizations frequently have to be weighed in the balance against the more diffuse interests of other stakeholders. Analysis of such issues thus draws on utilitarian modes of thought, as well as deontological principles.

Non-utilitarian consequentialism

Clearly there is a difficulty in adhering solely to one normative ethical position, and indeed the distinctions between them can be blurred. This is apparent if we consider the idea of non-utilitarian consequentialism suggested by Mackie (1977: 149–50). This refinement allows us to take account of consequences, but without adhering to the cold logic of utilitarian calculations. It enables explicit concern to be shown towards particular interests, rather than being slave to an ostensibly impartial method which in practice harbours value-judgments on, for example, the value of human life. In non-utilitarian consequentialism an action is evaluated in terms of its consequences, but these consequences are assessed in terms of principles which bear resemblance to those advocated by deontologists or are held by intuitionists (for example respect for human life, justice; see Raphael, [1981] 1994: 44). Thus such principles, as applied to the interests of particular individuals or groups, could override other, utilitarian, consequences, such as the financial benefits to a larger number of people.

Now, as Mackie noted, there can be considerable difficulty in distinguishing deontology from non-utilitarian consequentialism, largely because of problems encountered when we try to separate acts from their consequences. Here it is important to stress the deontological emphasis on moral agents' motives. For the deontologist, lying is wrong because, by definition, it entails the wilful misleading of another person. But consider the situation where a company launches an unsafe product. Arguably, the deontologist is concerned with the act of marketing rather than with the consequences of that action. In itself, the act of marketing the product may not be unethical in the eyes of a deontologist, unless there is an intention to mislead, through dishonest advertising and sales, thus causing or permitting harm. Such dishonesty would then be inherent in the act of advertising and selling of the product, and would reflect the motives of a business person who is well aware of the consequential implications of such behaviour. But in a case where no one in the company was aware of the life-threatening problems until after the adverse consequences had arisen, a deontologist would say that that there is no moral blame. Nevertheless, a situation has arisen of which we disapprove, on consequentialist grounds.

Consider the well documented case of the Ford Pinto, where it was known, before its launch onto the market, that the fuel tank was liable to rupture under certain conditions, with fatal results. There is little doubt that members of management were aware of the problems and the risks attached. They engaged in a process of self-justification, applying what seemed to be a utilitarian vindication for the decision to market the vehicle. This was based on a cost-benefit analysis: that the cost of anticipated casualties, valued in actuarial terms, was outweighed by the benefit to the company and its employees (Dowie [1977] 1987).

A host of issues can be raised concerning what to include in such a calculation: whether one can value a life, and so on. These reflect the objections to utilitarianism which I mentioned earlier; but that is not my point. My point is to raise the question of motives and consequences. In some situations one could say that the case against launching an unsafe product, when based on concern for human welfare, is, strictly speaking, based on a non-utilitarian consequentialist argument rather than on a pure deontological one, since there was never any intention to cause harm to people, and since this was not even anticipated. Only if those responsible were aware in advance of probable consequences, as in the Pinto case, would we be in the realm of deontological argument. Those responsible could then be accused of disingenuousness and deliberate negligence, even if not wilful intent to harm.

These matters are relevant to questions which I address later, especially in Chapter 8. To whom, or what, do we attribute responsibility? Can one attribute responsibility to an organization, as opposed to its members? Would that entail the evaluation of observable, but perhaps unintentional, consequences, rather than the subjectively understood motives and intentions of individual managers?

Altruism, emotion and character

A distinction between egoism and altruism is, if only implicitly, central to my argument in this book. Some discussion is called for at this juncture, however, in order to dispel the idea that there is a simple dichotomy between altruistic good and egoistic evil. While one may be in vague agreement with that position, the issues are not so clear-cut when we examine the concepts involved.

Egoism

Egoism reflects self-interest, not just in the material sense, but including such things as recognition, and also the 'enlightened' form where the motive behind concern for others is essentially self-centred. As a normative position, egoism is difficult to support. There are various versions from which to choose, but none is convincing (Baier, 1993). Possible candidates include the view that if everyone pursued their self-interest, the common good would be maximized. Yet Adam Smith, so often held up as the original advocate of this view, had premised his argument on the assumption that people were able to exercise some self-restraint in their economic and commercial lives; that 'Every man, as long as he does not violate the laws of justice, is left perfectly free to pursue his own interest his own way' (Smith, [1776] 1904: 184; in Book IV, Chapter IX). This is consistent with his earlier view that people should be able to demonstrate their 'moral sentiments' or impartial 'sympathy' with others' position (Raphael, 1985; Smith, [1759] 1976).

In another version, any possibility of altruism is denied altogether. This is psychological egoism; the view that, at root, all human action is self-interested, even if the intention is to help others. According to this view, people, whatever they do, have a hidden, perhaps subconscious, but self-interested motive; to win approval from others perhaps, or simply to feel good.

Altruism

Altruism is frequently posited as the alternative to, or opposite of, egoism. It is viewed as a concern for others, whereas egoism is defined in terms of self-interest. But on closer analysis altruism does not preclude concern for oneself. Thus

> to say that an act is altruistic is only to say that it involves and is motivated by a genuine regard for another's welfare; it is not to say that in performing it the agent neglects his own interests and desires. (Blum, 1980: 10)

So the relationship between egoism and altruism is not dichotomous. It is a 'behavioral continuum ranging from complete indifference to the interests of others (at one extreme) to complete responsiveness (at the other), with innumerable gradations in between' (Galston, 1993: 120).

Although we may talk colloquially of 'concern for others', 'service', 'duty' and other comparable ideas, if we agree with the statements above then it seems that some degree of concern for self is also permissible at the same time.

In a comprehensive analysis, Galston distinguishes between the objects of altruism and the motives for altruism. Rorty views moral progress as 'the ability to think of people wildly different from ourselves as included in the range of "us"' (1989: 192). But Galston, without denying the laudability of this view, raises the objection that any definition of altruism which recognizes everyone, including total strangers, as the objects of our concern, implies the possibility of conflict between acting in the interests of such others and in the interest of people to whom one is closer, such as relatives or neighbours. In that context Galston distinguishes between 'personal', 'communal' and 'cosmopolitan' altruism thus:

> *Personal* altruism is directed toward individuals near at hand, such as family members and friends. *Communal* altruism is directed toward groups of individuals possessing some shared characteristics: members of an ethnic group, coreligionists, and fellow citizens, among others. *Cosmopolitan* altruism, by contrast, is directed toward the human race as a whole, and hence toward individuals to whom one has no special ties. (Galston, 1993: 123)

On the question of motive, Galston notes three distinct types of basis for altruism: sympathy with others, or emotion (Blum, 1980), rationality (Nagel, 1970), and identity, or expression of self 'in which the customary boundary between self and others becomes indistinct' (Galston, 1993: 125).

The conflict between the various objects of altruism, referred to above, arises most obviously with the Kantian emphasis on universality. That position would lead us towards cosmopolitan altruism, although this can also stem from identity with humans in general. From the Kantian position, we would be expected to adopt a concern for others as a universal principle. Hill points out that from this perspective 'the possibility of altruism does not turn on what *sentiments* we have but rather on whether we can find adequate *reasons*, on reflection, for adopting at least the modest maxim of beneficence' (1993: 18).

However, that maxim doesn't help us out of the types of dilemma alluded to above. Nor does it tell us what precise form this concern might take in its realization. This is to repeat earlier remarks about the inevitable imprecision in such a theoretical formulation. The same sort of problem arises with utilitarianism, where not infrequently the larger number of people affected by an action, whose interests should therefore hold sway, would require sacrifices to be made by a minority (who may be closer to home). However, as we shall see later, utilitarianism, Kantian ethics, and variants of these, can do little more than point out different ways of thinking about situations; in themselves they do not provide practical solutions to our dilemmas.

Moral autonomy, emotion and gender

The relationship between emotion and ethics deserves much more treatment than I am able to provide here, as does the role of emotion in organizational life specifically (Fineman ed., 1993; Oakley, 1992; Peters, 1973; Solomon, [1976] 1993a). Emotional forces are important in heightening awareness of moral issues, in securing commitment to values, and in energizing the individual towards appropriate action. Moreover, a distinction between emotion and Kantian rationalistic moral duty, as two different bases for altruism, parallels Kohlberg's distinction between the conventional and the post-conventional (or autonomous) levels of moral development. Kohlberg's use of the term 'autonomy' is very much based on the Kantian definition, in which moral agents are viewed as detached from their own feelings, inclinations and personal attachments, while they engage in an impartial, unemotional application of ethical principles.

According to Blum (1982) Kant saw moral reasoning and decision-making (especially in the public domain) as the responsibility of men, with women playing a supportive, indeed subservient, role. Consistent with this and with his denial of any place for feelings in moral action, Kant saw emotion as a feminine characteristic. This is relevant to what has certainly been one of the most celebrated critiques of Kohlberg, one which is closely related to the question raised in Chapter 2, concerning whether or not the post-conventional level is indicative of a morally (as opposed to merely cognitively) more developed state. Here, Gilligan (1982) pointed out that Kohlberg's research was conducted with young male subjects. Based on her own research into women's responses to hypothetical moral dilemmas comparable to those used in Kohlberg's tests, she contended that there are alternative reactions to such issues, expressed 'in a different voice', both literally and in their content. She argued that the Kantian justice-based morality seen in Kohlberg's level-three reasoning reflects what is characteristically associated with rational 'male' thinking, devoid of an emotional impulse, dealing impartially with people in general, in the abstract. As an alternative, Gilligan referred to a distinctively 'female' morality of care, or compassion, for people to whom one is close, or for whom one feels responsible. This emphasis on relationships with particular people would not only recognize the possibility of an emotional response towards them, but, importantly, would require that moral responses and judgments recognize features of the specific context prevailing at the time. That would reflect Kohlberg's conventional level: 'living up to what is expected by people close to you' (Kohlberg, 1986: 488). And it would also suggest that such morality, rather than being developmentally inferior to that at the post-conventional level, should simply be regarded as different.

It must be stressed that Gilligan (1982: 2) did not claim a literal connection between gender and moral response. Moreover Rest (1986: 111–18) reported findings in which men as well as women were exposed to the same conditions and tests as in Gilligan's studies, without any significant variation emerging in the results. It may be that it is different ways of thinking, a masculinity–femininity distinction (Hofstede, 1980; Almond, 1990) which explains the contrast in responses, rather than gender as such.

Clearly, then, there are important reasons for examining the concept of autonomy in Kohlberg's thinking more closely. Certainly, Kohlberg adopts the Kantian position; but as Petrovich (1986) points out, he also implies a psychological interpretation whereby individuals can form their own opinions and principles rather than merely conforming to those around them. In other words, both concepts of autonomy (from 'self' and from 'others') are needed for people to act at the post-conventional level as defined by Kohlberg. They must be able to think in terms of abstract moral principles (the cognitive dimension in Kohlberg) and they also require the capacity to act against pressure from others if need be.

The practical implications of this should be spelled out. Were people to possess only the (psychological) capacity for independence from others' influences, without any moral restraint, then this would permit egoistic conduct; we would be back to Kohlberg's preconventional, amoral, level. So some sort of moral restraint is called for. But would that moral sense have to represent Kantian deontology? In another contribution from feminist ethics, Meyers (1987) observes that Kantian adherence to universal, impartial, principles is not the only mode of deliberation which meets the requirements of moral self-governance. Meyers questions whether adherence to such impartial rules really ensures the moral expression of persons' true selves. As an alternative, she offers the idea of 'responsibility reasoning' as a way of accommodating the morality of care. In this mode, people would ask whether they could take personal moral responsibility for their actions in particular circumstances. They would ask themselves: 'Could I bear to be the sort of person who can do that?' (Meyers, 1987: 151).

The virtues: character

What we are moving towards here is an emphasis on the character of the individual rather than the morality of a particular action. The question, 'what sort of person should I be?' as opposed to 'what should I do?', is the essence of virtue ethics. The ancient Greek philosophers, notably Plato and Aristotle, emphasized qualities such as wisdom (entailing knowledge and judgment), justice, beneficence, courage and moderation, the last of these referring to the need to hold other characteristics in balance. A re-emergence of interest in the virtues and personal character has been a feature of philosophical ethics in Western societies during the latter part of the twentieth century, perhaps in part due to concern at an apparent eclipse of moral values in society generally, and certainly due to a related and growing disillusionment with the applicability of modern, rationalistic, theories (Anscombe, 1958; MacIntyre, [1981] 1985; and see Jackson, 1996).

Until the 1990s, concern for the virtues made few inroads into academic business ethics, although there were notable exceptions (for example, Walton, 1988). This lack of impact may well have been due to the incompatibility between the perspective from virtue theory and managers' problem-centred orientation. As Klein has suggested, there appears to be a 'convergence of business persons' and analytic philosophers' attitudes' (1989: 61), while Larmore has observed that:

> Modern moral theory in its two principal forms, Kantianism and utilitarianism, has urged that what is morally right can be fully specified by rules. Indeed, this demand for a fully explicit decision-procedure was a reaction to what modern moralists perceived as the intolerable vagueness of Aristotle's appeals to [moral judgment]. (Larmore, 1987: 4–5)

Yet contemporary scepticism concerning the usefulness of consequentialist and deontological theory parallels that now expressed in many quarters with regard to the techniques and theories of management science. (On this latter point see Thomas, 1993.)

Virtue ethics has a significance which goes beyond specific ethical dilemmas and decisions. In particular, the focus on character means that qualities such as courage, beneficence and wisdom are relevant to leadership; and as Klein (1989) emphasizes, thinking in these terms provides a valuable perspective on the development of organizational cultures conducive to enhanced moral awareness among individuals. The virtues also relate to factors such as altruism, emotion in its relation to empathy, emotional self-control, and autonomy from one's own prejudices. These are all matters of relevance to the position I am adopting, especially regarding management development (in Chapter 12). Meanwhile, in the next section I shall consider the necessity for judgment in the resolution of moral dilemmas. This will anticipate a further practical development of that argument in Chapter 4.

The importance of moral judgment

For Aristotle, wisdom was the ability to see what is the right thing to do in particular circumstances. Thus, from the perspective of virtue ethics, one might talk of a person who possesses a sense of justice, rather than talking of a 'just' decision (Anscombe, 1958). As Walton observes, with virtue theory attention is shifted 'from the act performed to the performer of the act, from emphasis on thinking to emphasis on being, from the single act to the series of acts' (1988: 177).

This characteristic of the virtuous person entails the exercise of moral judgment, although as Larmore (1987: 19) notes, it is 'exemplary' that one cannot easily explain what judgment actually is. It does not entail the abandonment of moral principles, so much as bearing these in mind as one thinks about a particular situation. Such principles can provide us with reasons for acting one way rather than another. In the Aristotelian view, one learns to do this through practical experience; this is how one becomes a virtuous person. In short, we are left in a state of necessary uncertainty, trusting that in our wisdom we can adequately resolve each moral dilemma as it confronts us.

I shall try to recapitulate. The 'modern' ethical theories (consequentialism and deontology) are at the same time too precise and too vague. Too precise, because they each assume particular logical structures and underlying principles which lead to conclusions which are fundamentally different from those enabled by other, equally valid, perspectives. Too vague, because in the attempt to provide generally applicable formulations, they necessarily employ abstract terms such as utility, or respect for persons, which must then be interpreted in the concrete situations which provide the context for our ethical dilemmas.

Thus whatever the merits of these theories, they are not enough. What is missing is some sort of heuristic or framework which enables us to make sense of the detail of particular situations and to guide our judgment. This applies not only to decisions, in the sense typically depicted in management texts, but to our conduct more generally. To choices, for example, on how assertive or deferential to be in any given situation.

The idea of prima facie duties

Is there an approach which would help us here? As a starting point, one can go back to Oxford in the 1930s, where the Aristotelian scholar David Ross developed his theory of prima facie duties (Ross, 1930). This theory was for many years regarded as unfashionable, but has recently been the subject of renewed interest (Dancy, 1993a; Donaldson, 1989). It offers an approach to the handling of ethical dilemmas which will assume particular importance as the present argument unfolds.

A prima facie duty is, in essence, something which appears to us as a moral obligation, but which in the particular circumstances may be overridden by other ethical demands. Ross tells us that moral principles such as keeping promises, or not harming others, indicate prima facie duties, but it isn't a case of saying that one moral principle is 'right', or 'true', and another 'wrong'; they are all 'true', but, depending on the specific circumstances, some may emerge as more important than others in the resolution of a particular dilemma.

Ross called the chosen course of action one's 'duty proper' or 'actual duty'. I return to that later, but it should be noted that this would not be found in the answer to the question, 'to which prima facie duty should I give priority?' but in the answer to the question, 'what, taking everything into account, should I do?'

Ross (1930: 21) offered a categorization of prima facie duties, which I shall paraphrase as follows:

1 Duties resting on one's own previous acts; including (a) fidelity, as in keeping a promise and (b) reparation, or the duty to make good a previous wrong.
2 Duties of gratitude; in response to the (good) acts of others towards oneself.
3 Duties of justice; to prevent an unfair distribution.
4 Duties of beneficence; concerning an improvement in the condition, variously defined, of others. (Ross refers here to improvement in persons' 'virtue', 'intelligence' and 'pleasure'.)
5 Duties of self-improvement.
6 Duties of non-maleficence; the obligation not to harm others.

Ross stressed that this 'catalogue of the main types of duty . . . makes no claim to being ultimate' (1930: 23). Accepting the licence implied in this statement, the interpretation of prima facie duties which I shall employ here allows for anything which someone 'apprehends' (Ross's term) as such. It is this possibility – the apprehension of what people believe to be their prima facie duties – with which I am primarily concerned. Thus apart from those precepts familiar to students of Western ethical thought (for example, helping others, keeping promises, or redressing injustice) one could add such moral demands as the observance of specific holy occasions, or not taking interest on financial loans, as required according to Islamic or some other religious codes.

Plainly in so far as religious doctrine states that something is an absolute, it cannot, on a strict interpretation, be a prima facie duty, if that implies that it can be overridden. But my position is that the term prima facie does not preclude religious absolutes. It is just that while they are apparent at first sight, they will not be overridden unless, of course, two or more such demands were to conflict in a particular situation. The reasons for my all-encompassing definition will become more apparent later, but in general terms are to do with the need for a relatively simple and universally applicable approach to the *process* of dealing with ethical conflicts in management.

Following Aristotle, Ross maintained that we discover our prima facie duties for ourselves through 'moral experience' and we apprehend them intuitively. Now it is important, for what will be said later, to clarify what is meant by intuition in the sense used by Ross and other moral philosophers. It refers to the claim that we can know, through some sort of direct, non-empirical, awareness, whether an ethical principle or proposition is true or not; for example, that helping others is morally good, or that inflicting physical pain is bad. However it is not intended that the broader formulation being adopted in the present argument be confined to that philosophical meaning of intuition, and to that extent it departs from Ross's view. It is the *idea* of a prima facie moral obligation which is retained.

This process of moral learning, as one becomes aware of prima facie duties in concrete situations, is related to (but is certainly not confined to) what Kohlberg (1973) meant when he talked of the emergence of commitment to particular moral values and concerns following emotionally significant experiences. Thus for example the personal experience of being subjected to discrimination, unfairly, in your view, heightens your more general awareness of this type of inequity.

The critical point is that (perhaps barring religious absolutes as alluded to earlier, which would take us into a different realm) for virtually any principle, or prima facie duty, one can think of, one could also think of situations in which one feels that such a duty would be overridden by some other factor. So none is absolute; and what is more, no single normative ethical theory can tell us in advance what we ought to do in any anticipated circumstances, since we will need to know much more about the detailed context when the situation arises.

> There is no general ranking of the different types of prima facie duty, and since different moral principles express different prima facie duties, there is no general ranking of moral principles. There is just a shapeless list of them, which is no more than a list of the things that make a moral difference, a difference to what we should do. (Dancy, 1993b: 221)

Thus while we may feel certain about our 'apprehension of the self-evident *prima facie* rightness of an individual act of a particular type' (Ross, 1930: 33), we have, at least initially, no such certainty about our actual duty in a concrete situation; this will come down to judgment in the specific circumstances prevailing.

Moral concepts and moral context

The uniqueness and complexity of many ethically significant management situations means that any moral principle that is going to be some use is going to have to cover a variety of different [specific] situations, and in so doing it must give an incomplete description of the [general type of] situation it is intended to cover, leaving unspecified those areas in which they are allowed to differ. (Dancy, 1993a: 92)

Consider the application of the moral precept 'keep promises' in the following case. I have (rashly) promised an unemployed acquaintance that I will find him work in my business. As the owner, I have the right to do this, so there is no problem in that respect. But, of necessity, I have been rather vague; I cannot tell what sort of job it will be, nor what sort of contract I will arrange. I have not anticipated the possibility that some quite unexpected circumstance could arise which overrides the original promise; for example, if a serious financial downturn leaves me struggling to honour contracts to existing employees before I can even contemplate taking on new staff. The general promise might appear fairly unambiguous, but the detailed context could confront me with all sorts of difficulties and dilemmas of an embarrassing nature.

Dancy bases much of his thinking on Ross's theory of prima facie duties. In effect, it is these that constitute the necessarily vague principles, such that they need to be interpreted in the light of the actual circumstances. But what is it about a particular situation which enables us to say that, for example, the obligation to keep a business appointment should, or should not, take precedence over the duty to help a sick neighbour? For Dancy, this is understood in terms of the 'salient features' of the situation: the seriousness of the neighbour's condition, whether other sources of help are at hand, the importance of the appointment, whether or not it is too late to postpone or cancel it, the degree of inconvenience for the other party if one does call off, and so on.

All of these features of the situation lend to it what Dancy calls 'ethical shape'.

To see a feature as salient is to see it making a difference to what one should do in the case before one. Since there are normally several different salient features, related to each other in various ways, a full view of the circumstances will not only see each feature for what it is but will also see how they are related to each other. Such a view will grasp the *shape* of the circumstances. From saliences we move to shape. A situation has a shape in the sense that its properties have a practically related profile. There are the properties which are here non-salient; they are as it were on the valley floor. Rising from that level are the various peaks, major or minor, which are the properties which make a practical difference to the case. (Dancy, 1993a: 112)

In short, the same ethical proposition, comprising moral concepts and principles, assumes varying significance depending on the salient features of any specific situation as perceived by the individual. Now recall that the principles implied in this (such as promise-keeping, or helping those in need) equate with Ross's prima facie duties. By that definition, such principles are in themselves all equally valid, and, in the actual situation confronting one, it would be wrong to say that one or more are 'true' and others are not. They are all true, otherwise one would not have identified them prima facie. So the idea that in prioritizing *one* among a number of such conflicting 'oughts' means that the others are no longer 'oughts' also, is untenable.

This is what Dancy means when he addresses the problem of one's actual duty in the particular circumstances by introducing the idea of 'defeated reasons'. Defeated reasons are those prima facie duties which have been overridden by other ethical considerations, but which, as Dancy points out, are nonetheless important to what one does, and how one does it.

> For instance, I have to break some bad news to my sister. The distress I shall cause her is not sufficient reason for me to keep silent; as a reason against, it is defeated. But it still makes a difference to how I should break the news to her, when and where I should do it and so on. So it remains in the picture as a practically relevant consideration, even though it does not count among those features of the action which reveal why I do it. It is not a reason for doing it, but it is a reason for doing it this way rather than that. (Dancy, 1993a: 116–17)

In other words, such 'defeated reasons' still affect the manner in which one goes about one's business; the timing of decisions, the demeanour adopted in conveying information regarding, say, redundancies, or the precautions one might take to guard against harm to particular interests.

Conclusion

My concern in this chapter has been with the applicability of ethical theory to management practice. Much of the theory traditionally offered as the basis of business and managerial ethics teaching is rationalistic; it appears to offer an exact approach to resolving moral dilemmas, inviting independent reasoning by the individual and stressing the ideals of impartiality and detachment from one's own emotional ties. This may be termed a 'morality of justice'. However it has been argued that this represents a particular and not necessarily typical mode of thought, and ignores the significance of specific moral demands from those in one's own immediate circle; a 'morality of care'. That objection is consistent with a further problem, which is that the more rationalistic theories invariably require interpretation in actual situations; in other words, there is a need for contextualization and moral judgment. Each of these positions, the morality of justice and the morality of care, has some merit, and the judgmental process can draw upon the insights which each offers, depending on the particular situation in question. Such judgment, and also the likelihood of dissensus among people in organizations and a consequent need for dialogue, can then be more systematically considered. I shall turn to that in the next chapter.

4 Moral Judgment and the Management Process

The argument in the previous chapter leaves us musing over the place of modern, consequentialist and deontological, ethical theory. Such theory is still the stock in trade of many books on business and management ethics; and educational programmes still explore the possibility of its use. For example Chryssides and Kaler offer a 'checklist for moral evaluation', which requires, among other things, that one should calculate 'the utility and disutility of actions' and apply 'the test of universalizability to motives' (1993: 106). Many other business ethics texts include some sort of model for ethical decision-making (for example Treviño and Nelson, 1995; Vallance, 1995). In essence, these invite us to define the situation and the issues, and then to follow some sort of ethical reasoning process so as to arrive at a decision. In this chapter I offer an approach which, while retaining the idea of structured, systematic, analysis, is based on the theory of prima facie duties and judgment. I then recognize the pluralist, often political, nature of organizations by considering the need for dialogue amongst those involved in ethical issues.

Most attempts at formulating an 'ethical decision-process' for business and management ethics are symptoms of a tendency to cling to the ideal of some sort of instrumental rationality, impelled by the belief that if we follow those steps, this consequence (an ethical outcome) will result. It is the same tendency, noted in the previous chapter, which led to a favouring of modern ethical theories over virtue theory in business ethics. In our intellectualization of the process we struggle to maintain an appearance of being in control, yet we admit that it isn't really how things are done in practice. This has provoked a variety of critical responses, as I have already indicated. Duska points to the similarities between the Aristotelian position and postmodernism, suggesting that: 'We are all postmodernists trying not to be. Time after time we see that applying ethical theories to particular situations or practices doesn't result in any answer' (1993: 243). And Collier suggests that: 'Textbooks . . . present these competing and conflicting theoretical approaches in a way which leaves the student as bemused as the business practitioner' (1995: 144).

It is true that ethical theory can help us to identify the problem, and also to test different possible courses of action involving what are often competing moral principles. In a sense, therefore, normative ethical formulations such as Kant's categorical imperative or utilitarianism can be used in an instrumental fashion; they tell us that 'if we do this, then these principles (for example, fair treatment of all employees) will be violated', or 'those consequences (which will be more or less ethically acceptable to us) will result'. But any such modern ethical theory, because it must 'cover a variety of different situations' (Dancy, 1993a: 92) still demands interpretation in the concrete circumstances. Also, the very fact that the principles involved in different theories are liable to be in conflict means that, taken as a whole but lacking coherence, modern moral philosophy cannot in itself tell us which course of action to choose. There is no agreement on which is the best; each formulation has its own weaknesses and strong points, and as a result more than one theory may be useful in its own way in handling a particular case.

Rationality, intuition and judgment

The idea of a 'rational decision-process' practised by managers dies hard, and it is not surprising that so many people interested in business ethics have found this seductive. For example, Soler states that: 'Not only do businesses act – they act *rationally*, according to a rational decision-making procedure' (1990: 197). Certainly organizations have formal procedures, for decision-making, planning, financial control, and so on; but the individual manager's actual day-to-day activity is largely reactive, without much opportunity to use theory in an instrumental manner, in advance of action. The nearest that many managers get to that rational approach is to follow a few simple principles and practices that have served them adequately in the past. Thus Cederblom and Dougherty suggest that: 'It is more common for people simply to act in ways that have become ingrained in their character than to deliberate over what actions are right and wrong' (1990: 67).

This may, perhaps, be understood in terms of intuition. Not the ethical intuition as in Ross's theory concerning the apprehension of prima facie duties, so much as the manner in which previous experiences, including formal learning, can accumulate as taken-for-granted knowledge, which is then drawn upon without any conscious recollection of its origins in the past life of the individual manager (Agor, 1986). According to Isenberg

> intuition is not the opposite of rationality, nor is it a random process of guessing. Rather, it is based on extensive experience both in analysis and problem solving and in implementation, and to the extent that the lessons of experience are logical and well-founded, then so is the intuition. (Isenberg, 1984: 86)

This, yet again, moves us in the direction of judgment as an essential element of the management process. Mintzberg has said that managers 'use the word "judgment" to refer to thought processes that work but are unknown to them. "Judgment" seems to be the word that the verbal intellect has given to the thought processes that it cannot articulate' (1976: 54).

In the field of applied ethics, also, Jamieson (1993) has discussed the problematic relationship between moral theory and moral practice. Moral theorizing, he points out, is an everyday activity, practised by people in general, not just academics. Moral theories are derived from this process, not the other way round, and thus anyone could generate a 'moral theory' relevant to this or that. But of course programmes in ethics for managers tend to refer to the theories which I outlined in the previous chapter, and it happens that, as fairly abstract systems of thought, such theories reflect what people in general may be considering as they assess their own dilemmas, label others as either more or less ethical, evaluate events, and so on.

Jamieson observes that while some hold to the view that abstract theories of ethics are not used in actual moral decision-making, this overstates the case. The process of continual evaluation and re-evaluation of one's own, and others', moral theorizing, results in 'theories or theory-fragments . . . [which, while they] may not play a starring role in moral decision-making . . . surely have some effect, even if indirectly, on our moral practices' (Jamieson, 1993: 480). All of this suggests that there is a case for including ethical theories in management education programmes. The processes of moral sense-making, reflection, theorizing and intuition, not uncommon among people generally, can extend to managers specifically (Snell, 1993: 194–6), and can inform both their apprehension of prima facie duties and judgment as to their duty proper.

In this context it is important to note a distinction between circumstances in which people have to react instantaneously, or at least very quickly, to situations, and those circumstances in which they (or their advisers) have time to think, diagnose situations, reflect and decide. In many situations people do not have the time to take deliberative action. In other cases, such as the criticism or evaluation of others' plans when designing new systems of work-organization (often the responsibility of consultants), or the drafting of codes of ethics, there is normally an opportunity for reflection and deliberate ethical choice.

Awareness, conceptualization and the judgmental mode

An approach to managerial ethics which is based on the idea of prima facie duties seems to get closer to the way in which people in organizations do actually think about moral issues (when they think about them at all). This view has been confirmed by a number of practising managers with whom I have discussed it on part-time academic programmes. Nevertheless, it also seems that exposure to the various normative theories of ethics introduced in Chapter 3, and to discussion of all sorts of substantive ethical issues, do still provide valuable conceptual resources for the handling of ethical dilemmas. Surely someone who is aware of the different perspectives offered by deontological and consequentialist reasoning will be alert to alternative arguments in a way that others may not? So when considering the agenda for ethics education, or the provision of guidance for practitioners, this does not mean one has to abandon these theories, so much as reappraise their function and potential.

Unlike the linear process indicated in the typical decision-model, I am now suggesting that the process of working on ethical issues and dilemmas entails four broadly defined activities as elements in the whole. But the whole is oscillatory or iterative; one engages in the different activities almost simultaneously, and, importantly, while what follows in this section concerns what may be termed a 'judgmental mode', there is also a need for a 'dialogic' mode in the context of organizational pluralism and moral dissensus, which will be considered in the next section.

The four elements of the judgmental mode are:

- *apprehension*: the recognition of prima facie duties;
- *conceptualization*: making sense of the detail of the situation; identifying 'salient features' (Dancy, 1993a); contextualization;
- *reasoning*: considering different perspectives on the situation, which could be derived from ethical theory. This helps with conceptualization and with the articulation of 'reasons' and 'defeated reasons' (Dancy, 1993a) which will inform a choice of overall action. However, such use of theory is quite likely to be a rationalization, after the event, and may be used in 'story telling' to support the position adopted;
- *judgment*: this permeates the whole process, especially the eventual selection of a course of action.

Apprehension

The distinction between issues and dilemmas, noted in Chapter 1, is important (Toffler, 1986). An issue in itself need not indicate a dilemma; it is more general than that, indicating something of moral significance, on which one may hold a view. Discrimination, employees' job security, and product safety, are examples of issues, and when they are present in concrete situations they give rise to what we may construe as prima facie duties apprehended by management; for example to remove injustices, or eliminate life-threatening features of product design. Although these may seem fairly obvious when they are pointed out, in reality they are not always so clear. Furthermore, while ethics programmes for management devote considerable attention to resolving dilemmas, where two or more moral demands are in conflict, in practice moral conflicts often remain latent. That is, some, but not all, of the issues implicated are recognized by those involved. Thus a capacity for 'apprehension' (Ross, 1930) of all the issues, and the moral demands which these impose, should be encouraged. The tensions that arise if these responsibilities or duties conflict constitute dilemmas, which calls for a course of action, or, in Ross's terms, 'duty proper'.

Conceptualization, reasoning and judgment

This overall process demands appreciation of the shape of the situation. As described in Chapter 3, one can identify some dimensions as more salient (more important) than others. These more important features will then inform action; although 'defeated reasons' still play a part (Dancy, 1993a: 116).

Consider, for example, the following case. I am the manager of a sales office with fifteen staff. I am summoned to the managing director's office, where, in a meeting with the heads of two other sales departments, together with the human resources manager, ideas for a contraction in company staffing are suggested by the managing director. Discussion is amicable, reasonably informed and focused on the argument that merging two or three of the sales departments will allow for a reduction in staffing. This is seen as the only way to make the necessary savings at a time of great financial stringency for the organization. An agenda for further consideration is agreed, and a second meeting is arranged for early in the following week. In that meeting various matters concerning the fair treatment of staff, and other ethical implications of the overall situation, will be considered. It is also agreed that the situation, being so sensitive, must be kept confidential until a clear decision is reached. The whole process has the aura of a systematically conducted analysis, although for at least one of those involved the emotional impact of such a morally significant situation is that manager's first work-related experience of this sort.

Two days later, in my own office, one of my senior staff, John, tells me that he has heard that there is going to be a reorganization and redundancies. I have an instant dilemma. A jumble of thoughts passes through my mind. While some sort of intuitive process is doubtless going on, and ideas about ethics punctuate this, in no sense is it indicative of the detached reasoning of the case workshop or the textbook problem. I know that if what John has told me really were news to me, I would express genuine surprise or denial. Unless I feign such a response, I am likely to break the confidence placed in me by my senior colleagues. But I also know that I am unlikely to be able to enact this pretence convincingly; I tend to believe that honesty is the best policy, and it would be too obvious to John that I was hiding something. In any case, the thought also crosses my mind that I should not lie to John. That is both a matter of principle and of prudence, therefore, since even if my lying were convincing, John would discover the truth sooner rather than later.

I ask John how he came to hear this story, and he tells me that he overheard the other two sales office managers talking about it. Quickly reckoning that (fortunately for me) John will not be asked to take redundancy, I decide to confirm what he claims to know. I request that he also says nothing to anyone else, and reassure him that as far as I am concerned he need not worry about his own job security.

What is going through my mind here? The issues are (1) my obligation to keep the matter confidential; (2) the principle of telling the truth to John; (3) concern for the consequences of (a) revealing the truth to John and (b) not doing so, only to be 'found out' later (presumably) for having shown a lack of trust in him, and being disingenuous to say the least.

There are at least some elements of self-interest here. Both of the points under (3) but especially (b) reflect a concern for my own image; I don't want to be accused of breaking an agreement with colleagues, nor do I want John, and perhaps others, to accuse me of lying. But (1), (2) and (3a) are, in some sense or other, prima facie duties: to keep a promise; to tell the truth (and to demonstrate trust in another); to protect the organization from needless disruption and damage to morale (although one might ask why it matters whether staff know in advance about the likely reorganization).

These prima facie duties are in conflict: hence my dilemma. Now as I have indicated, one can place a cynical interpretation on my actions; but I want to show how this sort of situation can be understood in terms of an ethical analysis, even if that is, in effect, conducted intuitively. So what are the salient features of this situation? Apart from the issues already outlined, I am particularly conscious of the following: the relatively short time before the matter will become public knowledge anyway; the fact that John is extremely unlikely to be made redundant, thus making it easier to talk to him about it; and the fact that I regard him as a reliable and responsible individual.

My principal reason for conceding that what he has heard is true is a desire not to lie or to display a lack of trust in him. A reason for *not* being truthful, which is defeated, is that I had entered into an agreement to maintain confidentiality. But this reason is recognized, nevertheless, in several practical respects: I ask John to maintain the confidence; I feel that it is less serious than it would be were a long period of time anticipated before the decision is made public; and I am able to reassure John regarding his own position.

This is based on a true episode. It demonstrates the imprecision and, in this instance, simultaneity, with which the components of the judgmental process are enacted. It is an attempt to impose some structure on something that was in large measure an intuitive decision, in a time-critical situation. But I think it demonstrates the way in which prima facie obligations are apprehended, how some sort of sense is made of the circumstances, and reasons for acting one way or another are weighed up, affecting the actual manner in which the situation is handled.

Furthermore, incidents such as these are learning experiences. They can enhance one's ability to make sense of situations, and provide specific concepts, which are of more general value for use on future occasions. In this case, one conceptual insight to emerge concerns 'trust'; in particular, the basis on which I decide whether or not to trust John in the circumstances. (The concept of trust is the subject of Chapter 5, when I shall return to this case, so I will not amplify the point here.) But it is only after the event, on reflection, that such conceptualization is articulated. It is a rationalization; and it must be recognized that even the interpretation in terms of morality, which is placed on such actions, can mask other, self-interested, motives. There is often an inescapable ambiguity in such action, concerning whether or not it really reflects a moral motive, or sense of obligation. This point is raised periodically in this book; but as a reason for ignoring the potential for ethical judgment, it is defeated.

Concepts may also emerge from the literature in any area of management, business or other substantive field. As such, they are derived from both theoretical reflection and empirical research. Real experiences such as that described in this case, serve a comparable function to empirical work in this respect. They stimulate inductive processes leading to the identification of important dimensions and variables applicable to a whole class of situation, in much the same way as, in social research, Glaser and Strauss described 'the discovery of grounded theory' (1967: especially Chapter XI).

Thus such concepts enable debate over moral issues and dilemmas (whether actual or case-based) to proceed, frequently using everyday language which nevertheless harbours implicit ethical-theoretical positions. This is consistent with the fact that in practice people in organizations seldom make explicit use of unfamiliar ethical jargon, although of course this does not preclude such technical language being introduced in formal teaching situations.

In any actual case, to attempt to force our interpretation of a situation into particular conceptual frameworks is contentious and fraught with epistemological difficulties, but the value of such conceptualization is precisely that: it opens up debate. In the coming chapters I shall explore some substantive areas where the literature has provided such concepts. It should also be mentioned that judgment enters into the identification of salient features and their prioritization; and that modern ethical theories provide arguments and reasons, perhaps entering the process in an intuitive manner as described earlier. So there may still be an element of reasoning, but this often takes the form of rhetoric in the context of dispute and dissent, which takes me to the other main strand in this discussion.

Pluralism and discourse: the dialogic mode

In Chapter 1, I noted the pluralist, political, nature of organizations. An inescapable feature of this is verbal interaction. Management is, among other things: 'Negotiated, involving bargaining over the boundaries, content and style of work . . . [It is] [i]nteractive, involving a high level of face-to-face communication' (Hales, 1993: 14). 'Organizations are created, sustained and changed through talk,' says Mangham (1986: 82) and he adds that:

> It is through words that members of organizations negotiate, it is through words that they appeal, persuade, request, coax, cozen, assign, declare, debate, agree, insult, confer, teach, advise, complain, irritate, anger, correct, socialize, recruit, threaten, promise, praise, ridicule, condemn and dismiss. (1986: 82)

This mingling of politics and discourse gives rise to a number of possibilities. To suggest three, which probably overlap: dressing up an argument in the language of ethics to hide an ulterior, perhaps self-interested, motive; engaging in politics out of genuine moral concern, a pragmatic approach to ethics where the end justifies the means; and restricting oneself to the organizationally acceptable language of productivity and efficiency, while harbouring an ethical concern for the implications of the discussion.

In the first type of situation individuals may dress up their personal, self-interested, aims, in moral language. Echoing points already made concerning rationality, rationalization, and the use of theory to justify action, it is worth noting the contribution in this respect by writers on public policy. Pelz (1978), for example, has observed that administrators and managers may use theory in a 'symbolic' or 'legitimating' manner, to publicly support – or justify to others – a decision taken on different, hidden, grounds. Similarly, a theory may be used to justify objections to another's policy. Such modes of theory-use are, of course, rational; but one must ask, rational for whom?

In the second type of situation, actions labelled by observers as 'political' may be sincerely motivated by ethical beliefs (Burns and Stalker, [1961] 1966: 145; and see Chapter 9 in this book). So 'virtuous' behaviour and ethical reasoning, as something personal, may be in pursuit of goals and values which may or may not be accepted by others in the organization. What appears to others as self-interest, but is presented as a moral case, may be genuinely felt as such.

Third, it is important to appreciate how the moral implications of conversation in organizations are frequently obscured by efforts to convey an impression of rational deliberation, referring to policy plans, the need for control and effectiveness, and so on. If someone is questioning the procedure by which a contentious decision on company reorganization was arrived at, she may be very conscious of the implications of this decision for employees' working conditions, but, significantly, does not make this explicit in moral language. To do so would shift attention from 'organizationally' acceptable matters to more partisan considerations. This may be a political gambit, but sometimes an underlying desire to voice concerns in explicitly ethical language is inhibited by the culture of the organization; 'moral muteness' prevails (Bird and Waters, 1989).

These possibilities serve to remind us that most people in organizations have not been exposed to academic ethical theory. They use everyday language rather than the technical vocabulary of ethics, employing words such as fair, unfair, right, wrong, dishonest and trustworthy. And they use common-sense judgment in the context of some sort of private, homespun moral reasoning.

The need for attention to moral discord

The contrast between everyday language and the lexicon of academic ethics indicates the danger of losing one's audience. Thus it is often maintained that books on business ethics should be written in more accessible language, in so far as they are produced for managers and management students. But that very point, and with it the associated call for authors to aim at satisfying managers' desire for simple, 'rational' decision-models, raises a further issue.

As is pointed out in a number of recent sources (Collier, 1995; Nielsen, 1990; Rossouw, 1994) the striking deficiency of many business ethics texts is this reliance on a conception of rationality which is unrealistic in the face of moral discord; and if one person insists on what is, in effect, a utilitarian position, while another insists on a Kantian position, then moral discord is what one will face. As MacIntyre has argued, the kind of Enlightenment reason which is assumed in management science, and which many managers hope to find in guidance from moral philosophers, 'can speak only of means. About ends it must be silent' ([1981] 1985: 54). One might add that since even means are value laden, and their choice also raises moral issues, such means-related scientific rationality would only be morally uncontentious where there was consensus on ethical concerns amongst those affected.

Texts on corporate social responsibility, which emphasize concern for issues (such as environmental pollution) rather than the handling of dilemmas, do often refer to the need for employee involvement in discussions over such matters as the drafting of codes of ethics (for example Clutterbuck et al., 1992; Manley, 1992). And most texts on business ethics do make some mention of possible disagreement over ethical issues, usually referring to differing viewpoints and to the need to appreciate these. But consideration of this matter rarely extends beyond such brief remarks; what is needed also is attention to processes, approaches or methodologies which can help in the management of such conflict. Thus some discussion is called for here of what I have labelled a 'dialogic mode' of managerial ethics.

Conversation and story-telling

Before mentioning specific methods for handling ethical conflicts in organizations, a word is needed on language and conversation itself, as the essence of social interaction. This area of enquiry has generated a long tradition of research, coming from different directions such as the philosophy of language, ethnomethodology and conversation analysis (Shotter, 1993). Writers such as Mangham (1986) and Boden (1994), both of whom have highlighted questions of politics and conflict in management, have addressed the question of language, talk and conversation in organizations specifically. There is also the study of organizational 'scripts' (Gioia, 1992), managers' moral talk (or lack of it) (Bird et al., 1989; Bird and Waters, 1989) and stories (Watson, 1994).

Dancy, discussing the handling of moral discord in actual situations, refers to an 'appeal to rationality', but he does not mean rational in the instrumental or scientific sense, on which I commented above, so much as something like reasonableness in listening to what others have to say. He maintains that one relies on the 'persuasiveness' of one's story to convince others, rather than 'trying to browbeat them with principles of rational choice or judgement' (1993a: 114). 'Rationality here is not to be seen as essentially related to the ability to construct or respond to arguments. It is more like the ability to listen to and appreciate a story' (Dancy, 1993a: 114).

Dialogic approaches: intervention, management style and discourse

Clearly, therefore, an approach to managerial ethics which takes account of social interaction, conversation and language, is a necessary supplement to the judgmental mode described earlier. Such an approach is found in what I call the dialogic mode, where one is dealing with protagonists representing conflicting interests and concerns. In this, were one to ask the commonsense question, 'what are the issues?' some parties would emphasize one concern or point of view and others would support an opposed concern. Now if these different concerns, or issues, had been apprehended by a single person, we could describe them as indicative of prima facie obligations and the conflict would appear as a dilemma, especially in so far as the competing claims of these different concerns were roughly equal. Such an individual would then engage in the judgmental approach. So, in the dialogic mode, the ideal is that all individuals should entertain all the issues, not just those to which they are initially committed. They then share the dilemma and proceed in the judgmental mode collectively.

There is a diversity of theories and methods available, and I do not intend to contribute much more to this literature other than outline the general theme and draw attention to its place in the field of management ethics as a whole. These methods bear comparison with a number of other approaches to changing and developing organizations, and methodologies for conflict resolution and problem-solving; and some of the latter embody ideas comparable to those contained in my judgmental mode. However, while the dialogic mode emphasizes individuals' leadership or management roles, the other methods I have in mind are often put forward for consultancy-based interventions. Examples are Process Consultation (Schein, 1987, [1969] 1988), Action Inquiry (Torbert, 1987), and Critical Systems Thinking (Flood and Jackson, 1991).

So far as approaches for the handling of ethical conflict are concerned, one particular point to note concerns the degree to which such conflict is seen as resolvable rather than inevitable. In some cases the aim is the attainment of moral consensus, while in others the view is that this is neither possible nor required, even if it is a desirable ideal. People would settle for a limited accommodation of their differing ethical views together with some practical, if restricted, progress towards resolving the substantive issues and dilemmas involved.

What I will do now is to outline some thinking specifically addressed to the handling of moral dissensus in organizations. This will provide a cue for some of the discussion in later chapters.

Nielsen (1990) contrasts his *Dialogic Leadership* approach with McGregor's Theory Y style (McGregor, [1960] 1987) and some other human relations approaches (for example, Coch and French, 1948; Likert, 1967). In the latter, the relative lack of mutual dialogue, and largely functional nature of the leader's concern while listening to subordinates, means that people may arrive at a practical solution without agreeing on any ethical matters involved. Often, it is in effect a technique for manipulating people into acceptance of organizational goals and values (Hart, 1988). In Dialogic Leadership, however, the ethical ideals underpinning the process transcend the limited needs of individuals or even of the organization as a whole. Concern is for moral obligations to a wider community. (I return to this in Chapter 6; and as I note in Chapters 10 and 11 it raises questions about the ontological status of organizations, their 'boundaries', and stakeholder interests.) Nielsen builds on the idea of Socratic dialogue, emphasizing open-mindedness, initial opinions held by others, the problems with these others' views, invitations to the others to consider alternatives, and mutual search for appropriate action which might even be at a cost to the participants and to the organization. In short, one becomes

> a different type of leader-manager. Instead of focusing on controlling or mastering others, events, issues, ethics or being, we serve a process, a process of dialogic ethics action (praxis) and dialogic search for potential truth (epistemology). (Nielsen, 1990: 769)

Subsequently, Nielsen refines this in terms of *I am We* consciousness (Nielsen, 1991). This is based on the ideas of the eighteenth-century American Quaker merchant and social reformer, John Woolman, and on Bernard Lonergan's distinction between the unity of two subjects 'in their response to a common object' and their 'being united in a transcendent, common consciousness of a prior "we"' (Nielsen, 1991: 651). Distinguishing it from other forms of dialogue (Socratic, Buberian) the essence of Woolman dialogue as propounded by Nielsen is a five-step process. This entails:

1. 'I's' first motion toward the 'other' is respectful, friendly, warm.
2. 'I' explains and explores with 'other' mutual commonalities of experiences, principles, and/or concerns.
3. 'I' asks 'other' for help in exploring issue and/or feeling entanglements (individual – cultural, technical, etc.) of positives–negatives, goods–bads through expressions of feelings, inductive experience based reasoning, and/or deductive principle based reasoning.
4. 'I' and 'other' explore in each 'other's' framework potential experiments for disentangling positives and negatives.
5. 'I' clearly and gently explains 'I's' experience/perception of entanglements and potential disentangled experimental solution, does not press, and waits for experimental results, good/fairness/light in 'I/other' to grow and emerge. (Nielsen, 1991: 652)

In a subsequent paper Nielsen points out that people reflect different traditions, have different perspectives and thus 'see different aspects of a story such that, in effect, there are several stories operating, not one objective story' (1993: 261). And Rossouw, following the relativist argument that competing ethical positions can be equally valid, argues that an alternative (to modernist) rationality is called for. 'This alternative or post-modernist rationality simply accepts multi-culturality and moral dissensus as an integral part of the contemporary world. Moral dissensus is no longer seen as an unfortunate development, but rather an interesting phenomenon' (Rossouw, 1994: 14).

Nielsen and Rossouw thus remind us that there are many situations, not least intercultural, where agreement on moral principles is not achieved, even though one may reach an accommodation in terms of a practical response. Both of these authors are concerned with what they claim are postmodern perspectives on this issue. However the relationship between postmodernism and ethics is sufficiently problematic (are we talking about postmodernism, or post-modernism; and is there a difference?) to justify the suggestion that our discussion is, for the time being, best pursued without the added complication of further exploration in that territory (Rasmussen, 1993).

Although he builds on the concept of an ideal speech situation, Rossouw departs from Habermas in that he allows for disagreement on validity claims for moral principles and norms. He assumes the possibility of moral dissensus, does not insist that we seek to overcome it, and proposes instead: 'Rational interaction . . . with a more modest aim than consensus' (Rossouw, 1994: 17). This rational interaction approach requires participants who have a stake in the actual moral issue involved, and who are prepared to discuss it 'in a rational and tolerant way'. Rationality here 'allows for arguments in which values, culture, religion, emotions, etc., are taken into consideration' (Rossouw, 1994: 17), while tolerance calls for respect for other stakeholders as moral agents who have a valid contribution to offer in the discussion, without necessarily being expected to give an account of any moral theory or tradition that may inform their position.

Of course, notwithstanding the 'more modest aim', one may hope that conflicting parties will reconsider their positions as a result of dialogue, through becoming aware of different points of view. These contrasting viewpoints might, as I suggested earlier, lead to recognition of additional prima facie duties which would then assume more or less importance in the overall search for a way forward. In short, combining Rossouw's and Nielsen's statements, we come back to Dancy's appeal for reasonableness; for rationality in the sense of an 'ability to listen to and appreciate a story' (Dancy, 1993a: 114).

Conclusion

Theory generally finds its way into management practice through the medium of intuitive, sometimes habituated, responses to situations, this almost invariably requiring an element of judgment. Thus theory does have an impact, even if this is not always recognized. The process by which managers may appreciate and resolve ethical dilemmas can be understood in terms which are similar to the apprehension and weighing up of prima facie moral demands, a process which is largely judgmental and intuitive. It is based on a conceptualization of the overall situation, and an appreciation of different perspectives and reasons for acting one way rather than another.

Importantly, the reality of management situations also requires that we recognize that there is frequently conflict and dissensus over moral issues, and thus a need for dialogue in an effort to arrive at an acceptable way forward. There are many approaches or methodologies which have been developed to help with such situations in the management context, although we also need to accept that, on occasion, it may not be possible to reach agreement on ethical issues in organizations.

PART TWO   MORAL ISSUES IN ORGANIZATIONS

---

5   Trust and Distrust in Organizations

The ethics of trust is an essential and pervasive feature of individual and organizational development. Issues involving trust in organizations are innumerable, but obvious examples concern the granting of responsibilities to employees, the communication of confidential information, and the demand for openness in debate and negotiation. Both substantive and procedural ethical issues are raised here, and thus this chapter fulfils two functions: it offers an analysis of trust as a moral concept, and it provides an opportunity to explore the judgmental and dialogic modes which I introduced in Chapter 4.

The centrality of trust in social relations

The maintenance of trust is essential for the coherence of any social system (Trusted, 1987: Chapter 7) and organizations are no exception to this truism. As Nash has said: 'Nearly every business decision and activity inherently has a moral aspect or significance. Many of these are variations on the quality of trust' (1990: 26). Until fairly recently, however, explicit and prominent reference to the topic featured less often than one might expect in academic writing on the subject. Writing as a philosopher, Baier observed that she searched in vain for such work. 'The question, "Whom should I trust in what way, and why?" has not been the central question in moral philosophy as we know it'; she added that:

> One would expect contractarians to investigate the forms of trust and distrust parties to a contract exhibit. Utilitarians too should be concerned with the contribution to the general happiness of various climates of trust, and so be concerned to understand the nature, roots and varieties of trust. (Baier, 1994: 96)

While Luhmann observes that:

> Trust has never been a topic of mainstream sociology. Neither classical authors nor modern sociologists use the term in a theoretical context. For this reason the

elaboration of theoretical frameworks, one of the main sources of conceptual clarification, has been relatively neglected. (1988: 94)

Nor has discussion of trust as an academic concept been prominent in the
field of management. Exceptions include Fox (1974b) who highlighted the
syndrome of low-trust relations resulting from the imposition of bureaucratic
controls in organizations, Culbert and McDonough (1985) who placed trust
at the centre of their analysis of political behaviour in organizations,
Fukuyama (1995) on cultural differences, and a collection edited by Kramer
and Tyler (1996) which reflects a recent interest, within the academic management and social science communities, in the dynamics of trust in
organizations. Other writers on management have made passing reference to
trust, as can be discovered from a glance at book indexes; one could name
Bennis and Nanus (1985), Greenleaf (1977), Nash (1990) and Watson (1994)
as examples, each with their own particular perspective.

Overall, an apparent lack of explicit discussion on this subject may be
because the concept of trust overlaps with so many others, such as confidence,
promise-keeping, obligation, cooperation, social exchange and reciprocity.
If one includes its treatment in these related terms, the coverage has been
quite substantial (Michalos, 1990). As a concept, it invites a multidisciplinary
analysis, and indeed those sources which do explore it at length represent a
variety of paradigms and emphases (see, for example, Gambetta, ed., 1988).

Of late, the rising tide of popular concern about ethics in public and business life has borne a scattering of journalistic and professional references to
trust. Two issues, perhaps two sides of the same coin, are harboured in this
concern; first, persons' willingness to trust others, and second, the keeping of
trust. Much of the recent writing to which I am alluding has been inspired by
Francis Fukuyama's *Trust: The Social Virtues and the Creation of Prosperity*
(1995) and his thesis concerning the social and economic benefits of a high-
trust society. Essentially, this represents a concern with the first of the two
issues to which I refer. On the other hand many columnists have focused on
specific episodes, such as the collapse of Barings Bank in 1995 (for example,
Stock, 1995), and on the need to put systems in place which act as a fail-safe
when we are let down by those in whom we had faith. Thus we are reminded
that while there is a moral demand (in the Kantian sense) to show respect for
people by trusting them, we also have a duty to those who may be affected by
the consequences should things go wrong if such trust is misplaced. Typical
of the overall public concern with current trends is this statement on the
wider cultural context for corporate ethics:

> Given that it is more and more difficult to build longstanding relationships, people
> need to know that they can have confidence in the people they encounter. Trust and
> reliability are becoming valuable commodities in a fast moving world. And once a
> reputation for trustworthiness is lost, it is difficult to restore. (O'Sullivan, 1995: 15)

In management, trust is central to leadership, work design and organization,
yet as a subject for conceptual and theoretical enquiry it is still relatively
incoherent. When considering ethical aspects of the internal management of

organizations, trust is especially significant in relation to the Kantian principle of respect for persons. To trust someone is to recognize his or her abilities and potential; it is to help in that person's development. This is germane to the question of work organization which I discuss in Chapter 6. That it may help the organization's development is, from the Kantian standpoint, incidental, although it is still an important point for management to heed. Trust is also relevant to several other aspects of organizational life which I address in other chapters: fairness and non-discriminatory practice, the idea of the organization as a moral community, and the dialogic aspects of working on moral issues and dilemmas.

Conceptualizing trust and distrust

The explicit development of concepts and theories concerning trust is, as I have said, relatively recent and disjointed. Nevertheless, some important ideas and distinctions may be noted.

Implicit and explicit trust

A distinction between implicit and explicit trust is perhaps the most fundamental, in that it alerts us to the way in which trust is suggested in so many other concepts. As a theoretical point it extends, in practice, to innumerable concrete situations. Blau ([1964] 1986: 94) distinguished between specific and non-specific obligations reposed in those who are trusted. Specific obligations are spelled out explicitly in formal agreements and bureaucratic edicts. Nonspecific obligations are implicit in general social and moral relations, and in organizational discourse, but may also arise within the specific parameters of a broadly defined role. This distinction between diffuse, or non-specific, and other more precisely defined types of obligation was also noted by Fox (1974a), who argued that non-specific obligations depend on trust for the maintenance of reciprocal relations in the workplace, this being what he termed a high-trust situation. Elsewhere, Fox devoted considerable attention to the syndrome which can come about as a low-trust, high-specificity, bureaucratic relationship develops (Fox, 1974b). This is one of the more pervasive themes encountered in the subject.

Vulnerability, risk and uncertainty

At this point I notice the unclear interpretation of the word, for there are some who in everyday parlance assume that 'to trust' entails total confidence in another, while many academic writers insist that trust necessarily means that some uncertainty is present (see for example discussions by Gambetta, 1988; and Horsburgh, 1960). This ambiguity signals a complex area of analysis, and what follows is an attempt at simplification sufficient for present purposes. To this end, I shall focus on three aspects of the complexity indicated, which contribute to a definition of the concept and help identify its ethical significance.

The idea of *vulnerability* refers to those respects in which one could suffer harm should one's trust in another prove unfounded. This is something to which Baier pays particular attention, because it is the realization of such vulnerability that reminds us, often too late, of the taken-for-granted trust-based nature of our social interactions and relationships. Thus Baier states that trust 'is accepted vulnerability to another's possible but not expected ill will (or lack of goodwill) toward one' (Baier, 1994: 99).

Then there is *risk*. According to Deutch, distinctive features of trust are: a choice of actions or an 'ambiguous path', such that one of these options could result in a harmful outcome, such outcomes depending on another's behaviour; and where the possible harm is greater than the benefit one seeks through the trust relationship (Deutch, 1962: 303). As Luhmann says, 'Trust is only required if a bad outcome would make you regret your action' (1988: 98). And this risk, of a worse outcome than one could have secured were one less trusting, is not the same as the probability of its occurrence. On that question of *uncertainty* Gambetta states that 'trust is particularly relevant in conditions of *ignorance* or uncertainty with respect to unknown or unknowable actions of other [persons]' (1988: 218). Thus the more constrained the other party, the less the likelihood of the risk arising and exposing one's vulnerability.

This takes us back to the possibility of total confidence. Strictly speaking, one can never have total confidence that nothing unexpected will happen, although doubtless it is easier to predict the intentional actions of a reliable friend than the possibly frustrating circumstances in which they may have to act. But one can argue that, by implication, the greater the uncertainty the less control there is over the other, and the more one can then regard one's trust in that person (if we are talking of individuals) as indicative of moral respect for her or him; one trusts that they will not let you down. And it may also indicate concern for the other person, in that, as I amplify below, such trust contributes to their moral development.

The ethics of distrust

Much of the emphasis in the literature tends to be on 'trust' rather than 'distrust'. For example, of the eighteen papers in Kramer and Tyler (1996) the titles of fifteen refer to 'trust', while only two refer to 'distrust'. The significance of this is that while so much discussion concerns conceptual clarification, the necessity of trust for social cohesion, or the ethics of *trustworthiness*, the act (or mental state) of (dis)trusting others is also of profound ethical concern. This has important consequentialist relevance, in that pervasive distrust does not make for a better world (Michalos, 1990). And in so far as one does distrust other people, it makes a difference, from a Kantian standpoint, whether one is questioning their motives, integrity, or other facet of their moral qualities, or whether one's doubts about their reliability rest simply on uncertainty as to their competence in a technical sense. That may be closer to a utilitarian position, in that it concerns their ability to contribute to the system. Associated with this, it also makes a difference whether one is passing judgment on someone in a particular situation, or in situations in general. Thus one can identify four 'ideal-type' possibilities (Maclagan, 1990b: 64):

1 *Distrust in general on grounds of motive.* This indicates a general and negative moral evaluation, implying that someone is self-interested or deceitful.
2 *Distrust in a specific context on grounds of motive.* This need not be such a serious moral criticism as in (1). The individual may be supporting a different set of values and interests from oneself in that particular situation, and indeed may feel strongly that he or she is morally right, but this would still give grounds for others to exhibit distrust. Examples might typically arise in the context of organizational politics.
3 *Distrust in general on grounds of competence.* This is barely a moral evaluation of the person, unless one holds that 'being incompetent' is morally reprehensible.
4 *Distrust in a specific situation on grounds of competence.* I maintain that this is not normally a moral evaluation of the person distrusted, but more probably refers to the suitability of the person for that role or task.

The idea of a distinction between distrust of someone in general, and distrust in relation to specific circumstances, is derived from Horsburgh (1960). An important part of his argument seems to be as follows. There is a form of trust which he called 'therapeutic' and which has a beneficial, developmental, effect on those in whom it is reposed. 'Open prisons, the more successful reform schools, and even such organisations as Alcoholics Anonymous all testify to the power of this kind of trust' (Horsburgh, 1960: 348). Thus he maintained that the nature of the trust relationship is 'one of the main ways in which one individual can affect the moral growth of another' (1960: 350). If we then argue that there is a moral obligation to recognize others' potential as moral agents, even if this seems optimistic in the light of their past conduct, it surely follows that we must endeavour to display trust in them.

On my other distinction, between motive and competence, Baier similarly differentiates between 'well-meant but ill-judged or incompetent attempts to care for what is entrusted [and] ill-meant and cleverly disguised abuses of discretionary power' (1994: 104).

Interpersonal and systemic trust relations

A pervasive underlying distinction in business and management ethics is that between individual action and systemic behaviour (see Chapter 8). The latter may amount to the impersonal, organizational, analogue of individual moral action, resulting in institutionalized outcomes which are ethically questionable. Thus it is that Fox noted that

> quite apart from personal trust or distrust between particular people, there can be said to be 'institutionalised' trust or distrust which is embodied in the social arrangements, decisions and policies which men seek to impose on each other. (1974a: 99)

These institutionalized relations need not necessarily mean that particular individuals stand accused of lack of trust, although perpetuation of unsatisfactory situations becomes a managerial responsibility. Nor, however, can we say that there is anything particularly virtuous in routinized, repetitive arrangements which amount to 'mutual predictability' (Baier, 1994: 136). Such trust, if that is what it is, ceases to have any moral quality.

High-trust and low-trust cultures

A final general observation on the ethics of (dis)trust is provoked by Fukuyama's recent book on low-trust and high-trust societies (Fukuyama, 1995). Leaving aside his utilitarian argument that the latter are more conducive to economic development, what can nevertheless be added is that trust 'is implicit in the codes of all societies' (Trusted, 1987: 84). Even if families or communities in remote areas of rural America or southern Italy are distrustful of outsiders, there are inevitable trust relations and moral expectations *within* those social groups. The ethics of *keeping* trust, therefore, may be a universal norm, albeit 'ultimately bound up with social customs and codes' (Trusted, 1987: 84).

By contrast, to return to the different matter of placing one's trust in another person, here the argument is much more susceptible to relativistic considerations. The case for the moral-developmental function of trusting others is a powerful one, although the practical efficacy of such an approach will doubtless vary between contexts and cultures. But another facet of the same concern for fellow humans is found in the sense of disrespect which some may feel at being, as they experience it, distrusted. And here I maintain that there will be cultural variations. In high-trust societies people expect to be trusted, and in the organizational context this suggests that violations of that expectation are likely to be interpreted by people as a sign of others' lack of respect for them (Fox, 1974a: 98). But in other contexts (low-trust societies, and some organizations within high-trust cultural settings) such expectations, of responsibility, discretion and so on, may not exist. People may not feel offended by this situation; but do we nonetheless regard it as demeaning and ethically unacceptable?

Interpersonal trust in organizations

In the literature on trust in organizations one can discern two main perspectives: one clearly managerial, or functionalist, and the other critical. For writers in the first category, the essential concern is with organizational effectiveness. Their interest is in the creation of high-trust relations through organization development and leadership (for example, Bennis and Nanus, 1985; Filley, 1975). Then there is a smaller number whose concern is with an essentially Kantian respect for the individual (for example, Fox, 1974a, 1974b). From this standpoint, to trust people, although it entails a degree of risk, may facilitate individuals' moral and personal development. It therefore indicates a prima facie duty for management to give discretion and responsibility to employees.

The functionalist view

The functionalist position is utilitarian, although concern for the individual's development, and concern for others in the system, are not necessarily incompatible. Writers on organization development see no conflict between the need for improved trust relations in the interest of institutional effectiveness, the personal development of individuals, and a commensurate respect for persons (for example, Culbert and McDonough, 1985; Filley, 1975). However, it is this concern for the wider system, or for particular parties within it, which also provides a moral justification for *not* trusting someone; for exercising caution, when the nature of the risk and the probability of its occurrence seem too great.

Coercive and corrupt trust relations in organizations

While keeping trust, as with promise-keeping, is commonly regarded as morally good, at most it is so only on a prima facie basis. The management philosophy which calls for loyalty and unquestioning commitment to official policy and programmes may be challenged here, just as it is when the possibility of principled dissent and whistleblowing is considered (see Chapter 9). As Baier (1994: 126) points out, we cannot ignore the wider social network of which specific trust relations are often a part, and this applies particularly in organizations. Beyond any trust between specific individuals or groups are further relationships which may be affected: with the public, consumers, shareholders and others. Where the consequences of organizational activity are ethically unacceptable, viewed in the light of those other interests, there may be a justifiable case for individuals to break their trust relationship with colleagues or with management.

Baier also observes that: 'Where the truster relies on his threat advantage to keep the trust relation going or where the trusted relies on concealment, something is morally rotten in the trust relationship' (1994: 123). Thus managers who rely on threats to employees, often associated with increased specificity and formalization of direction, cannot justifiably expect further cooperation on grounds of trust and respect alone. Furthermore, when, for example, Bennis and Nanus assert that trust is the 'emotional glue that binds followers and leaders together' (1985: 153), one is entitled to be sceptical, since it would seem that a number of other factors relating to the hierarchical structure of organizations, and influence processes therein, could be operating.

Further critical observations

Nichols and Beynon (1977) described the introduction by management of a new system of work, the 'New Working Arrangement' (NWA) at a UK chemical plant, ChemCo. In essence, the NWA replaced time rates and bonuses with a form of measured day work, together with various plans for the involvement of workers, such as job rotation and enrichment. The new system depended on the creation of a high-trust climate amongst management and workers (Nichols and Beynon, 1977: Chapter 11). But as they observed: 'Trust rarely arises out of compulsion' (1977: 175), and they argued that in this case there was compulsion because, due to the lack of alternative employment, the workers had not really chosen to work for ChemCo.

Now this raises fundamental issues concerning the difference between the ethics of organizational relations and the ethics of capitalism as a system. Nichols and Beynon offered, in effect, a moral critique of the latter, entailing the proposition that any trust which is built up is 'corrupt' (Baier, 1994: 123), because of the inherent coercion of labour by capital. It is a moral dysfunction of the capitalist system. Nichols and Beynon argued therefore that in such circumstances employees are under no obligation to demonstrate loyalty or to discharge their responsibilities to the organization. This argument requires further analysis. If such constraints on employees really are systemic, and no one can alter them, or even act in a discretionary manner within them, then trust is barely a relevant concept. Such coercion is, then, hardly the fault of individual managers, who, on Nichols and Beynon's own admission, would be similarly constrained (1977: 175). But in so far as coercion and constraint is even to some extent attributable to specific managers, or is within their control, then its perpetuation has the effect of reducing the uncertainty for management, and diminishing the moral quality of any presumed trust which they might have in their employees. It can also be argued that inequalities in power create situations in which weaker parties to a relationship may trust the more powerful not to harm them; or indeed to help them.

A fundamental assumption in this book is that individual managers do have some 'leeway' to choose how to act, how to conduct themselves, before the 'ultimate influence of economic necessity' takes over (Anthony, 1986: 193). So in practice, assuming the possibility of managerial discretion, it *is* individual managers who, collectively and individually, adopt strategies and styles of management and leadership. A coercive relation may thus exist, although the power resources available to different parties will often be unequal and usually latent. Employees may exploit a trust relation by, for example, disguising shoddy work. As Baier notes, if revealed, this would justify managerial action in response to the breach of trust. Clearly a great deal depends on the motives and perceptions of those involved. Managers introducing job enrichment schemes, or delegating tasks to subordinates, are aware of their authority and latent power, yet may have a genuine desire to help staff develop their abilities or experience greater freedom than before. How such behaviour is viewed by employees will colour their reaction; a cynical view of trust as manipulation will encourage distrust and perhaps lead to commensurate action by management.

The more explicitly formalized, contractual, specific and coercive the system of management control, the greater the tendency for trust to break down, if indeed it ever existed, with employees seeking to circumvent the rules and exploit the loopholes. The less coercive and the more discretionary the working environment, the more the system depends on trust, shared values and norms. In ChemCo, the NWA was a deliberate attempt to move from specific to non-specific controls; from low-trust to high-trust relations between management and employees. It implied a degree of managerial trust in personnel who, it was assumed, would share management's values.

The managerial need for employees to share a set of values which support officially recognized goals is inescapable. There are few circumstances, except in the most precisely defined work situations, in which employees cannot to some extent place their own interpretation on norms, and circumvent or bend the rules if it suits them (Selznick, 1948). Typically, therefore, managers see an important form of control in the inculcation of values and norms, something which Selznick (1957) saw as a function of organizational leadership. (This has been attacked as 'manipulation' by various critics of the human relations school, as I note in Chapter 6.) So even in apparently high-discretion roles, employees may be subject to styles and methods of leadership which indicate a desire for control by managers who feel that individual employees are unwilling to contribute on the basis of their own authentic and prior commitment to the values and goals of the organization.

Managerial controls as a symptom of distrust

This argument has even greater force when presented in relation to bureaucratic controls. In one of the more substantial theses on trust in organizations, Fox (1974b) discussed high-trust and low-trust work relations, arguing that formalized controls reflect management's lack of trust in subordinates. (A correlative argument, normatively oriented in favour of the creation of high-trust organizations, is found in the work of organization development writers such as Tannenbaum and Davis, [1969] 1983, who advocated the dismantling of bureaucratic systems.)

To exemplify his point, Fox drew upon a number of studies in the sociology of industry and organizations and in industrial relations (for example,

Flanders, 1964; Gouldner, 1954a; Guest, 1962). Of these, Gouldner's well-known work is particularly relevant, for two reasons. First, it predated Fox by two decades in identifying lack of trust as a reason for managers' use of bureaucratic control in organizations (Gouldner, 1954a: 137, 179). Second, in a succession of papers written in the wake of that earlier empirical study, and in conjunction with his critical reappraisal of functionalist social theory, he developed an explicit interest in morality (for example, Gouldner, 1960, [1973] 1975a).

The events discussed by Gouldner (1954a, 1954b) took place in a gypsum plant, an outpost of a larger company, very much tied into its local and rather isolated community. It was managed in an easygoing fashion by Old Doug; an 'indulgency pattern,' as Gouldner termed it, characterized by 'leniency'. Specifically, in this instance, leniency meant: meeting workers' expectations that there should be no close supervision, that they be given a second chance if they made a mistake, that rules be applied flexibly, as when making allowance for employees' domestic circumstances, and that workers could use company equipment for private use.

It was against the background of the 'indulgency pattern' that, when Doug died, the owners of the factory installed a new manager, Vincent Peele. Peele was appointed with instructions to increase productivity. He recognized the expectations of head office, and the power they had over him. ' "I appreciate their [head office's] confidence in me", he said, "and I want to show it" ' (Gouldner, 1954a: 72).

Peele was an outsider, unencumbered by pre-existing bonds with the work-force and their community. While he could have tried to maintain his predecessor's informal style of management, he chose instead to do two things: to invoke the formal rules, and to introduce new staff of his own choosing to supervisory positions, people whom he trusted. As Gouldner explains, this was the easiest way forward for Peele. Because he was an outsider, who apparently felt considerable anxiety in his new role, his appointment was resented from the outset. By appealing to the formal rules laid down by head office he could deflect criticism of himself personally; and he also needed quick results. Yet, as indicated above, he did have a choice: he could have tried to build trust between the workers and himself. He had inherited commitments made by Doug and he faced the question of whether or not to honour these. Had he done so, that might have helped him establish good relations, but it could also have impeded the quick commercial turn-around which head office expected.

Instead, as well as enforcing the rules, he was constantly to be found walking around the plant:

> the men resented his continual presence, feeling it to be an expression of distrust. A sample [-room] worker stated this succinctly:
> 'Doug *trusted* his men to do a job. Vincent doesn't. Doug didn't come around so much. He *relied* on the men'. (Gouldner, 1954a: 87)

Overall, Peele distrusted the existing workers, largely, it appears, on grounds of 'motive' rather than 'competence'. He was concerned that they would take too much advantage of any freedom granted. Now what is the moral justification for this position? Peele's immediate concern was for his own reputation in the eyes of senior management. He felt under pressure to get quick results, and he assumed that tightening up on discipline would achieve this. This is understandable, although it may seem self-centred and ethically less desirable than the creation of a high-trust situation over a longer term. One could also reflect on Peele's interaction with the workforce generally; were there aspects of his demeanour which were morally questionable, such as the manner in which he kept close watch on people at their work? All of these matters would, for a balanced view, have to be weighed up against concern for the organization as a whole, for the other stakeholders, which would appear at first sight to justify the intention behind head office directives, the aim of which was to reduce the private use of company property and other waste of resources.

Reciprocity, trust and beneficence

Baier (1994: 114–15) speculates that discussion of trust in Western moral philosophy has failed to explore the variety of possible forms which this can take, partly because of a male-dominated contractarian perspective which, in the main, assumes reciprocal relations between equals. Yet there are many situations in which weaker or dependent persons trust those who are in a stronger position, although the latter have no obligation, based on reciprocity alone, to meet this.

Gouldner's gypsum plant study had encouraged him to reflect on problems of power and dependence in relation to functionalist sociology (1959, 1960). His starting point was in Parsonian social theory (Parsons, 1951) and in the assumption that a mutually gratifying exchange relationship, that is, reciprocity, is essential for social system stability. Gouldner's analysis inclined him to question the need, for system stability, for equality in such mutual relations; for a necessary symmetry of reciprocity. The basic formulation of the idea of reciprocity fails to allow for the possibility that weaker or less advantaged members of a system cannot themselves reciprocate, and therefore would not receive help in the first place. Referring to the 'indulgency pattern' in his earlier study, Gouldner suggested that:

> There seems little question but that what I had called the 'indulgency pattern' is *not* a form of *reciprocity* but, rather, is a contemporary expression of a different norm – a norm of *beneficence*. It contributes to the stability of factory social systems precisely insofar as it allows workers to receive *more* than they are legally owed under their union contract or is customarily due them in their worker-status. ([1973] 1975a: 265–6)

Gouldner emphasized an altruistic tendency in such beneficent action, which means that managerial leniency intentionally designed to elicit goodwill and performance from employees would be excluded, since that would imply anticipated future returns for the organization; a step towards reciprocity, or enlightened self-interest by the employer. 'The norm of reciprocity *justifies* an obligation to help another on the grounds that he has or will help you; the norm of beneficence justifies the obligation to help on the grounds of the other's *need*' (Gouldner, [1973] 1975a: 285). Trust enters into the beneficent relationship in two respects. First, in that the weaker members of a system trust others not to harm them, perhaps even to help them; and, second, because the truster hopes that any latitude, privileges or concessions granted (which are not motivated by the expectation of reciprocation) will not be abused.

Trust, control and professional work

The management of those employees who have specific knowledge and skills raises particular issues relating to trust. As Baier says:

> If one stands over one's builder, watching and querying every move she makes, she may well refuse to finish the job, since what self-respecting builder would put up with such apparent lack of *any* trust in her professional skill and standards of care? Is she, the builder, not supposed to be the one with the know-how? (1994: 139)

Typifying such 'control as distrust', there has during the 1990s been a tendency, particularly (but not exclusively) in some UK service institutions, to impose increasingly bureaucratic controls on professional staff. It has affected banking (Braid, 1994; Harrison, 1993), the Civil Service (Hugill, 1994a), and other areas such as police, health services and education (Caulkin, 1995; Mulgan, 1995). While clearly associated with financial cutbacks, this appears to go beyond any obvious need for budgetary control or coordination. It is seen in some attempts at measuring performance, even when this is inherently difficult to do without diverting attention and energy from less measurable but more fundamental activity. An example of this is found in routine police patrol work, where the more effective officers are at crime prevention, the less evidence there is of good performance as measured in reports of incidents and in clear-up rates.

Of course in some cases performance measures act as an incentive, and are introduced for that reason. There is also the argument that, over time, such monitoring and assessment may change organizational cultures such that there is greater focus on performance goals. The tendency towards such bureaucratization has been described (and justified) in terms of introducing 'business methods' into the public sector; on that point I simply observe that the business ethics consultant John Drummond was by no means the first to say that companies in the future will be 'high trust, low cost'; they will be less dependent on bureaucratic controls than in the past, not more so (quoted in O'Sullivan, 1995: 15). Decades of research show that knowledge-based employees (professionals, technical experts) resent such controls and do not (or cannot?) perform well under such conditions (Hales, 1993: 160–5; Hall, 1968).

Thus the utilitarian reasons against such institutionalized distrust are strong. But there is also the criticism that lack of trust generally is insulting to people, unless there are good grounds for basing one's judgment on their lack of competence or lack of motivation. Overall, the ethical significance of this is that high-trust relations between management and relatively autonomous employees, the intrinsic motivation of the latter, and their potential for a service orientation towards their work, are liable to be undermined and replaced by a self-interested, instrumental orientation, where something closer to 'working to rule' can become the norm. The syndrome evident here resurfaces periodically in later chapters; for example, when discussing the effect of formal controls on employee motivation (Chapter 6) or codes of ethics (Chapter 11).

A matter of judgment

I return now to the case of my conversation with John, which I introduced in the previous chapter, concentrating this time on trust as a concept. Of course an adequate contextualization of the situation I faced would call for a wider range of insights than can be provided by the concept of trust alone. For example, since that dilemma was fundamentally concerned with the issue of staff redundancy, one would want information on those individuals who might be affected, their vulnerabilities, the alternatives open to them should they lose their jobs, and the range of options open to management. These would be salient features of the overall situation understood in terms of concepts such as fairness and discrimination.

Concepts in context

I shall view the case, as before, primarily from my own position as John's supervisor. It happens to be quite a complex situation, demonstrating the way in which an apparently two-person trust relationship is embedded in the wider context of other such relationships, where trust may often be implicit rather than explicit. I had faced a dilemma as to whether or not to admit the truth to John; that the rumour he had heard was correct, and that redundancies were in the offing. Focusing on trust, what is the nature and context of this dilemma?

Most obviously, and in some respects explicitly, I have a prima facie duty to maintain the trust of my managerial colleagues, and, by implication, to protect the coherence of the organization and the interests of a majority of stakeholders. (It was assumed by the management group that a premature leak of information would cause a damaging loss of morale.) But then there is a non-specific, implicit, trust which my own staff have in me, which might suggest that I should be involving them in discussion. So I also wonder whether I should have dissented from the managerial decision. Should we bring all the staff into the discussion immediately? Or do we work on the assumption that they trust us to be fair in our deliberations?

Moreover, after I had spoken with John, I wondered whether I was putting him in an awkward position. Would he feel obliged to share his information with other colleagues? Or is this covered by the fact that he had originally heard the rumour from a source other than myself, so that this is not my responsibility? This concern raises the possibility that the trust I repose in John is coercive. Am I taking advantage of my formal position when I ask him to maintain strict silence? Reflecting on this, I feel assured that it was not my intention to take advantage of my position as John's supervisor. I felt that I was relating to him as a friend, but of course he might see things differently.

This raises a further insight: there are actually two elements to the trust I placed in him. First, there is the rumour itself: that there will be reorganization and redundancies. Can I reassure myself with the thought that it didn't take me to tell John this? Or should I be reminding him that he should keep this to himself, even though he already knew? If I take that line, which was implied in my conversation with him, then I would be acting in my role as member of the management group which took the decision; in a sense I would be compensating for the indiscretion of my managerial colleagues. The second element is that I have asked John to keep confidential the fact that I personally had confirmed the rumour. This is where our relationship as friends rather than as superior–subordinate is relevant. The trust I place in John is corrupt if I am using my hierarchical position to pressurize him, simply in order to protect myself from my own vulnerability; to ward off the threat to my reputation in the eyes of other managers.

The possibility of coercive trust prompts the additional question of my own options, or indeed those of the managing director. Do any of us have a choice? Is trust a relevant concept? But we do have choices on at least some matters, such as the procedures to be followed, the decisions on who is to be made redundant, and the communication of such information. On these matters, at any rate, staff place their trust in us.

This initial attempt at making sense of the situation invokes the following concepts: the variety of groups and individuals affected, or wider social network; the implicit, non-specific trust which these relationships entail; the 'content' of the trust I repose in John (what do I trust him with?); the role I adopt as truster (authority figure, or friend?); and power relations in the organization generally.

I could also ask why I trust John. Or why I might not. The basis of my trust in him seems to be twofold. First, on competence, I regard him as 'reliable and responsible'. Second, on the question of motive, I happen to believe that he has integrity, in general. But if I sought further reassurance in these particular circumstances, perhaps it is that since I can tell him that he will not be affected personally, he will have less reason to spread the rumour further; to think in these terms is to introduce a micropolitical perspective. This said, however, John's very integrity might incline him to talk with his own colleagues, with a view to their interests as potential victims of the emerging situation.

I have mentioned my vulnerability at a personal level, and also that assumed by the management group concerning the stability of the organization. But what of the risks involved when I trust John? These are understood in terms of those vulnerabilities, set against the advantage to me of trusting him. Again, it is necessary to distinguish between my personal situation and my membership of the management group. From the former position my advantage in trusting John is that I avoid any subsequent reproach from him, which would surely arise were he to discover that I had been dishonest. The risk is that fellow managers discover that I had broken the trust they had placed in me. Which of these outcomes is worse is a moot point; a matter of judgment, although I could argue that my maintaining good relations with John is important for the organization. (I am ignoring the point that two of my senior colleagues also seem to have been indiscreet, if less deliberately.) From my standpoint as a member of the management group, there seems to be no immediate advantage in trusting John, whereas the risk would be that the rumour is now confirmed, and as such John might reveal this to all the other staff. On the other hand, this vulnerability may be lessened by the very fact that John already has some information, albeit unconfirmed. Finally there is the question of my uncertainty, and here I feel that the likelihood of John letting me down is slight.

In a case such as this, concepts of vulnerability, risk and uncertainty are indicative of intuitive processes, rather than any carefully thought out rationality. On this occasion, and viewed in those terms, I suspect that my action in trusting John is close to being a rational choice, rather than a risky trust situation. There seems to be a degree of self-interest involved, protecting my reputation with John. If, however, we look at it in terms of prima facie duties, it is worth noting that my trust in John could be construed as developmental, or 'therapeutic' (Horsburgh, 1960). And as such it would fall under Ross's prima facie duty of beneficence, concerned with an improvement in another person's condition (Ross, 1930). That prima facie duty would then have to be weighed against conflicting duties of fidelity to the management group, and perhaps an obligation not to cause harm to others by allowing needless alarm to circulate prematurely. Which interpretation is appropriate would depend on my thoughts and motives at the time. And they are incompatible. If I am going to be guided by a prima facie duty of beneficence, and other prima facie duties to employees, would I not be arguing for all my staff to be consulted, implying mutual trust in the dialogic process?

Conclusion

Doubtless readers will have their own interpretations to place on this case. Doubtless also, there is much more detailed information that would be needed to make an informed judgment. But what I have tried to do here is show how conceptual and theoretical developments connect with the process of judgment in the face of ethical issues and dilemmas. Furthermore, apart from decisions as to what to do, one must not ignore matters of dialogue and demeanour. Throughout my exchange with John, my language, bodily signals and timing of communications were all liable to convey impressions of trust, uncertainty, power, friendship and other morally significant facets of our relationship.

In the next two chapters, other aspects of organizational life – concerning work, motivation, fairness and discrimination – will be discussed. There also, interconnections with the dialogic and judgmental modes of handling morally significant situations will be noted.

6 Work, Employment and Motivation

The responsibilities of employees, as opposed to those who manage them, are perhaps not what spring to mind when one refers to the ethics of work. For much of this chapter, however, I shall consider the view that people in organizations have a responsibility to society; that they cannot simply hide from the wider moral implications of their work, uncritically doing as they are told. In that vein, I shall then offer a critique of motivation theories as typically construed in the context of management. I shall suggest that such theories are essentially concerned with the control of employee behaviour, implying the manipulation of individuals' moral values in relation to their task and its context. What we have, therefore, are competing paradigms of work organization: one concerned with respect for individuals' potential as moral agents, the other with the control and regulation which, to some extent, is required in all organizations. The juxtaposition of these competing perspectives presents the sensitive manager with an ethical dilemma, the essence of which concerns the question of psychological manipulation. I shall conclude, therefore, with some comments on that issue, and on the alternative possibilities for open dialogue.

Varieties of work ethic

A starting point is to consider why people work at all; in particular, I shall base my overall argument on the proposition that traditional norms of hard work and self-interested instrumentality in employment situations, uncritically accepted, may have adverse and ethically significant implications, including lack of concern for the social and environmental consequences of organized activity.

Much work in organizations is experienced as alienating and stressful. For long associated with manual labour, this now extends to managerial and professional occupations also. In many cases a contributory factor is the long hours worked, something which should be considered in relation to the numbers who are unemployed (McCrystal, 1996) or reluctantly part-time (Durham, 1994) and the safety risks sometimes involved, as with long-distance truck drivers (Woolf, 1995). Of course, these sorts of problem are frequently attributed to the economic pressures faced by organizations, and most employees have little option but to work as required by management, or risk redundancy. But in some cases an underlying factor is that employees themselves assume the need for particular employment, or are motivated by a combination of 'workaholism' and indiscriminate pursuit of specific levels of income and status, which perhaps they should question. Their position in the organization, their earnings, and their visible consumption patterns, possessions and lifestyles all contribute to their sense of self (Dittmar, 1992) and very often it is these things which they feel they must sustain.

Yet when people ask the question, 'why work?' the distinction between the actual activity itself, and the employment relationship, must be borne in mind. Since the 1950s, repeated evidence from the USA has suggested that many people would wish to remain at work (that is, in their employment) even if this was no longer essential for financial reasons (Gini and Sullivan, 1987; Morse and Weiss, 1955). Yet while work does of course often provide non-remunerative benefits for individuals, such as a feeling of involvement in useful activity, and a sense of identity, there are other spheres outside the traditional employment relationship which can fulfil the same functions: various types of part-time work, recreational and voluntary activities. Thus it is fruitful to distinguish between, and question, the different functions of work and employment. Of course most people need to earn an income; but how much, and why, and to what do they subject themselves (and others) in order to realize their personal goals? Could they perhaps obtain the same satisfaction in alternative activities? As we approach the millennium, increasing numbers of people are asking these questions.

The Protestant ethic

Concern for the general issue of working hours is not new. Bertrand Russell (1935) argued that not only could technology enable a reduction in working hours, thus removing much toil and drudgery, but that the leisure time thus available to individuals could be used in satisfying their intellectual curiosity, writing, and voluntary public service, all of which would have a civilizing influence on society.

Russell's view was an explicit challenge to the idea of a (Protestant) work ethic. It is characteristic of those involved in manufacture and trade, the owners and managers of businesses, to subscribe to beliefs which justify their hard work, and which legitimize their demands that employees should, likewise, engage in diligent labour. Such beliefs assume the status of an ideology, or 'ethic', in the sense that they comprise a social morality or imperative. For those in northern Europe and North America particularly, the earliest manifestations of this were in terms of, or reminiscent of, the sixteenth-century Protestant work ethic (Bendix, 1960: Chapter 3; Buchholtz, 1983; Weber, [1904–5] 1930).

Weber's thesis that Protestantism contributed to the rise of capitalism (through the twin moral imperatives of wealth accumulation through work, and an ascetic prohibition on its consumption) is something I shall leave aside, not least since it has been subject to a degree of criticism (for example, see Tawney, [1926] 1938: Chapter 4, n. 32). What seems indisputable, however, is that such Protestant beliefs did affect the attitudes of the entrepreneurial and managerial classes, who saw hard work as a moral duty. This sowed the seeds of a secular paradigm which has affected both managerial theories and industrial cultures in the West. The emphasis on wealth accumulation, either as a means to the spiritual end of salvation (in the original version), as a measure of personal status and success, or, latterly (and in contradistinction to the Protestant position) as a means to material consumption, which itself helps to sustain the capitalist system, has thus generated several variants of the work ethic (Furnham, 1990; Jackall, 1988: 7–10).

A radical perspective

> The authoritarian-obsessive-hoarding character that had begun to develop in the sixteenth century, and continued to be the dominant character structure at least in the middle classes until the end of the nineteenth century, was slowly blended with or replaced by the *marketing character*. (Fromm, [1976] 1979: 145)

Like Marx's alienated worker, but more self-consciously, such individuals become commodities, adapting and changing to meet the needs of the employment market, unaware of any more fundamental ends in life, unconcerned with the wider social and environmental implications of their work for the organization, or of their consumption patterns beyond it. Individual success is understood in terms of organizational status occupied and salary earned, rather than in terms of actual performance in one's job. This is especially true when performance is hard to measure. In such situations, success (that is, obtaining positional status) may be achieved through the 'presentation of self' (Goffman, 1959) or the marketing of one's 'personality' (Fromm, [1976] 1979: 146) rather than by any evidence that one can do the work competently.

Since the 1970s, the environmental debate has posed perhaps the most serious challenge to this consumption-driven work ethic (Fromm, [1976] 1979; Goldsmith et al., 1972; Gouldner, [1973] 1975b; Heilbroner, 1974; Lansley, 1994; Passmore, 1974). But that specific concern is just part of the threat to the dominant paradigm. In the past few decades there has, more generally, been growing unease with an outlook which ignores the non-material and moral implications of work (Nicholson-Lord, 1995). Increasing interest in what is variously labelled 'downshifting' (working fewer hours for less income) and 'voluntary simplicity' (Ghazi, 1996), affirms that concrete changes are taking place. Developments such as the ethical consumer and investment movements, and heightened concern for the morality of business generally, are indicative of a closely related tendency. While no single alternative 'ethic' can be identified which describes this revision, the terms, 'post-materialist' and 'professional' come to mind, and, in the context of ethics, I shall encapsulate these in the idea of an 'ethic of responsibility'.

An ethic of responsibility

With the secularization of the Protestant ethic, employment, as opposed to the task itself, became all-important. The nature, content and wider social implications of the latter lost their significance as both the product and the consumer were treated in an instrumental fashion, reflecting an essentially self-interested orientation at both organizational and individual levels.

Several sources have pointed to this distinction between self-interest and ethical concern for others in the context of organization and work. Halmos (1970) drew to our attention the ideal of a service orientation, which had been assumed by earlier writers such as Follett ([1925] 1973) and Tawney ([1921] 1961), who were concerned with the professionalization of business and management. Mohr (1973) suggested that insufficient attention is paid to outward-looking, 'transitive', aspects of organizational activity: the contribution which people in their work roles can make to society, and the personal fulfilment they can derive from this. He suggested that the 'occupation of transitive roles . . . may well be a sine qua non of successful long-term social living' (1973: 481). Roszak equated alienation with the giving up of personal responsibility for one's work; such responsibility being 'the crucial distinction that separates mere employment from true vocation' ([1978] 1981: 228), and where vocation, or calling, refers to the 'well crafted and the ethically right' ([1978] 1981: 230). He stressed the significance of such responsible concern for others, and particularly for ecological matters. People should ask: 'Is the job honest and useful? Is it a real contribution to human need?' ([1978] 1981: 234).

Fromm's distinction between 'having' and 'being' as modes of living reflects 'selfishness and altruism as two basic character orientations' ([1976] 1979: 9). *Having* is defined in terms of the acquisition of material and symbolic possessions, and controlling other living things. This is seen in the Protestant ethic and its legacy. 'Existential having' refers to the prerequisites for physical survival, similar to Maslow's physiological needs (Maslow, 1943). By contrast, 'characterological having' is a product of social norms. Thus the ego is something one has, providing an identity, boosted by one's status, by other more specific possessions, and manifest in the image which one wishes to convey to others. In this mode of living goods are acquired as much for their symbolic significance as for their functional usefulness.

Being entails the abandonment of egocentricity, selfishness and desire for possessions. It means giving expression to one's faculties and one's need for relationships, pursuing courses of action other than those guided by unfettered self-interest. Unlike the egoistic having mode of living, 'being has as its prerequisites independence, freedom, and [significantly] the presence of critical reason' (Fromm, [1976] 1979: 92). In Chapter 3, I rejected egoism as an acceptable normative theory of ethics, while suggesting that those other moral theories which one might consider would all at least imply some concern for others, a tendency towards altruism. While egoism is consistent with having, being is consistent with a view of employees as responsible moral agents:

individuals who on occasion must exercise moral judgment rather than simply comply with orders or conform to a role (Maclagan, 1991b).

As indicated above, having and being can be viewed as ideal-type character orientations, towards which people may tend. Fromm maintained that most people have potential for both, and that they can be influenced one way or the other by their social environment. Moreover, it is important to note that Fromm was not arguing for a dismantling of the industrial system. Production and consumption are necessary, but what must be questioned are the motives behind such activity and its ethical and ecological acceptability. Management theories should recognize these possibilities, especially the potential for being. Instead, they usually reflect particular, positivistic assumptions about human nature and behaviour, viewing this as coloured by the having mode of living, and assuming that it is predictable and controllable. Nowhere is this more evident than in theories of work motivation, to which I now turn.

Feeling responsible and being motivated

People in organizations engage in all sorts of actions which could be said to be 'motivated', apart from purely task-related behaviour; for example, political activity and expressions of dissent. Hence much of the coming discussion, although heavily slanted towards the relationship between the individual and the actual job, has wider implications for our appreciation of behaviour in organizations.

A fundamental distinction is that between content and process in motivation. Content theories emphasize needs that people are presumed to have (Maslow, 1943) and the connection between these needs and the rewards available from work and employment. Process theories focus on relationships between persons' values, cognitions and actions, but, importantly, leave unanswered the question as to what precisely is valued (that is, the content). This remains to be identified in particular situations, and is significant for reasons which I outlined in Chapter 2. There, I noted the way in which overt behaviour is often ambiguous, and one cannot always tell what underlying values incline someone to act one way rather than another.

A second fundamental distinction is that between determinism and freedom. Most theories of employee motivation incorporate deterministic assumptions, according to which behaviour in organizations is caused, and is therefore in principle predictable and controllable. But other theories of motivation, especially process theories, are more obviously compatible with the view that people can choose, and act accordingly. In so far as I am addressing the question of employees' moral potential, therefore, I am assuming this second position, emphasizing freedom rather than determinism.

The best-known process theory is expectancy theory. There are several variants (for example Vroom, 1964) but all share a common proposition that the strength of a tendency to act in a certain way depends on the strength of an expectancy that the act will be followed by a given consequence (or outcome) and on the value or attractiveness of that consequence (or outcome) to the actor. (Lawler, 1973: 45)

As Carter and Jackson observe, 'Expectancy Theory has received a great deal of attention, but with a marked resistance to the possibility that subjectivity cannot be confined to the context of productivity' (1993: 99). To realize the true moral potential of employees as humans, this possibility must be recognized. To be epistemologically valid, such theory must accommodate the underlying values to which the specific individuals in question subscribe, which inform their actions, and which may provoke within them a sense of moral responsibility for the implications of their work.

Human motivation also entails an energizing factor which helps convert such values and personal goals into action. It is proposed here that this energizing factor is often emotional, especially where there is a moral concern present. This is not inconsistent with a judgmental approach to ethics, since moral concerns and aims may be arrived at in a thoughtful manner but the desire to realize them be emotively charged. Indeed, the words 'motivation' and 'emotion' are from the same root in the Latin *movere* (to move), a point also noted in a useful discussion on the subject by Richard Peters ([1958] 1960: 37).

It is worth lingering with this theme, on the idea that 'energizing' implies an emotional dimension to motivated action. Fineman (citing Argyris, 1964; Likert, 1961; Pfeffer, 1981) observes that many writers on organizational studies have

placed human beings and their subjectivity, nearer centre stage . . . Yet, when we look closely, the people presented are emotionally anorexic. They have 'dissatisfactions' and 'satisfactions', they may be 'alienated' or 'stressed', they will have 'preferences', 'attitudes' and 'interests' . . . [but] [o]ften these are noted as variables for managerial control. (Fineman, 1993: 9)

Fineman continues by observing that even the more recent and 'influential anti-rationalist writings of [Tom] Peters and Austin (1985)' present human emotion at work in a normative vein, as '"oughts" for managerial success'; indicative of enthusiasm for admired companies and their products. So it seems that even as the people depicted are transformed, over generations of theoretical writing, from mere bodies to human beings with feelings, they remain objects to be manipulated in the pursuit of productivity and profitability.

The values which inform individuals' motivated action may be influenced by organizational factors and work experience, as I noted in Chapter 2. But we cannot assume that they are invariably consistent with those approved by management. They may not even relate directly to the task, let alone the pursuit of productivity. People in organizations pursue, in a motivated fashion, all sorts of other personal goals, some selfish, some altruistic, some messianic; self-aggrandizement, hassle avoidance, whistleblowing, and the politics of strategy formulation and implementation reflecting sincerely held beliefs.

Motivation as management control

From a moral point of view these other employee values, feelings and motivations are important. Yet, as my comments regarding expectancy theory indicated, managerial theories of motivation, and associated prescriptions for organizational and job design, incentive systems, leadership and supervision are, if only implicitly, deterministic theories of influence and control. They are grounded on unanalysed assumptions as to what people seek from their work, such as financial rewards, companionship or intrinsic interest. They also presuppose that managers can manipulate the means of satisfying these presumed needs, so as to elicit productive behaviour from individuals, but that is problematic. For example, with attempts at motivation through job enrichment, one often has to know in more detail what will actually prove satisfactory for particular individuals. So what is clear is that the various assumptions about human nature, which are central to such management theories – 'rational-economic', 'social', 'self-actualization' (Schein, [1965] 1980) – can, in themselves, be interpreted from a subjectivist perspective, recognizing human potential for moral action. But the demands of the somewhat deterministic, control-oriented paradigm out of which such theory has emerged precludes recognition of this, or at least it is ignored as being irrelevant to the theorist's primary interests. Nor has concern for human moral potential been helped by a social scientific tendency to ground concepts in what is observed, rather than in what could be. Many people may be concerned about ethical issues, but don't reveal this in the workplace. Thus theories, in so far as they reflect how people are, reinforce 'moral muteness' (Bird and Waters, 1989) and fail to alert researchers to other possibilities.

Few concepts in management theory offer a better illustration of these points than the term *responsibility*, and since this also is central to much that I shall say in later chapters, it merits further attention.

Responsibility: an example of conceptual ambiguity and deficiency

The term 'responsibility' has several different meanings (Downie, 1971: Chapter 3; Walton, 1988: 20–34). One can talk of people being accountable to others, occupying formally defined roles; or being responsible for something in the sense of having caused or allowed it to happen; or simply having a sense of responsibility. For the present, I shall draw a distinction between responsibilities which are defined for one by others, and those which one assumes oneself, which one feels. The first category I shall regard as 'objective', in that the observer could identify them in, for example, organizational job descriptions. The second category I regard as 'subjective'; it may include instances of the first when these are recognized by an individual employee, but it refers essentially to personally defined obligations which may well go beyond the circumscribed limits of formal organizational edicts.

In Chapter 5 of his novel *The Grapes of Wrath*, John Steinbeck's evocative portrayal of the squatters' eviction from their smallholdings by representatives of a bank, illustrates what it means to be responsible, in these two senses:

> The owners of the land came onto the land, or more often a spokesman for the owners came. They came in closed cars, and they felt the dry earth with their fingers, and sometimes they drove big earth augers into the ground for soil tests. The tenants, from their sun-beaten dooryards, watched uneasily when the closed cars drove along the fields. And at last the owner men drove into the dooryards and sat in their cars to talk out of the windows. The tenant men stood beside the cars for a while, and then squatted on their hams and found sticks with which to mark the dust.
>
> In the open doors the women stood looking out, and behind them the children – corn-headed children, with wide eyes, one bare foot on top of the other bare foot, and the toes working. The women and the children watched their men talking to the owner men. They were silent.
>
> Some of the owner men were kind because they hated what they had to do, and some of them were angry because they hated to be cruel, and some of them were cold because they had long ago found that one could not be an owner unless one were cold. And all of them were caught in something larger than themselves. Some of them hated the mathematics that drove them, and some were afraid, and some worshipped the mathematics because it provided a refuge from thought and from feeling. (Steinbeck, [1939] 1951: 30)

People may feel responsible for the conduct of their formally defined role, in the sense of being accountable to their employer. They may also feel, in a more intensely personal, emotive, sense, responsibility for the consequences of such action. This is a different sort of responsibility. The bank's agents did not take the policy decision to evict the tenants, nor to intentionally cause them harm. But some still had feelings of responsibility, in the sense of complicity, while others disclaimed any sense of guilt, maintaining that they were compelled to act as they did, that they had no option, perhaps taking refuge in the 'mathematics' or in the diffused responsibility of a group (Collins and Hoyt, 1972; Festinger, 1957).

In essence, the point is that moral values, which could of course be positive rather than negative, enter into persons' appreciation of situations. They can indicate prima facie duties; as reasons for acting one way rather than another they may therefore affect the course of action followed and the manner of its conduct. Hence the demeanour adopted by some of the 'owner men' in the case above. They may have carried out their official responsibilities, but not with any great enthusiasm; while some showed as much kindness as they could to the tenants. And of course in other situations, employees might simply refuse to comply.

The concept of responsibility in management theory

Most of the major traditions in management theory are conceptually deficient with regard to such possibilities (Maclagan, 1983). The term 'responsibility' is almost invariably defined in terms of actual or implied formal role requirements and obligations. One would hardly expect it to be otherwise, so long as such theories are, at root, intended as recipes for eliciting employee performance in line with specific managerially defined goals. This is plainly the case with classical (Fayol, [1916] 1949) and scientific management (Taylor, 1911) theories. But it is also apparent even where there is explicit reference to responsibility as a subjective state felt by employees, as in the human relations tradition. For example, Likert suggested that a successful leader 'endeavors to build and maintain in his group a keen sense of responsibility for achieving its own goals and meeting its obligations to the larger organization' (1961: 171–2).

The concept of self-actualization is especially interesting, since in its original formulation it was a morally neutral reference to the development of an organism's potential, irrespective of context (Goldstein, 1939). Yet one need only consider the actions and attitudes of Charles Strickland, (anti?) hero of Somerset Maugham's *The Moon and Sixpence* (and the author's licensed personation of Paul Gauguin) to realize how someone in pursuit of his private mission, while clearly self-actualizing, was not obviously acting morally. Impervious to the criticisms and entreaties of others, Strickland abandoned his wife, family and career as a stockbroker to satisfy his obsession with painting, to which everything else was subordinated.

Management theories based on the idea of self-actualization fail to do justice to human moral potential (Blackler and Brown, 1978; Harrison and Pitt, 1984; Maclagan, 1983). In particular, such theories do not allow for employees' moral evaluation of the nature of the product, and its social significance. This has been noted by a number of writers. For example Anthony has suggested that:

> If it is the setting and purpose of work rather than its content that is important, it suggests that changes to increase self-actualization by enriching, enlarging, or rotating jobs, are not likely to achieve their end. Improvement in the content of jobs is of little account if the job itself is seen as a detached activity, unrelated to reality. (1977: 284)

While Perrow, commenting on Argyris's (1962) concept of the 'mature', self-actualizing, individual, remarked that this assumes that self-actualization 'would be on organizational terms' and he went on to say:

> Though Argyris and others note the creative aspect of conflict, there is little in their work which suggests that a proper form of self-actualization might be to organize employees for better working conditions, to advocate more ethical advertising practices, or to expose the cover-up of unjustified expenses in government contracts. Nor, presumably, would it be mature to oppose the development of chemical warfare techniques in a chemical firm or a nonprofit research laboratory, to be in favor of mass transit rather than private automobiles at General Motors, to oppose price-fixing techniques at General Electric, or to call for better testing of drugs and more accurate advertising in a pharmaceutical firm. (Perrow, [1972] 1979: 114)

In defence of writers such as Argyris (1962, 1964) and Herzberg (1966) perhaps employee concern for the wider social implications of their work was less likely in the 1950s and early 1960s than in more recent decades. But attention to such matters is something which nowadays we might expect from employees, or would-be employees, who adhere to what earlier I termed an 'ethic of responsibility'. Nord et al. point out that 'inquiry about work values must be historically grounded and sensitive to changes in work over time' (1990: 257). So if we wish to influence research and practice, towards recognition of employees' moral potential, then 'strategic conceptual choices' (Dachler and Enderle, 1989) must be made; the conceptual adequacy of theories must be constantly reviewed if they are to be empirically and praxiologically valid. As Nord et al. suggest:

> concepts about work values are deficient because they fail to encompass a number of components individuals might want from work. For example . . . the relationships between producers and customers and the nature of the product relative to its ability to satisfy important human needs have received little attention in the study of work values. (1990: 288)

One approach to work design which does to some extent harbour this potential is offered by Hackman and Oldham (1980), for whom the 'experienced meaningfulness' of work refers to 'something that "counts" in one's own system of values' (1980: 73). They associate this with the job characteristics of 'skill variety', 'task identity' and 'task significance' (1980: 77). Identity refers to 'doing a job from beginning to end with a visible outcome' (1980: 78) while the significance of the task is defined as: 'The degree to which the job has a substantial impact on the lives of other people, whether these people are in the immediate organization or in the world at large' (1980: 79). In their Job Diagnostic Survey instrument, designed for administration to job incumbents, Hackman and Oldham made an explicit effort to capture this concept of significance, by asking respondents for an assessment of the extent to which their job affects 'the lives or well-being of other people' (1980: 279).

However, for Hackman and Oldham, another crucial factor influencing motivation is 'experienced responsibility'. This is associated with 'autonomy' as a job characteristic, defined as: 'The degree to which the job provides substantial freedom, independence, and discretion to the individual in scheduling the work and determining the procedures to be used in carrying it out' (Hackman and Oldham, 1980: 79). This represents what earlier I called an 'objective' definition of responsibility, understood in terms of job descriptions or other formal specifications. Thus subjective and objective elements are combined in Hackman and Oldham's theory; a confusion of paradigms, with the concept of responsibility as a *subjective* state either ignored, or implied in their definition of meaningfulness. Yet even when employees have little workplace autonomy or discretion in the formal, 'objective', sense, they could, depending on their strength of feeling regarding the issue in question, experience a subjective sense of moral responsibility. The passage from Perrow, quoted above, indicates the type of situation where this could arise. That this may not depend on 'autonomy' can be inferred from this next example.

> In a dirty old factory in Blackfriars during the war a job came in one day which consisted of painting a large quantity of metal 'Ds' – the letter D stamped out in metal. These were put onto trays, sprayed with paint, and dried, and two women had the job of turning them over so that they could be painted on the other side. Hour after hour, and day after day they turned these things over and were at screaming point with boredom, when by chance the foreman, who was walking through the shop, said that these 'Ds' were for labelling drinking water for the troops fighting on the second front in Normandy. Obviously, this changed the

whole meaning of the job; they were doing something of national importance and began to enjoy it. (Klein, 1963: 6–7)

The argument can be summed up by considering two dimensions. First, an 'objective' conceptualization of work design: the degree of discretion allowed in the formal role. And, second, a 'subjectivist' conceptualization of the basis for employee motivation: concern for self or moral concern for others. The objective dimension is central to a great deal of writing on the organization of work. It refers to the formal, managerially defined, responsibilities attached to a role. In many past theories concerned with understanding employee attitudes and behaviour these were seen as constraining, if not determining, factors (for example, Blauner, 1964). The subjectivist dimension refers to a concept of motivation which accommodates an ethic of personal responsibility. People may be concerned with self or with others; but, importantly, this need not be affected by the formally defined amount of discretion or responsibility in the job. Where they occupy a high-discretion role, people may be motivated by concern for others; alternatively they could be quite selfish or narcissistic in their pursuit of self-actualization. Or they may be motivated mainly by financial gain. In low-discretion roles, they may seek and find financial rewards for themselves alone, in pursuit of a miserly or hedonistic private existence; alternatively they might tolerate a routine assembly-line job because of its importance for society, or for the income, as the only way to earn enough to support a family. And in any type of job we may find the employee who, recognizing the distasteful impact of the product or process on society, experiences a negative feeling, a sense of revulsion or demotivation.

Having responsibilities and being manipulated

In turning the focus onto managerial responsibilities in relation to employees, it is critical that one recognizes the ethical context for this, which is concern for the wider range of stakeholders who are affected indirectly by such internal issues. The concept of trust, introduced in Chapter 5, is relevant here. For example, while participation and the empowerment of employees is a marked trend in late twentieth-century management practice, this can have adverse consequences for organizational performance if it impedes efficient decision-making (Maier, 1967; Vroom and Yetton, 1973) or results in irresponsible conduct by employees (Gandz and Bird, 1996). To some extent, and clearly in the second case, such matters are also a responsibility of employees themselves. Thus it is sometimes unhelpful to separate managerial and employee obligations; there are situations where everyone involved has prima facie moral duties which must be considered and acted upon.

In the discussion to follow, I will focus on two broadly defined traditions in management thought. One of these is represented by classical and scientific management, although these are actually different in their detailed emphases. The other is represented by human relations, which can include 'organizational psychology' in the form of job enrichment (Schein, [1965] 1980; Silverman, 1970).

Viewing these theoretical traditions as strategies of control or influence over employees, one may note two key features: *hierarchy* and *manipulation*. These are connected, since hierarchical forces, in various respects, underpin manipulative tendencies. The difference between the strict hierarchical control and direction, epitomized by Taylor (1911), and the participatory human relations approach emanating from Elton Mayo's researches in the 1920s (Roethlisberger and Dixon, 1939), and others such as Lewin (1951) is important. Paradoxically, participation as a management strategy may be even less acceptable from an ethical standpoint, since its potential for psychological manipulation could indicate a greater threat to individual thought and moral judgment than is the case with impersonal controls. Furthermore, the need for attention to this manipulative tendency extends to the management of managers, since they are more likely to occupy discretionary roles and be involved in participative processes.

Hierarchy and bureaucratization

In Lewis Carroll's *Through the Looking Glass* (Chapter 9), one finds the following exchange between Alice and the Red Queen:

> 'Please, would you tell me –' she [Alice] began, looking timidly at the Red Queen.
> 'Speak when you're spoken to!' the Red Queen sharply interrupted her.
> 'But if everyone obeyed that rule,' said Alice, who was always ready for a little argument, 'and if you only spoke when you were spoken to, and the other person always waited for *you* to begin, you see nobody would ever say anything, so that –'
> 'Ridiculous!' cried the Queen . . . .
> (Carroll, [1871] 1947: 262)

But the Red Queen couldn't think of a suitable response, and she changed the subject! Alice may have assumed a practical concern, yet her argument is also Kantian in its ethical implications. One could not universalize the rule and, as Green (1986) observes, the same logic applies to Taylor's scientific management. On a strict Kantian basis, management cannot justify deliberately treating people as a means, to the extent of depriving them of the purposeful element in their actions. The opportunity to express one's intellectual and moral potential is something which each human is entitled to at work as elsewhere; it is part of what we mean by 'respect for persons'. These concerns are at the heart of many critiques of Taylorism and related management methods; among philosophers such as Schwartz (1982), for example, and in the sociological literature following Braverman (1974).

However, as Raphael ([1981] 1994: 56–7) notes, the second formulation of Kant's categorical imperative states that one should treat people as an end and never *merely* as a means. It is the word 'merely' which is important here. So Raphael argues that where people enter freely into an agreement, such as an employment relationship, each must recognize the other's desires and right to a free choice. This suggests that if someone wishes to work purely for financial rewards, with no concern for any intrinsic interest or value in the work, that is his or her concern. People are individuals and vary in their reactions to routine work. So if it is possible to select individuals to suit the job, rather than the reverse, as MacKinney et al. (1962) advocate, then one may argue that the ethical case for efficiency (lower resource consumption; more widely available, lower-priced goods) should take precedence.

A number of counter-objections, both Kantian and consequentialist, can be raised here. Kant's categorical imperative to treat people as an end, to respect their humanity, applies to oneself as well as to others, and we might argue that those who subject themselves to bureaucratized working conditions violate this rule. Moreover, research has shown that routinized, low-discretion working conditions can have an adverse effect on mental health (Kornhauser, 1965; Newell, 1995). Since not all employees are aware of their own potential, or do not always appreciate the possibilities for stimulus in more enhanced work unless they have been exposed to it (Daniel, 1973), those with influence would have to encourage the provision of such opportunities, including drawing attention to its social significance.

Finally there is the argument from 'political efficacy': that participation at work (or in other institutions) encourages political participation in society generally, and is therefore a force for democracy (Pateman, 1970; Srivastva and Cooperrider, 1986). As Schwartz (1982) observed, further evidence relevant to this argument is found in Kohn and Schooler's (1978) report on the relationship between the complexity of persons' work and the development of their thinking capacity. Their research indicated that among people of equal intellectual ability, those who experience undemanding jobs early in their careers fail to develop mentally compared with those in complex jobs. As a result they are disadvantaged in the labour market, and may have a lower ability to cope well with non-work demands and to participate in society generally.

Participative arrangements and the possibility of manipulation

Like responsibility, 'participation' is a poorly defined term, the variants of which have significantly different moral implications (Dachler and Wilpert, 1978; Pateman, 1970). A vast amount has been written on the subject, and I shall only dip into it as appropriate. Dachler and Wilpert (1978) offered a conceptual framework including discussion of four major value-positions found in the literature: democratic, socialist, human growth and development, and productivity and efficiency. Democratic theory is represented by Pateman's (1970) thesis, mentioned above. The socialist position refers to employees' self-management of organizations, and is clearly relevant to work and motivation, especially where this reflects an ethic of responsibility, since employees then have control, collectively if not individually, over such matters as the nature of the product. This position is also relevant to the question of organizational governance, as I note in Chapter 10. But regarding the ethics of employee relations, it is the human development and productivity-oriented theoretical traditions which are customarily associated with motivation and workplace organization, and I shall dwell longer on these perspectives.

An explicit primary concern for productivity and efficiency, including the management of change, lies behind much participative management theory. Here a distinction may be drawn between individual and group-based participation. The former category refers to styles of leadership and supervision; for example Tannenbaum and Schmidt (1973), Vroom and Yetton (1973) (and see Bryman, 1986, for an overview). In the case of group participation, early studies (for example, Coch and French, 1948) are still regarded as seminal, even though new ideas like quality circles are now more familiar (Bernoux, 1994).

Theorists concerned with human growth and development focus on participation as a way of countering the adverse psychological impact which hierarchical, bureaucratic organizations have on employees. Included in this category are Argyris and Herzberg, mentioned earlier in relation to job redesign, and McGregor ([1960] 1987) who saw participation in terms of individuals' varying degrees of involvement in decision-making. But as I also noted, the manner in which such theorists' work is defined and circumscribed in terms of organizational values and goals creates an ambiguity. So despite their best intentions, such theorists are typically trying to serve two masters, seeing no incompatibility between their humanistic concerns and those of efficient management. Indeed McGregor quite explicitly saw 'management by integration and self-control' as 'a deliberate attempt to link improvement in managerial competence with the satisfaction of higher-level ego and self-actualization needs' ([1960] 1987: 61).

In general, then, there has been, and still is, a widely supported belief that such arrangements can satisfy both productivity criteria and those of human growth and development. (For overviews see Blumberg, 1968; Hales, 1993: Chapter 6.) However, such attempts at satisfying both the goals of management and the presumed needs of employees are frequently based on an inadequate conception of people as human beings, and are liable to result in stunted growth. While managers may like to believe that their style of leadership, their attempts at eliciting motivated behaviour, are ethical, this can be questioned. They can ensure that attention in participatory situations is focused on formally defined organizational goals, and, within such parameters, psychological manipulation arises because in group situations there may be pressure on individuals to conform. More generally, the fact that people have shared in a decision makes it cognitively harder for them to dissociate themselves from it, or to act in a contrary fashion. This whole issue was placed in a wider social context in the important contribution from Pateman (1970: 69). Other landmark sources on this and related themes are

Bendix (1956) on managerial ideology and Baritz (1960) on social scientists' complicity in such ideological and epistemological bias.

Of course, the manipulative potential of participative management may be harnessed to secure the commitment of employees to what would be widely regarded as an organization's beneficial contribution to society. Following Mohr (1973), Burns (1978) suggested that people could be stimulated to greater heights of motivation and morality by being encouraged to focus on organizational purposes. While we should recognize the largely public sector context which Burns was addressing, it is worth noting that his ideas were adopted by Peters and Waterman (1982) in their chapter entitled 'Man waiting for motivation'. Peters and Waterman recognized the role of service as a motivating force; they referred to 'love of product' and 'the dominating need of human beings to find meaning and transcend mundane things' (1982: 76). What I have suggested in this chapter is that this will depend on the employees' evaluation of the product and the productive process. However, assuming that we are talking of influencing people in the interests of apparently laudable goals, is this acceptable? Or is any manipulation wrong? Unless employees' critical capacity is fostered, the ideas of writers such as McGregor, and Peters and Waterman, are ethically questionable. The motive is little different from that of any other attempt at managerial control. There may be occasions when a consequentialist analysis would seem to support such influence, where the ends justify the means, but if one has to generalize, then managers have a duty to be aware of the moral issues involved.

These issues can be complex. To encourage employees to focus on the manifest importance of an anti-viral drug may well deflect attention from aspects of its production and testing, or from side effects in its use. Only full access to information, and critical reflection regarding all relevant concerns, will counter the potential for distortion, whether by those convinced of the product's value, or by its opponents. As I noted in Chapter 4, there is a substantial contemporary literature on participative problem-solving and conflict-management processes, designed to counter such bias and manipulation. I referred particularly to Nielsen's (1990) 'dialogic leadership', which is aimed at avoiding such tendencies and putting ethics onto the agenda in open discourse between management and employees. In the context of the current discussion, Kelman's (1965) paper on manipulation should not be overlooked either. Kelman spelled out steps that can be taken by social researchers and consultants to minimize the likelihood of such influence. Translated to the context of organizational management, these suggest the following rules. First, that managers should seek to increase awareness of possible manipulation, by making explicit their own values and encouraging reaction from employees. Second, that in order to facilitate resistance to manipulation, employees' values should receive at least an equal hearing to those of management. And third, that in order to encourage participants' freedom of choice, the full range of options or policies available should be brought forward and explored, and then discussed in a supportive setting.

Conclusion

My discussion has differed from most others on this topic, in that I have been concerned with the ethics of employees' motivation, and not solely with moral aspects of managerial influence and control. I have tried to argue that the values and subjectively defined responsibilities of each member of an organization are potentially significant for the wider society in which that organization is located. Both as producers of goods and services, and as consumers, people are implicated in activities which may have social and ecological importance. As producers, or employees, not only does this suggest responsibilities, but it indicates possible (de)motivating factors.

That perspective is indicative of a particular theoretical standpoint, or paradigm, which is radical humanist (Burrell and Morgan, 1979) or critical (Alvesson, 1987). But while certainly there are issues of environmental concern, of public safety, of illegality, employee health and so on, to which members of organizations should be alert, their more familiar responsibilities to stakeholders remain. For example, taxpayers, customers and shareholders have legitimate expectations concerning service, reliability and return on investments, which are met through efficient and effective organization. And the morally aware employee, however radical in some respects (such as preparedness to speak out against dishonest marketing methods), may at the same time recognize, as another ethical demand, an obligation to contribute to the efficient and careful manufacture and delivery of the products or services involved.

This latter is the manifest concern of those whose thinking and theorizing reflects the 'productivity and efficiency' (Dachler and Wilpert, 1978) or 'functionalist' (Burrell and Morgan, 1979) paradigms. Thus different value-orientations or paradigms are indicative of competing (moral) concerns. Ethical issues and dilemmas are indicated as a result. In the context of the present chapter these dilemmas are conspicuous in a more specific tension between a desire to maintain control over decisions or decision-outcomes, and respect for employees' moral development. Management may believe that this tension can be dealt with either by excluding personnel from decision-making entirely, or by some sort of participative arrangement through which to recognize employees' concerns. The ethical case for exclusion, or minimal involvement, resides in the need, on occasion, for quick, efficient, decisions: this would entail what Srivastva and Cooperrider call a 'chain of consent' rather than a chain of command (1986: 707). In other instances, that type of hierarchical control is unjustified, indicative, perhaps, of a lack of trust in subordinates. Instead, some sort of open and non-manipulative dialogue would be called for in the context of identifying and resolving ethical issues and dilemmas; what, in Chapter 4, I called a 'dialogic mode' for handling ethics in organizations. Those involved, whether individually or in groups, would be aware of prima facie moral obligations to immediately affected parties (including, of course, personal interests such as one's own dependants) as well as more distant stakeholders affected by organizational activity. They would then, through discussion with others, arrive at a judgmental decision. Such participation reaches towards the goals of involvement in 'honest and useful' work (Roszak, [1978] 1981) and 'political efficacy' (Pateman, 1970) and contributes more to human moral development than is indicated in the work of most self-actualization theorists.

7 Equality and the Management of Differences

People in organizations, as in life generally, harbour a wide variety of personal differences: physical, sexual, intellectual, racial, cultural. The reasons for such differences are manifold, complex and in some cases poorly understood. In this chapter I shall clarify issues concerning the significance of such individual differences and categorizations: the nature of discrimination and harassment, the extent to which such action is deliberate or otherwise, and whether it is attributable to specific individuals or systemic in nature. These issues frequently demand a moral response by management and others: the removal of barriers to equal opportunity, changing the criteria for preferment, examining the distribution of organizational rewards and resources, reconsidering procedures for policy formulation and decision-making, and the cessation or prevention of harassment and victimization. Sometimes this may suggest conflicting prima facie moral duties: to the disadvantaged individuals or groups, but also to stakeholders generally. Thus positive action is invited where concern for particular individuals' or groups' needs is judged to override other, functional, considerations. As with Chapters 5 and 6, this chapter has a dual function. For while it is primarily concerned with matters of equity, it also provides an opportunity to demonstrate the need, in the judgmental approach to handling ethical issues and dilemmas, for an adequate conceptualization of the situations faced. So I shall quite deliberately emphasize, and indicate how we can use, particular concepts and conceptual frameworks.

Differences between people

Some differences reflect genetic factors present at birth, and others indicate traits, habits or characteristics which have been acquired subsequently. Within the latter category, sociologists would refer to ascribed and achieved characteristics, the former stemming from the circumstances into which one is born, in which one is raised, and over which one has little or no control. Innate differences include age, sex, physique, coloration, some aspects of health and, arguably, individual variations in intelligence. Ascribed features include the effects of initial educational opportunity, social and economic background, religion and related characteristics, such as some deeply ingrained values. These are not normally the result of conscious choices or effort on the part of the individual. By contrast, acquired or achieved characteristics include knowledge, skills, qualifications and other manifestations of self-conscious personal and intellectual development. Also included here may be habits (addictions?) such as smoking, diet and other aspects of lifestyle, in so far as these can be said to be self-induced, which may be a problematic assertion given the influence of home, subcultural and economic background in these respects.

Due to these differences between people, and especially the genetic and ascribed factors, absolute equality is unrealistic. Instead, we have inequality, explained in terms of differences which constitute sources of personal advantage and disadvantage. While some of these factors affect matters such as housing, health and education (themselves the bases of difference), the particular focus in this discussion is on their manifestation in the context of work. Because of their differences, people may have varying degrees of success in obtaining and retaining employment, with obvious economic implications. Their experience of work can also be affected, as seen in harassment, victimization and exclusion from processes of organizational decision-making. A key point in all of this is the distinction between what are obviously individual characteristics, and those which are common to a whole category of people, such as women, members of a racial group, or graduates in general. This is important because of the tendency for people to stereotype others. Not only may the stereotype be quite inaccurate, the perpetuation of a myth, but to typecast people in this way is unfair to individuals as individuals.

Of course, as Williams (1962) has stressed, one obvious respect in which people are equal is as human beings. If one assumes that we all have a capacity to feel pain, a need for self-respect, and a potential for moral thought, then in terms of respect, rights, justice and fairness there is a moral demand to treat people reasonably and equitably. As sources of personal disadvantage, the characteristics which comprise bases for difference can be changed, or at any rate compensated for, during someone's life. And in so far as one can make allowance for or control such differences, one can approximate to a state of absolute equality between individuals in the sense that Williams noted.

However, we must bear in mind that there are differences between jobs (their place in the organizational structure, the type of work involved, and the remuneration attached), which are not the same as the differences between individuals. In the interests of organizational performance (itself a utilitarian ethical issue), management must ensure that the appropriate people are recruited and appointed to a wide variety of roles, and that they engage in the appropriate behaviour. For example a scientific research department requires staff who have relevant knowledge and experience, and people will be selected accordingly. But the same laboratory may have sound safety reasons for banning smoking on the premises (quite apart from health considerations or concern for non-smokers). Policies such as these may sometimes have contentious discriminatory implications; can one refuse to employ smokers, or ban the wearing of garments specific to an ethnic group?

All such moves raise issues concerning the justification for specific

managerial decisions. These lead into the question of prejudice and unfair discrimination, and beyond that, to harassment, bullying and the real effects of
such behaviour for all concerned: anger, stress, illness, resignation among
victims; and poor morale, diminished performance, inadequate quality of
work and possible safety or security risks for the organization and its public.
Thus organizational policy and development must both address the management of differences in the interests of functional performance, and also
deal with questions of bias and prejudice which can inform demeanour, discourse and decisions, may sometimes be unconscious, and sometimes be
institutionalized in corporate culture or procedure.

It is hardly possible to discuss this subject at the organizational level without some appreciation of the societal context. In particular, differences
between individuals in terms of their economic class and social status are, in
large measure, the manifestation of a reciprocal relationship between organizations and society. This takes the form of a syndrome, whereby specific
differences and inequalities, ranging from educational background to physical characteristics, form the basis for discrimination at the organizational
level. This in turn affects people's economic welfare, which tends to reinforce
the advantages and disadvantages with which they started, and also those of
their offspring.

Explanations for social inequality

Sociological explanations for inequality in society can be divided into two
broad categories: functionalist and conflict-based. As an academic theory, the
functionalist mode of social explanation was especially characteristic of the
1940s and early 1950s. As a popular, ideological, justification for wage differentials in particular, it is still with us. Essentially, functionalism entails the
conceptualization of social systems as analogous to biological organisms,
adapting naturally to exigencies in their environment. Applied to questions of
economic inequality among individuals, the functionalist perspective was
epitomized by Davis and Moore, in their assertion that: 'Social inequality
is . . . an unconsciously evolved device by which societies insure that the most
important positions are conscientiously filled by the most qualified persons'
(1945: 243). In other words, 'the most important positions' command the
highest rewards, and the assumed economic and social necessity for such differentials provides a utilitarian ethical justification for income inequality.
However it would appear that large numbers of occupations are more or less
equally important, and any attempt to differentiate between them is, as
Parkin ([1971] 1972: 19) noted, simply a value judgment.

According to functionalist theory the device which ensures such outcomes
is the labour market. As an employment sector faces a recruitment shortage,
so market forces push up wages, attract people into that area and thus rectify
the problem. However this theory assumes a pure market, which it very rarely
is. Professions can restrict entry to their membership, so limiting their

numbers and the income levels of their practitioners. The collective bargaining process, both at national and organizational level and involving trade unions and employers, may entail an element of coercion by either side in a dispute; threats, strike action, redundancy, the closure of operations, and so forth. And senior executives can exercise their prerogative to award themselves considerable salary increases with, at least until a recent upsurge in public outcry on both sides of the Atlantic, little accountability to anyone except, perhaps, shareholders.

So in opposition to the functionalist explanation, we find an interpretation in terms of power and conflict (for example, Dahrendorf, 1959). Sociological debate here deals in the concepts of class and status as aspects of social stratification. Class, often associated with Marxist analysis, refers to material differences, to persons' economic resources, including opportunities to earn income. This must be distinguished from status, which Weber defined in terms of membership of social circles or occupational communities (Gerth and Mills, 1946: Chapter 7). Some occupations may be quite high in status but offer relatively low material rewards. This occurs particularly in the personal service professions, such as education, some branches of medicine, or the Church (which is why the professions proved awkward for Marxist analysis: see Johnson, 1972: 10).

Apart from the distinction between the two concepts, it is also crucial to appreciate the aetiological relationship between status and class. Membership of high-status groups or occupations is associated with access to influential elements in society, and with the acquisition of appropriate behavioural norms, both of which facilitate appointment to important higher-paying positions in society. And, as I note below, within organizations these factors are instrumental in giving rise to bias and discrimination, if only unconsciously, on grounds which may not stand up to close scrutiny; for example having attended a particular school. So if what we are really concerned with is people's life chances, then this requires a more comprehensive basis for analysis than that provided by economic class alone.

There are other important respects in which members of some social groups experience disadvantage due to their non-work situation. A prime example is seen in the case of women, in so far as they are expected to give priority to a domestic role. Because of those responsibilities, women's access to employment is often restricted to work which is part-time, low-paid, or both. Similarly, disabled people may be hampered by problems of mobility; and ethnic minorities, especially newcomers to a society, such as refugees, by problems of language or adjustment to an unfamiliar culture.

Organizational reinforcement of social inequality

Inequalities in the workplace are to a considerable extent bound up with these wider societal patterns. This is a two-way process. Managerial policies and decisions may appear to be constrained by social norms, even when this results in manifest unfairness; and what goes on in organizations affects and may reinforce the nature of society. The most obvious example of the latter point is the way in which the hierarchical nature of most organizations and administrative systems, in most societies, generates parallel class and status differences in their host communities. Yet it may not be feasible for the management of an organization to ignore occupational wage and salary differentials in society at large. Even if the rate for a particular job seems unjustifiably low in relation to the type of work involved, anything higher may threaten the viability of the organization.

There are other less obvious illustrations of this interaction of social norms and organizational policy. For example people with certain physical characteristics, defined by society as attractive, may be employed in advertising or other front-line dealings with the public, on the grounds that this is necessary if the organization is to present an appropriate image and compete successfully. In all such examples there are commercial or financial considerations, concerning the overall state of the organization, which themselves have ethical implications for stakeholders. The effect of large numbers of employers following the same policies is to create, highlight and reinforce such differences and inequalities at the societal level, which has implications for the social categories involved. However, such extant manifestations of the management of differences often rest on unquestioned assumptions and prejudices, and actually there may be scope for choice.

Discrimination in organizations

It is often assumed that acts of prejudice and discrimination are the result of consciously held tendencies to favour particular individuals or certain types of person compared with others. But much discrimination in organizations, as elsewhere, is unconscious and unintentional. And whether it is deliberate or not, discrimination may well be the product of unquestioned assumptions, beliefs and norms in society. Furthermore, a distinction can be drawn between discrimination by individuals, or groups of individuals, and situations where such bias or disadvantage is inherent in formal organizational policy and procedure. Thus one can conceptualize the possibilities according to whether bias is individual or systemic, and whether or not it is the deliberate product of consciously held beliefs. This is seen in Figure 7.1; but it must be stressed that in this figure both the dimensions 'individual – systemic', and 'conscious – unconscious' represent conceptual idealizations which have a heuristic value; they should not be regarded as clear-cut dichotomies.

Before looking at each of these possibilities a few additional comments are called for. First of all, I use the term discrimination in a general sense. It need not be confined to what one would normally regard as unfair or unjustifiable, but may include what are, arguably, ethically acceptable actions based on

Figure 7.1   *Deliberate and unintentional discrimination*

	Conscious or deliberate bias or discrimination	Unconscious or unintentional bias or discrimination
Individual or group action	1	3
Systemic or organizational effect	2	4

distinctions reflecting technical or other practical reasons (such as a requirement for specific professional qualifications). Second, only actual persons can be moral agents, although a discriminatory policy or outcome, as an unintended, perhaps implicit, organizational property, can of course be subject to evaluation in ethical terms. Particular individuals could then be held responsible for 'sins of omission' if they fail to initiate corrective action where this seems appropriate. Third, for each of the possibilities in Figure 7.1 one can ask several further questions. What is it about some people that sets them apart from others? What is at stake for the victims of discrimination? What sort of rationale, if any, is put forward by management to defend their actions?

I have already outlined the answer to the first of these questions, on differences. On the second, what is at stake for individual victims of discrimination may be position or status, material rewards, access to decision-making, or personal wellbeing. Discrimination in relation to positional matters refers to the selection, appointment and promotion of individuals, and also to transfers and changes in, or termination of, their contracts of employment. Material rewards include remuneration, and the award of bonuses or other benefits, although such differences are often associated with the position, rather than with the individual. Access to decision-making refers to situations where individuals or categories of people are excluded from decision-making processes, or not consulted on matters which affect them. Again, this may be a property of the position itself in relation to organizational structure and procedure, rather than personalized discrimination against particular persons. Personal wellbeing refers to discriminatory situations which affect the individual's physical or mental health. This includes 'violence' in the form of harassment, bullying and comparable treatment on grounds of one's 'difference'.

The question of a rationale to justify discrimination raises a host of complex issues. Individuals may act quite unofficially, or they may act in a formal capacity but allow personal prejudice to affect their interpretation of policy. In any event a plausible rationale may be presented, referring to such matters as efficiency, safety or indeed equity for others. But there are also situations where formal rules and procedures have the quite unintentional effect of disadvantaging specific categories of people. Here a distinction should be made between an unjust system, which is nevertheless administered consistently, and situations where the execution of policy or the implementation of rules is variable and unfair. In the latter case the action is that of particular individuals, reflecting their interpretation, and may well reflect personal prejudice as suggested above. There are also situations where physical or logistical arrangements can have a discriminatory effect if they present barriers to the equal treatment of different categories of people: for example the absence of lifts or ramps for the disabled.

Finally it must be stressed that the conceptualizations and typologies which I offer here are far from fully comprehensive. They represent one attempt at defining, in general terms, the various ways in which discrimination can occur, the reasons for this, and the ethical issues arising. Furthermore, although I am focusing on employee relations in organizations, it is worth mentioning a possible extension of the arguments to include all stakeholders, who, as I point out in Chapter 10, may have comparable rights to fair treatment.

Deliberate and unintentional discrimination in organizations

In Figure 7.1, *Cell 1* (individual/group – conscious/deliberate) we find those cases which spring to mind most often when people think of prejudice and discrimination: the conscious, more or less deliberate, sometimes malicious harming of others' rights and interests. This could be individual or group action. It could be provoked by almost any 'difference', but is most commonly associated with race and sex. It arises in relation to the denial of positional and material rewards, as well as access to decision-making. Most (but not all) instances of harassment and other violence also fall into this category. Discrimination by individuals can also arise through their discretionary interpretation of administrative rules. More generally, failure to correct systemic inequities arising from administrative or technological arrangements could be deliberate 'sins of omission'.

Discriminatory action will usually be justified by reference to a rationale, normally of a functional tone (that the discrimination in question supports organizational performance). But such arguments may be specious. If a manager prohibits smoking on the premises then the supporting case may be fairly strong, on health or safety grounds. But if it is argued that certain categories of people, such as members of a particular racial group, are unreliable, then this is likely to be unacceptable stereotyping, and unfair to the vast majority of the category in question.

The no-smoking decision, meanwhile, may become formalized in administrative rules. Thus in *Cell 2* (systemic/organizational – conscious/deliberate) we find the intentional and systemic organizational expression of such functionally justified discrimination. In this explicit, formal manifestation, there may be a clear rationale which justifies the policy, such as safety or health. But a more contentious example might be a policy of insisting on graduates only, or people below a certain age, for appointment to particular positions in an organization. Cell 2 could also include any deliberately induced element in the culture of an organization, intended to guide action towards some sort of discriminatory or selective outcome.

Planned, systemic, discrimination is seen most clearly in administrative rules, and can affect employees' interests regarding positional and material rewards and access to decision-making. Arguably, also, the overall rationale of technological arrangements can include a deliberate intention to employ certain types of personnel. This is a form of conscious discrimination, as in scientific management (Taylor, 1911) or in more recent innovations entailing the use of information technology (for example the displacement of programmers by systems analysts in Pettigrew, 1973).

With *Cell 3* (individual/group – unconscious/unintentional) we need to recognize unquestioned tacit assumptions, and also thoughtlessness or ignorance, in persons' actions. These assumptions may reflect the influence of society and of those elements of the organizational system, including its culture, which harbour unintended inequities and discriminatory tendencies. This indicates an overlap with Cell 4. Such unconscious discrimination can occur in relation to almost any issue, including harassment or other forms of hurtful conduct. These situations can arise out of ignorance or misunderstanding on the part of the perpetrator, who is thus not necessarily guilty.

Rowe (1990) introduces the concepts of 'microinequities' and 'microaggression' to describe apparently minor instances of prejudice, discrimination, harassment, and so on. Of course, if these were deliberate, they would be located in Cell 1, above. But Rowe's concepts are especially relevant in relation to unconscious or unintentional acts, which can undermine their victims through frequent, if apparently insignificant, occurrences. Despite the prefix 'micro', they are not trivial, any more than other 'everyday' moral issues are trivial (Waters et al., 1986). They are small instances of a more insidious problem. They do not always relate to obvious things like race, religion or gender, where consciousness of the issues may indeed be better developed; although of course they usually do. Quite often they concern less talked-about differences, such as the nature of persons' private lives. These things may set some individuals apart from the rest, and perhaps impede communication and mutual understanding between them and their colleagues. Meanwhile the latter are unaware of the harm and hurt which their actions are causing. Patterns of discriminatory, offensive or unwelcome behaviour are then perpetuated because microinequities and microaggression 'are in the air we breathe, in the books we read, in the television we all watch, and because we cannot change the personal characteristic that leads to the inequity' (Rowe, 1990: 155).

That people may be unaware of the distress they are causing can also be due to the peculiar sensitivity of the victim. For example, Rowe refers to the possibility that someone has witnessed or experienced sexual violence as a young child. As a result he or she may be particularly sensitive to innuendo, joking, comment or suggestion of a salacious nature, experiencing this as continuous, if slight, harassment, with deleterious personal consequences due to associations with the past: 'Like the dripping of water, random drops may do little damage; endless drops in one place can have profound effects' (Rowe, 1990: 159).

In *Cell 4* (systemic/organizational – unconscious/unintentional) obvious examples are found in the culture of the organization, where racist, sexist and other bias may be pervasive, which then influences individuals' unconsidered actions. Another not uncommon situation is where particular departments of organizations have reputations which may be unjustified or out of date, be the subject of adverse myth and argument, and their members suffer as a consequence. Such cultural bias may or may not reflect the relative functional importance of the departments in question, but it can lead to unfair conduct towards personnel in those areas, with real consequences, especially in terms of material rewards and access to influence over decisions. Cell 4 also covers cases of unintentional administrative and technological sources of discrimination. Sometimes these are so obvious that they are overlooked. For example, rigid nine-to-five hours of work in an office have a discriminatory effect on people who have unavoidable daytime domestic responsibilities. Once this problem is recognized, innovations such as flexible hours and childcare provision can be introduced as a solution. Similarly, technological and physical arrangements which preclude the employment of disabled persons are implicitly discriminatory. Yet all sorts of innovations can be used to obviate such difficulties, such as Braille and audio output for the visually impaired, and mechanical aids for those who have problems with dexterity and mobility (Coussey and Jackson, 1991; Grzeda, 1994).

The equitable organization

Inequalities in organizations, when these are perceived as unjust, foster distrust between management and those whom they manage. Such situations hamper cooperation and inhibit flexibility. Fox (1974a: Chapter 8) stressed that this essentially moral issue should be put forward against the argument that inequalities stimulate performance by providing a system of incentives. Recent research also demonstrates that in the management of managerial careers 'fairness of promotion procedures and the honouring of agreements' are vital to a satisfactory employment relationship (Herriot et al., 1994: 120).

Thus the justice, or fairness, of the actual *distribution* of benefits or advantages in any system must be distinguished from the fairness of the *procedure* by which such distribution is decided. The latter refers, in particular, to persons' opportunity to participate in the policy and resource allocation processes, the moral importance of which is stressed by many writers on management and business ethics (for example, Donaldson, 1989; Fox, 1971; 1974a; Srivastva and Cooperrider, 1986) and in ethics and political philosophy (for example, Rawls, 1972). I shall attempt to separate distributive and procedural justice, and deal with them in that order.

Distributive justice

'Everybody is in favour of justice, but not the same interpretation of it' (Raphael, [1981] 1994: 67). Two different interpretations of justice can be identified. One emphasizes individuals' *merit* (or lack of it), and calls for them to be treated accordingly, as they deserve. The other concept of justice starts from the assumption that one should help those most in *need*, in order to redress the disadvantages they face.

The concept of need is a reminder of the question of social inequalities. It was also discussed in the previous chapter, with reference to Fromm's ([1976] 1979) notion of 'existential having'. As such, it can be connected to the question of a minimum acceptable provision (of income, health and welfare, education, and other social goods) which will vary between societies (although there are specified levels recommended by, for example, the World Health Organization and the European Community). Such provision may be regarded as a right, and may be legally so in some cases. Thus the more disadvantaged members of any system (a society or an organization) would be entitled to some sort of special consideration in order to compensate them, and to bring them into line with the acceptable level.

The merit theory of justice reflects utilitarian ethics. It calls for the reward (or punishment) of people because their actions are useful (or harmful) to society or to organizations. Market forces operate on this basis, putting a high value on those people whose contribution is most in demand, although one may question whether 'the market' necessarily has a monopoly of wisdom about what is good for society. Furthermore, in the case of employment, other factors, notably power and conceptions of fairness, also affect the level of remuneration which different occupations and individuals can command.

Rawls (1972) maintained that the introduction of social and economic inequalities is only justified if they produce increased benefits for the whole system, and if those who were previously the most disadvantaged are no worse off as a result. Thus an inequality can be justified if it contributes to social utility, as in the merit theory outlined above. But within this overall increase in utility, priority is given to the needs of the least well off. In short, differential rewards to the most fortunate are not offered on grounds of desert, but as an incentive. Rawls's theory has wide relevance, applying to any distribution of resources in society, material or symbolic. Many such situations are complex, since a variety of factors combine to produce inequality, and, as with utilitarianism, while the boundaries of the system may appear fairly obvious if we are talking about a nation state, this is much more problematic when applying the theory at the organizational level. Nevertheless, according to Scanlon, Rawls's approach can be seen most clearly in situations involving 'the creation of new jobs or offices to which special economic rewards are attached or [involving] an increase in the income associated with an existing job' (Scanlon, 1975: 192).

Equitable pay

Distributive justice is relevant to the allocation of any scarce resource in organizations, but I shall concentrate here on remuneration, not least because the ethical aspects of comparability, especially regarding the salaries of senior executives, have come to the fore recently.

'Equal pay for equal work' is, in principle, entirely fair. The problem is that not all work is equal. Thus what is really needed is some basis for comparability between what are sometimes very different occupations and jobs. This is especially relevant to comparisons between 'men's work' and 'women's work'. (The belief that there is such a distinction raises other ethical issues, to which I have alluded already in this chapter, such as the accessibility of particular types of employment to women.) Typically, the criteria used for comparing dissimilar jobs reflect the demands placed on people in their work, and perhaps the investment they have had to make to attain such positions. These criteria include skill, responsibility and training required, as well as the danger or disagreeableness involved (Benn and Peters, 1959: 138; Simon, 1988: 364).

In practice, such comparability is immensely difficult. One need only consider industrial relations bargaining and pay settlements to see this. The arguments used in such situations concern fairness; they are 'moral arguments' (Clegg, 1979: 248). However Simon (1988) suggests that, over time, the attainment of a 'reflective equilibrium' (Rawls, 1972) on matters of comparability is possible, involving an alignment of principles and intuitions through a process of considered dialogue and mutual judgment.

In recent years, both in Britain and in the USA, a great deal has been said, in the press and elsewhere, concerning the increasingly high salaries of corporate executives. The Archbishop of Canterbury was a prominent critic of this trend in several statements in 1992. Perhaps the most publicized instance in the UK was that involving British Gas chief executive Cedric Brown (£475,000 per annum in 1994), but in fact even more striking examples could be found among fund managers in the City of London (Blackhurst, 1995). Pay differentials have emerged as a major issue at a time when income inequalities in Britain have reached new extremes for the period since World War II (Barclay, 1995). For example, the relative treatment of UK civil servants and nurses provoked great outcry in February 1995.

As Sampson (1995: 314–19) points out, apart from moral outrage among the population at large, apparent abuses of power by industrial leaders has implications for other stakeholders in their organizations, such as pension funds, and all of this has provoked calls for enquiries into corporate governance (see Chapter 10). The specific question of remuneration is part of the broader agenda here, and in the UK the Greenbury Report called for greater disclosure of executive salaries (Greenbury, 1995). However, significantly, there is now some evidence of a new form of comparability emerging: between executives. Disclosure of high remuneration packages for some may lead to demands from others for similar rewards (Rodgers, 1996).

Rawls (1972) argued that any inequalities in a social system must benefit the least well off under conditions of equal opportunity for all. On this basis one could justify inflated salaries for some only if the situation of the worst off is protected, if not improved. Rawls called this the 'difference principle'. Yet, in general, pay increases for the leaders of industry have frequently been accompanied, indeed enabled, by redundancies in the middle and lower reaches of their organizations.

The defence offered by companies for their executives' high levels of remuneration has tended to refer to compensation for risk-taking, and more recently, to the need to attract and retain top-quality managers. Meanwhile the Greenbury recommendations pointed to the need to relate salaries to performance. Both of these positions reflect the merit theory of justice. Thus a link between top salaries and the problematic question of performance-related pay (PRP) is forged (for comment on this see Jebb, 1996). PRP has received much attention. While organizations seem determined to introduce such schemes, perhaps because they appear to offer an effective control mechanism (Proctor et al., 1993), some research suggests that they may do more harm than good (Kohn, 1993; Thompson, 1993). The problems with PRP are considerable. Attributing credit for performance, not least with executive tasks, is often hard to determine precisely. There is a danger of goal-displacement as the more measurable criteria are emphasized, or the more easily attainable are pursued by employees. The attribution of performance to specific individuals in a collective situation can be problematic, while the alternative of group-based performance measurement can raise the issue of alleged 'free riders' who are felt not to deserve as much as the others. Where performance cannot be objectively assessed, problems of bias may enter into the judgments of those responsible for evaluating others' work. And, as I indicated earlier with the reference to Fox (1974a), all of these things can provoke rancour, inhibit cooperation, and lead to demotivation by those who feel unfairly treated.

Procedural justice

The 'difference principle' is one of two principles which Rawls maintained would be chosen by parties to an imaginary situation, known as the 'original position'. This is designed to ensure a fair basis to a just society. (The other principle is that individuals have an equal right to liberty, provided that they do not intrude on others' similar rights.) The hypothetical original position has a strong Kantian flavour of impartiality. In it, people agree on principles of justice behind a 'veil of ignorance'. That is, they do not know what position they would occupy in the future social system, or even to which values they would subscribe. But this idea of people acting behind a veil of ignorance is inadequate in itself, because, in reality, one would need to ask how they come to be in such a position in the first place. As Scanlon suggests:

> To complete the argument some motivation for the construction of the Original Position is required, ideally a motivation which connects the device of choice behind a veil of ignorance with intuitively plausible arguments for a pluralist form of social cooperation. I believe that this further motivation can be found in Rawls' theory in the notion that a person's good is to be identified not with the particular goals and commitments which he may at any given time have adopted but rather with his continuing status as a rational agent able to adopt and modify these goals. (Scanlon, 1975: 171)

In reality, people will also be affected by social influences, which threaten their autonomy as rational moral agents. And while sometimes in organizations such influences may be an unplanned effect of systemic, institutional arrangements, at other times they may be deliberately brought about by management, in pursuit of the specific goals that the institution in question was set up to attain. Now this is in conflict with Rawls's principles of liberty and distributive justice. In the first place, it suggests manipulation; and, second, it suggests an unequal distribution of access to decision-making processes. What is at issue here is not merely the procedure for arriving at a just or fair distribution of, say, financial rewards. What is also of concern is the extent to which people are allowed to participate in this procedure. And just as a particular substantive distribution (for example of pay) may be based on a rationale reflecting either a utilitarian or an egalitarian argument (or, alternatively, reflecting someone's personal prejudice), so access to the decision-process itself will reflect, to a greater or lesser degree, a (Kantian) concern for persons' rights to be involved therein.

I have already rehearsed these arguments in the previous chapter, and as with the conclusion to that discussion, the way forward here is by means of open and non-manipulative dialogue. This will incorporate the judgmental process, including the conceptualization needed to make sense of situations and help arrive at solutions. So far in this chapter I have suggested ways of distinguishing between different forms of discrimination, and commented on theories of justice. Now I shall present a particular and more practical approach to the conceptualization of discrimination and equal opportunity in real situations, which goes some way towards reconciling the twin concerns of utility and fairness.

Criteria of relevance and surmountability

Any instance of discrimination depends essentially on the presence of obstacles which hinder individuals, or categories of people, who seek a particular 'good' (Westen, 1985). These obstacles, which relate to persons' different characteristics, may be assessed as more or less 'surmountable' by the individual, and more or less 'relevant' to the functioning or goal-attainment of the organization or institution (see Figure 7.2). Where they are not relevant or are insurmountable, employers have a moral duty, and, increasingly, a legal obligation, to remove them or to take some other positive action to help people overcome such difficulties. This refers to Cells 2, 3 and especially 4, in Figure 7.2.

Figure 7.2   *The relevance and surmountability of obstacles to equal opportunity*

	Obstacle surmountable by individuals	Obstacle insurmountable by individuals
Relevant	1	3
Not relevant	2	4

However, both surmountability and relevance are hugely problematic notions in this context. Strictly speaking, insurmountable obstacles are limited to innate factors such as date and place of birth, skin colour, or sex. On the whole, there is little one can do to change these. Surmountable obstacles refer to factors such as educational qualifications, marital status, religious belief, minimum age, style of dress and some personal habits or mannerisms. But things are not so simple. First of all, many of these barriers, particularly those classed as surmountable, are better represented as a continuum; how reasonable is it to expect someone to change their marital status, divest themselves of dependent children, abandon their religion, or to gain a university degree? There is a measure of difficulty or sacrifice involved in these, often reflecting more profound factors such as the individual's location in the economic structure of society.

The concept of surmountability here is comparable to Williams's concept of 'operativeness'. Williams said that 'there is a distinction between a man's rights, the reasons why he should be treated in a certain way, and his power to secure these rights, the reasons why he can in fact get what he deserves' (1962: 122). For example, even if people have equal rights to redress from the law, it may well be that only some can actually avail themselves of the courts if it costs money and if no financial aid is forthcoming from public funds.

Returning to the organizational context, a number of questions are raised. First, one must ask whether or not people can overcome such obstacles unaided. If they cannot, is their employer (or potential employer) willing and able to facilitate this? For example, by offering more flexible hours of work to a single parent with young children. A second and even more problematic question concerns the idea of relevance. Questioning the relevance of an obstacle means that one has to consider very carefully whether the organization is justified in adhering to a policy, or in retaining some other arrangement (administrative or technological) which has a discriminatory effect on certain categories of actual or potential employees.

Using Figure 7.2 as a framework, various examples can be considered. The first of these concerns a chain of shoe shops where management had imposed a two-tier pay system, with a bonus of 15 pence per hour (in 1995) being paid to those employees who did not smoke (Goodwin, 1995). At first sight this falls into the 'relevant – surmountable' category. But it is problematic, particularly with regard to relevance. The general manager claimed that there had been evidence in the past to show that prior to the introduction of this policy, fifteen years earlier, smokers had a higher rate of absenteeism. He claimed that since then staff had become healthier and that this had contributed to company profitability. Allied to general trends towards no-smoking policies, this appears to be a justifiable argument. However there was no really rigorous scientific testing of the assumption that attendance at work, let alone profitability, was due to a reduction in smoking among staff. What was even more contentious was that staff who only smoked socially, outside their working hours, were also denied the bonus. This may be consistent with the claim that the management concern was with employee health and an assumed relationship between that and productivity; but then such an argument could be extended to other aspects of employees' private lives, which, in general, would not be regarded as grounds for this sort of discrimination. It would be better to judge staff on their attendance record, if that is the real issue, rather than on tentative associations between that and the propensity to smoke outside working hours.

My second case seems to fall into the 'not relevant – surmountable' category. In 1992 a young male employee was dismissed by a large supermarket chain because he had grown his hair almost to waist length. Now it may seem entirely feasible for someone to have his hair cut, but why should he, unless hair length is a crucial issue with regard to the performance of his task? Yet this was not obviously the issue; rather, the company was reported as saying that it 'wanted its employees to have a "conventional" hairstyle' (Dyer, 1994). Given that women were allowed to grow their hair to a similar length, the company's action was subsequently ruled to be a breach of the Sex

Discrimination Act. And even if hygiene factors were relevant, there are ways of overcoming that, such as the provision of headgear.

Third, we have the 'relevant – insurmountable' category. Some examples of this are quite clear, such as people with physical disabilities. In such cases there is often legal backing for the argument that employers should help with circumventing the problem, for example through the provision of suitable facilities. As I have touched upon this already I shall not dwell on it further. Some cases within this category are more problematic, however, and this very point means that they might equally well be considered under one of the other cells in Figure 7.2. Hence my caution, that this figure is no more than a heuristic.

For example, people in some safety-critical occupations, such as airline pilots, have to retire at a specified age (an insurmountable barrier). This is because of an assumption that as one gets older the possibility of physical incapacity, including sudden collapse, increases. It is relevant, but since people age at different rates it may nevertheless seem unfair in some instances. So should it be health that is the criterion, rather than age? If so, age would be reclassified as a non-relevant criterion.

Certainly, in many occupations 'ageism' provides good examples of the 'not-relevant – insurmountable' category. This is increasingly being recognized, although in the UK it is proving hard to legislate against organizations' stipulation of upper age limits in the recruitment process (O'Sullivan, 1996a). Many other cases of this sort (for example concerning race, sex or disability), at least where equal opportunities legislation and policies are in place, tend to be manifestations of personal bias, or the unintended consequences of administrative or technological arrangements as I have mentioned earlier. Sometimes, however, more complex and problematic situations arise. In one case, a large company operated a graduate management training programme, which effectively made it very difficult for non-graduates to progress beyond a certain level in the hierarchy. However, the organization helped those who wished to attend a local university so that they could gain a degree through part-time study, some of this being in the evenings. One woman in her thirties, who was single and had a disabled parent living with her, felt that she could not take on the additional burden of this part-time study. Yet she felt that her non-graduate status was an unfair barrier to her career progression in that company, of questionable relevance as a guide to her potential.

Positive action

Singer maintains that a policy which focuses solely on equal opportunities 'rewards the lucky, who inherit those abilities that allow them to pursue interesting and lucrative careers. It penalizes the unlucky, whose genes make it very hard for them to achieve similar success' ([1979] 1993: 39). But we need not confine the issue to genetic differences. In effect what Singer is saying is that there are *fundamental* differences between people, as I noted early in this chapter, including aspects of their social and economic background. And policies of equal opportunity at the point of entry to an organization, or in relation to subsequent discrimination (promotion, transfer, access to decision-making, and so forth) do not normally take account of these genetic or ascribed characteristics.

The solution to this is positive (or affirmative) action. This refers to all those things which organizations can do to help people overcome problems of minority ethnic background, disability, gender and other manifest disadvantages in particular contexts. Some of these solutions – technical and administrative innovations such as facilities for the disabled – I have described already. Other action includes: explicit encouragement to specific minority groups to apply for particular work; encouraging them to undertake training; raising people's consciousness regarding discrimination generally, including harassment; and cultivating an appropriate organizational culture (Pemberton, 1995). I do not intend to explore technical and legal aspects of this; there are specific sources to which one can refer on such matters (for example, numerous publications of the Equal Opportunities Commission in the UK; Coussey and Jackson, 1991; Shaw and Perrons, 1995).

In its more extreme manifestation, such action involves giving preferential treatment to members of disadvantaged social groups or categories. In the UK it is illegal to positively discriminate in favour of members of particular groups in the actual selection process. Nevertheless 'positive discrimination' (also known as reverse discrimination) raises important questions. Viewed as redress for past injustices, it compensates a group or category of people, rather than specific individuals. But can a group have moral rights? It was specific individuals who were disadvantaged previously, yet now we are suggesting favouring others (albeit from the same group or category) over 'innocent' members of a different class which until now has been favourably treated. So is it a logically flawed policy? It would be acceptable if all we were talking about was the elimination of a prior injustice, but it seems that we are doing more than that; we are, perhaps, replacing it with another, different, injustice.

Furthermore, it can be argued that for positive discrimination to be justified, it has to be shown that such inequity really did occur in the past. For example, if there are few women or members of ethnic minority groups in a particular occupation, this does not prove that there has been discrimination. It may be that few have applied for this work, or that those who have applied were not as well qualified as applicants from among males or the ethnic majority. However, in response to this, one can ask *why* more women, or those from minority groups, have not applied in the past. The answer may well be that members of such groups have been discouraged (at school, perhaps) by a popular view that the occupation was not suitable for them. Thus one argument for positive discrimination is that what it is really intended to do is to redress an imbalance in the culture of a system. Members of disadvantaged groups will continue to suffer for as long as there is a scarcity of role models to encourage them, and a dominance, in the institutions of society, of views and values held by other categories of people (Sher, 1975).

This, in effect, would be to invoke criteria of need and equality as relevant grounds for discrimination, whereas up to now in this discussion the notion of relevance has been construed in terms of utility (for the institution in question) and individual merit in relation to such goals. Consider the following possibility, which represents an argument found in Singer ([1979] 1993: 44–51). An employer decides, for reasons which are as much to do with such social or ethical policy as with corporate performance in the conventional sense, to deliberately favour non-white job applicants. The whites who lose out as a result will doubtless argue that they have been discriminated against, since they think they were better qualified (and let us assume that in a technical sense they were). But what does it mean to say they are better qualified? The idea of 'qualification' refers to some assumed criteria relating to the goals of the organization. So, if the organization introduces a new goal or policy in order to help redress the previous injustice or imbalance – and there is no reason in principle why an organization's goals should not reflect an ethical or social policy, should those who govern it so choose – then why should the white applicants complain? All they can do is challenge these revised goals, which could be a hard case to argue.

So when the criteria of relevance underlying acts of discrimination are considered, these need not be confined to conventional definitions of organizational goals. To assume such technical, functional factors, as is so often done and as I have done for much of this chapter, is to restrict the possibilities. Organizations pursue social goals, and indeed these are not incompatible with their other 'survival' goals when viewed over the longer term, since there may be an element of enlightened self-interest involved. Thus positive action, perhaps even positive discrimination, has a part to play in this process of social development. Nevertheless, such discrimination, as opposed to 'weaker' forms of positive action, raises significant problems when applied in formal organizations. It is worth suggesting that since the disadvantages which positive discrimination is designed to overcome tend to reflect persons' circumstances in their birth, childhood and years of full-time education (or lack of it) there is a good case for saying that it is particularly in those contexts (social policy generally, and especially education) that positive discrimination should be enacted.

Conclusion

A significant strand in this chapter has been a recurring reference to the organization–society relationship. Not only do societal factors affect individuals' chances in the employment context, but organizations can reinforce or counteract these tendencies. It would be too simple, therefore, to say that concern here is for the fair treatment of employees only; the policy issues raised clearly affect a more diffuse population.

This is one example of moral concern for the social and environmental impact of organizations. Such concern provokes questions regarding individuals' moral values and sense of personal responsibility, a theme which has already been addressed in the context of motivation, but also raises crucial issues concerning the relationship between individuals and their employing organizations. That is the particular focus of the next two chapters.

8 Organizations and the Attribution of Responsibility

A key concept in business and management ethics is *responsibility*. But in organizations this is often difficult to pin down. It is not always easy to distinguish individual volition from systemic behaviour, yet it is important to do this if one is to employ terms such as culpability, blame or praise. Furthermore, to talk of an ethical or unethical organization, apart from the conduct of its members, is problematic. From the moral-developmental perspective, therefore, I suggest that we should focus on the people in organizations; on their moral values and responsibilities, while recognizing the systemic forces to which they are exposed.

A vignette from John Steinbeck's *The Grapes of Wrath* illustrates the initial issue addressed here. Some tenant farmers are arguing with the representatives of a bank, who are evicting them from their homesteads. The tenants want to know who they are dealing with, as they seek to defend what they see as their land. The bank's representatives retort:

> 'We're sorry. It's not us. It's the monster. The bank isn't like a man.'
> 'Yes, but the bank is only made of men.'
> 'No, you're wrong there – quite wrong there. The bank is something else than men. It happens that every man in a bank hates what the bank does, and yet the bank does it. The bank is something more than men, I tell you. It's the monster. Men made it, but they can't control it.' (Steinbeck, [1939] 1951: 32)

Is it the bank's representatives who are acting? Or is it the bank itself? Or is it the result of pressures in a larger (capitalist) system? There is a tendency for people to talk of organizations as if they can act in much the same manner as do humans. We say that 'the Government has raised taxes', that 'the University has introduced a new degree in management' or that 'Union Carbide was responsible for the Bhopal chemical plant explosion'. Such language and ways of thinking entail both reification, treating something which is really an abstraction as a concrete entity, and anthropomorphism, attributing human characteristics to this entity. This tendency confronts us with meta-ethical issues. For example, in the literature on business ethics one often finds reference to 'ethical organizations', or organizations as 'moral persons', but does this make logical sense? Can organizations be regarded as moral agents? Can they, as opposed to their members, be blamed or praised? Such questions are fundamental to much of the discussion in later chapters: on moral dissent, on social responsibility and on organization development.

I shall argue that organizations cannot in any literal sense be moral agents. But one can see that individuals in organizations, managers and others, frequently have sufficient discretion to enable ethical deliberation and choice.

Thus where organizational systems harbour characteristics or generate consequences of which we disapprove, responsibility may be attributed to particular individuals for those outcomes, or failing that, we may expect them to take corrective action after the event.

Legal safeguards and moral responsibilities

Any comprehensive discussion of this subject must make some reference to the legal context. Incorporated associations, such as business corporations, have the status of legal entities. This means that such organizations can be treated as distinct from their members, and can be sued under civil law in their own right. As a result they may be required to pay financial compensation to the victims of their negligence. However, there are those who would seek to hold corporations criminally liable in serious cases which have involved loss of life. This is very problematic. First, it implies punitive action against the organization, and it is questionable what this achieves; one cannot imprison a company, while fining it seems less satisfactory than ensuring financial compensation to those entitled to it, something which is enabled by civil law anyway. Second, as I explain later, it is in any case often extremely difficult to apportion responsibility and blame in the organizational context. Examples of cases where this problem has arisen are well documented; they include the capsize of the ferry *Herald of Free Enterprise* at Zeebrugge, in 1987, and the *Piper Alpha* oil rig and Clapham rail crash disasters, both in 1988.

Nevertheless, a number of academics have pursued the idea of 'corporate moral personhood', which would enable criminal action to be brought against offending organizations by treating them in the same way as individuals. Now this idea of the corporation as a moral person may be a useful metaphor, but that is all that it is. In the legal context it could facilitate possible innovations such as, in the UK, the Law Commission's recently published recommendation that a new criminal offence of 'corporate killing' should be created (Law Commission, 1996). However, at various points in this book (for example, with regard to corporate social responsibility in Chapter 10, and codes of ethics, in Chapter 11) I raise the objection that external constraints, or threats of punishment, do not make for moral development. In Kohlberg's terms, what is generated is a self-interested, or perhaps conformist, reaction to external pressures. In other words, if the behaviour of organizations is shaped by such threats of legal action, then while they may *appear* to be ethically acceptable, this is not necessarily indicative of a genuine moral concern among their members.

Meanwhile, if one draws a distinction between punitive and prophylactic measures, there is much to be said for a trend in the latter direction. So far as legal mechanisms are concerned, what is really needed is legislation, or more effective enforcement of existing legislation, to ensure that proper arrangements are established which may prevent untoward things happening in the first place.

Peter French has put forward the idea of 'Enforced Corporate Responsive Adjustment' (ECRA). His 'Principle of Responsive Adjustment' (PRA) states that 'after an untoward event has happened, the persons who contributed to its occurrence are expected to adopt certain courses of future actions that will prevent repetitions' (1992: 12). ECRA requires a corporate defendant to 'prepare a compliance report that spells out what steps it has taken or will take by way of internal discipline, modification of existing compliance procedures, and, as appropriate, compensation to victims' (1992: 170). A second-stage judicial hearing would then either acquit or convict the corporation, depending on whether or not it had taken the appropriate measures as 'responsive adjustment'. As French points out, this would place responsibility for such corrective and preventative action on the managers of the corporation.

There is ample evidence that many disasters result from poor management practice and from failure to learn from past events (Toft and Reynolds, 1994; Turner, 1994). Most of the literature on the subject concerns fatal accidents, but the same logic can apply in respect of innumerable other instances of harm to the public and to employees. For instance, the Barings Bank collapse in 1995 had similarities with the Zeebrugge disaster (initial focus on a lower-ranking individual; subsequent appreciation of possible management deficiencies also; consequent increase in ambiguity over who was responsible).

The intensity of public feelings over loss of life, over severe financial loss for innocent pensioners or investors, or large-scale redundancies in a single-company town, may eventually stir those responsible for an organization's activities so that, to use the well worn cliché, 'it never happens again' (though it often does). How much harder it is, then, to provoke the necessary response and learning where relatively minor damage is involved and there is no public outcry. The literature on this subject usually refers to matters sufficiently serious to capture national or even global attention; but of course many things happen in the workplace, internal to the organization, where the logic is the same, if not the level of attention by the outside world. Yet for the victims, such damage (industrial injury, defective products, poor customer service, offensive sales methods, small-scale pollution, and much else) is experienced as unethical conduct by organizations. One is reminded of C. Wright Mills's distinction between 'personal troubles' and 'public issues' (Mills, 1959: Chapter 1).

Thus people in organizations, especially managers, have moral responsibilities. These responsibilities go beyond the narrow, formal, definitions found in the job specification or organizational rule book (Maclagan, 1983). They encompass a moral demand to exercise imagination and empathy, anticipating things that might go wrong, apprehending prima facie duties, especially, in the context of the immediate argument, a duty of care.

The organization as a moral person

Although most of the philosophical debate on organizations as moral persons has referred specifically to business corporations, the theoretical and most of the practical issues raised have more general relevance. So I shall draw upon this body of theory as the starting point for my analysis.

The volume of literature on the subject is substantial (for example, Collier, 1995; Donaldson, 1982; Ewin, 1991; French, 1979, 1984; Goodpaster and Matthews, 1982; Haworth, 1959; Klein, S., 1988; Ladd, 1970; Pfeiffer, 1990; Velasquez, 1983; Werhane, 1985). Broadly speaking, there are two positions in this debate. On the one hand, a holistic, sometimes anthropomorphic, perspective from which organizations as wholes are viewed as the (moral) agents; on the other hand, a reductionist standpoint, whereby it can only be actual people, usually as individuals, but perhaps including small groups, who act and to whom responsibility is attributed. However within these two positions there are variations, reflecting additional points of clarification and raising further issues. What follows is an attempt to sort out these positions and identify some of the issues.

Anthropomorphism and organizational responsibility

There is an argument that organizations 'act', if one were to replace their existing members (or some of them) with different individuals, it would have no effect on the decisions then taken, or on other manifestations of organized behaviour (Haworth, 1959). Whether this exonerates individuals from moral responsibility is a moot point to which I shall return, since they may be viewed as simply conforming to the formally and socially defined meanings pre-existing in the organization (Silverman, 1970: Chapter 6; Kohlberg, 1969, 1981). But to return to the present argument, a number of writers, notably French (1979, 1984) have maintained that the presence of formally defined and enforceable roles and responsibilities, and policies, criteria and procedures for decision-making – what French (1979) called a Corporate Internal Decision Structure, or CID – justifies the attribution of moral agency to the corporations in which such CIDs are found.

Goodpaster and Matthews built explicitly on French's concept of an internal decision structure when they argued that corporations should be as morally responsible as individual people. They offered the two concepts of 'rationality' and 'respect for persons' as the features of a morally responsible individual, and projected this to organizations. Rationality here refers to 'lack of impulsiveness, care in mapping out alternatives and consequences, clarity about goals and purposes, attention to details of implementation' (1982: 134). Respect for persons refers to the Kantian ideal of treating people as 'ends', and to 'concern for the effects of one's decisions and policies on others' (1982: 134).

Goodpaster and Matthews then argued that organizations could show the same qualities as individuals. We can, they said, see differences between more and less responsible organizations in these terms.

> Some corporations have built features into their management incentive systems, board structures, internal control systems, and research agendas that in a person we would call self-control, integrity and conscientiousness. Some have institutionalized

awareness and concern for consumers, employees and the rest of the public in ways that others clearly have not. (Goodpaster and Matthews, 1982: 135)

However, they explicitly denied any suggestion that corporations are literally persons. They recognized an emotional dimension to human moral behaviour (1982: 134) which does not feature in their corporate analogue. As Ewin says: 'Corporations, as artificial persons . . . lack the emotional life without which there can be no possession of virtues and vices' (1991: 749).

The moral person as a metaphor

Referring to the use of metaphor in organizational analysis, Morgan pointed out that 'there is a close relationship between the way we think and the way we act, and that many organizational problems are embedded in our thinking' (1986: 335). Earlier, Landau had stated that: 'To take a metaphor literally is to create a myth, and the more conventional myths become, the more difficult they are to dislodge' (1961: 335). The 'organization as a moral person' is only a metaphor, but there is the danger that it can become a myth, of use to those who would focus on, and blame, the system, rather than look to those who should take responsibility for an organization's impact on society.

This attack on the 'moral person' as a metaphor for organizations would probably be equally effective with regard to other human or social analogues, such as 'brains' and 'cultures' (Morgan, 1986). (In any case brains could belong to evil people and cultures could encourage them in their wrongdoing.) So what about the machine metaphor instead? At least this has no pretence to moral virtue. Danley ([1980] 1990) suggested this perspective, pointing out that if one thinks of the organization as a machine, one which has gone out of control in some way, wreaking havoc and harm, one would hardly express outrage at the machine. One would look to those who designed it, or operated it, or failed to maintain it properly, or licensed its use. This, as Danley pointed out, is an especially useful perspective for those who are 'reform minded'; who wish to improve organizations.

French's CID model is a particularly good instance of the type of theoretical construct to which the machine metaphor applies. But of course organizations are much more than machines, or even brains. If French's 'corporation as a moral person' was confined to the CID, to 'the ethereal world of black lines and boxes', as Danley ([1980] 1990: 204) put it, then there would be very little for which to blame (or praise) the organization anyway, since so much actual behaviour in organizations cannot be accounted for in such purely formalized terms (Barnard, 1938; Selznick, 1948).

Systemic explanations or individual moral agency?

Essentially, the argument that it makes no sense to attribute moral responsibility to organizations is based on the assertion that this would amount to a 'category mistake . . . which represents the facts of mental life as if they belonged to one logical type or category (or range of types or categories) when they actually belong to another' (Ryle, 1949: 16). Since, as a meta-ethical proposition, only humans (and possibly some animals, especially cetaceans) have a capacity for moral awareness, plainly an abstraction such as a set of administrative arrangements cannot fall into this category.

One strong advocate of this position was Velasquez (1983). Stressing the distinction between fictitious legal entities and real entities, he argued that for an organization to have intentions or moral purposes, it would have to be a real entity, consisting of actual people in a structure of roles. Velasquez then asserted that since moral responsibility cannot be attributed to the structure in itself, it can only be attributed to the people who are party to these arrangements. He suggested three possible answers to the question of who is morally responsible for corporate acts. First, if particular members of the organization intended to bring about a corporate act, then they are morally responsible. Second, if particular persons designed a system (policies, procedures, technologies and other artefacts) intended to bring about specified consequences, then those persons are morally responsible. Third, an event may be the unintentional outcome of a combination of various different actions by members of the organization, in which case Velasquez observes that perhaps no one is morally responsible.

Variations in the attribution of responsibility for specific events

This third possibility accounts for quite a high proportion of organizational activity. In such cases, while no one may be morally responsible for bringing about the event, management are responsible for trying to prevent a recurrence. But there are also occasions where there has been negligence, or where people take calculated risks, in the full knowledge that certain unfortunate results may follow. These possibilities may be amplified along the following lines, although the complex variety of situations makes it difficult to provide a definitive catalogue.

1 *Unexpected, unintended events which are systemic in nature*   Here no obvious moral responsibility can be identified, but there is a danger that management may scapegoat particular persons who were causally implicated in an immediate sense.

2 *Unintentional errors and lapses by members of the organization*, which lead to unfortunate outcomes. Here, again, internal disciplinary action may be taken against them, even though there may be extenuating circumstances.

For example, in the Summerland leisure complex fire on the Isle of Man in 1973, which claimed fifty lives, a number of factors were identified concerning the construction and operation of the complex: unsuitable building materials used, lax building regulations, and scheduling its completion to meet the start of the new tourist season. For staff in the complex these amounted to systemic factors (as in [1] above), but in addition, the emergency exits were locked, the keys were mislaid and staff training with regard to fire safety was subsequently found to have been inadequate (Toft and Reynolds, 1994).

In the case of the *Herald of Free Enterprise* capsize at Zeebrugge, the assistant bosun was responsible for closing the bow doors under the supervision of the chief officer. As this was normally done while the ship sailed out of the harbour, by which time the chief officer had to be on the bridge, it meant that he had to be in two places at once. On this occasion the assistant bosun overslept while resting in his cabin. The chief officer waited for him, and when he saw a figure making his way to the door controls he went to his position on the bridge. In the event, he had mistaken someone else for the assistant bosun, who failed to attend to the bow doors. Clearly there was no intention here; but in the immediate aftermath of the disaster the most obvious target for criticism was the crew member who had fallen asleep, even though more considered investigation revealed a wide range of other factors (Boyd, 1990).

3 *Calculated risks taken by management* in the context of planning and resource allocation, including non-response to warning signs. For example in the well-documented case of the Ford Pinto, the vehicle was marketed in the knowledge that it was unsafe under certain circumstances (rear-end impact at twenty miles per hour). Similarly, before the Zeebrugge disaster, senior management had refused to authorize expenditure on equipment which could have reduced the risk, despite the fact that there had been an earlier instance when one of the company's ships had sailed with her bow doors open. Of course, such situations do not mean that harm was intended, but it is hard to defend those implicated against the accusation that they deliberately refrained from taking preventative action.

4 *Deliberate management decisions with regard to contentious issues* Here there is an expectation that particular outcomes will result, or situations prevail, which others regard as unacceptable. In these cases there is an intention that particular situations, sometimes known to be harmful, will result, or continue. For example, the suppression of research produced by a cigarette manufacturer's scientists pertaining to the health hazards of their products (*The Guardian*, 6 February 1996: 15) or by a pharmaceutical company, regarding the effectiveness of a drug (Reed and McKie, 1996).

5 *Deliberate action by members of the organization* acting in a manner which cannot be legitimized in official organizational terms. This last point, concerning the distinction between what can be viewed as organizational, as opposed to individual, is important when the question of internal organizational discipline arises, and I shall return to it below. Many such instances would be attributable to self-interest by employees, but this need not

be the case. For example in one case of a fairly serious fire, it was found that daily cleaning staff in the building were in the habit of jamming open the fire doors to help them carry equipment around. When a conflagration started it thus spread more rapidly than it would have done otherwise.

Problems of organizational and individual rationality

There are practical dangers in talking of the attribution of responsibility to organizations. For one thing, such reification leads to the elevation of corporate goals above personal values (Velasquez, 1983). Another point is that it can deflect attention from culpable individuals (McMahon, 1995; Velasquez, 1983). Danley stressed that ascribing responsibility to the organization may sever the connection between 'responsibility' and 'remorse, regret, compensation, or punishment' ([1980] 1990: 205). Managers may argue that 'it was the system' and nothing could have been done to prevent whatever happened.

Perhaps this second point is of less concern to the public, provided the organization as a whole can be constrained or penalized in some way, but it will be of concern for management in the context of internal discipline. Individual employees also have an interest in this matter, if they feel they have been unfairly blamed or scapegoated, and also if they are thinking of reporting events or blowing the whistle. These things apply not just in the context of major incidents where legal action might arise, but with minor instances also. This distinction between major and minor incidents leads into the subjectivity and ambiguity of evaluation. Some episodes or situations may be uncontentiously serious, as in fatal accidents. But other issues, such as the use of a particular sales technique, may strike only a few people as ethically significant. Jackall reports how while an accountant in one organization was greatly concerned about violations of proper conduct – 'irregular payments, doctored invoices, shuffling numbers in accounts' – these were regarded as 'small potatoes indeed, commonplaces of corporate life' by other managers (Jackall, 1988: 110).

In broad terms, there are two respects in which members of organizations are concerned with these questions of responsibility-attribution:

1   People have an interest in the extent to which events are caused by individuals' actions, rather than being justified or explained in official organizational or systemic terms. This has a bearing on internal discipline and the correct identification of those responsible, including management themselves. It is relevant to all members of the organization, including potential whistleblowers.
2   Where events appear to be the unintentional outcome of systemic factors, there is a need for understanding so that corrective action can be taken if possible.

In considering this distinction between what is 'organizational' and what is 'individual' I shall draw primarily on the theory of bureaucracy. My assumption (and here my reasoning is deliberately comparable to that demonstrated by French in his exposition on the CID structure) is that the formal system of policies, rules and procedures is the nearest we have to an unambiguous, some would say 'objective', statement of organizational values and intentions. Thus if individuals' actions conform to such formal criteria, they may be said to be 'organizational'. However, because of the ambiguity in such formal statements and in what counts as 'official', and because of the obscurity of persons' motives, it is often very difficult to tell what represents behaviour 'of the organization' and what is private, and individual.

An argument from bureaucratic theory

At this juncture, the theoretical starting point ought really to lie in Max Weber's analysis of bureaucracy, especially his much misunderstood concept of the 'ideal type' and the distinction between formal and substantive rationality (Weber, [1921] 1947: 8–29, 324–41). Of more immediate relevance, however, is the wave of research in the late 1940s and 1950s including Merton (1952), Selznick (1949), Gouldner (1954a, 1954b), and Blau (1955). The essential point is that systems of rules, procedures and measurements designed for one purpose (usually some form of control in relation to presumed organizational goals), interact with the cognitions, values, motivational patterns (Katz, 1964) and other characteristics of people in the organization to generate consequences which were not intended by the authors of the system. Such consequences, although an outcome of perfectly legitimate rule-following by employees, may lead to inconvenience, inequity, or worse, for others. Within this broad category of bureaucratic dysfunctions, a number of variations may be identified.

First, there is rule-following bringing about unintended consequences. This is the situation described by Merton (1952) where rigid adherence to the formal rules constitutes a displacement of emphasis, from concern for end-values, such as service to the public, to an inflexible attention to the detail of the rules or means. In Merton's analysis, the impersonality expected of bureaucrats plays its part in this process, giving rise to a psychological 'trained incapacity' or dysfunctional learning, and preventing any expression of personal sympathy for the peculiarities of the case in question.

Second, there is the effect of systems for control and incentive. Here employees may consciously, and often understandably, seek to attain specified performance targets, remain within budgets, or unquestioningly employ predefined formal decision-criteria (Blau, 1955: Chapter 3; Ridgway, 1956). In Blau's research in a government employment agency, the performance of staff who interviewed job seekers was assessed on the basis of the number of interviews which they held in a month. Because of this, people who were difficult to place, especially in times of job scarcity, did not receive the attention they required. Comparably, in most universities, teaching quality, despite its importance to the majority of stakeholders, generally takes second place to research, largely because of the pre-eminence of the latter among staff promotion criteria, and perhaps because it is more measurable (Jenkins and Gibbs, 1995).

Such goal-displacement is actually an outcome of role conflict. It is particularly apparent where pressure to attain specified targets, either individual or institutional, creates conflicts which lead to 'short cuts' and dangerous or improper practice (Bishop, 1991; Hosmer, 1987). For example a high proportion of road accidents in the UK result from sales staff and executives under pressure to attain deadlines, meet customers and attend meetings, driving without due care (BBC Radio 4, *Today*, 8 April 1996). This type of situation was also evident in a number of the cases referred to earlier, such as Zeebrugge, where there was commercial pressure to sail on time (Boyd, 1990). Successive studies have shown that administrative and organizational weaknesses of this sort (concerning communications, information systems, incentives, role conflicts and logistics) play a major part in such cases (Boyd, 1990; Shrivastava et al., 1988; Toft and Reynolds, 1994; Turner, 1994). But the same logic applies to the whole spectrum of events, from the very serious disasters which get the attention, to very ordinary episodes which are nonetheless ethically significant for some people.

This second type of dysfunction clearly stems from the entirely legitimate pursuit of self-interest by members of the organization; indeed organizational incentive systems are usually designed to exploit this motivation. By contrast, a third variation is where such self-interest motivates an exploitation of the rule-system. This is seen most obviously in 'working to rule'; a result of the 'apathy preservation' function of bureaucratic rules (Gouldner, 1954a). Yet even then, there may well be a moral justification for such action.

The effect of organizational culture and politics

The boundary between compliant or legitimate action and that which is illegitimate or irregular is usually very unclear. Formal rules cannot cover everything, and the resulting ambiguity permits discretion for individuals. As Barnard noted, there is a necessary element of personal choice in executive action (Barnard, 1938: Chapter 17; March and Olsen, 1976; Morgan, 1986: 128–31; Selznick, 1948). Indeed, as I note below, discretion in practice may extend to a questioning of the rules (even by those subject to them) and thence to their being changed. One cannot really appreciate these matters without taking account of the culture of the organization; yet where does one draw a boundary between official, legitimizing, values and norms, and behaviour which is non-legitimate and not sanctioned by those in authority?

Over time, the result of all of this is systemic behaviour which may be extremely hard to attribute to the conscious choices of specific people, certainly to present members of the organization. Often it represents longstanding, unquestioned, custom and practice which has emerged incrementally and has subsequently been institutionalized as necessary ampli-fications of formal rules and procedures (Selznick, 1948). There is a slow accretion of beliefs and myths, cultural values and norms, which are then taken for granted (Berger and Luckman, 1966) by new members of the orga-nization and may even be reinforced through programmes of induction and training. To some extent this may be viewed as the incremental formulation of policy, as in Gioia's 'script analysis' explanation for product recall practice at Ford in relation to the Pinto (Gioia, 1992), or the emergence of discrimina-tion against minorities and women at AT&T prior to the 1970s (Garrett, 1989; Werhane, 1985, 1989). In-depth studies of organizational life provide rich evidence of the processes which I have outlined (for example, Pettigrew, 1985; Watson, 1994).

Pettigrew observes that: 'The content of strategic change is . . . ultimately a product of a legitimisation process shaped by political/cultural considera-tions, though often expressed in rational/analytical terms' (1985: 443). The question of organizational politics will be addressed in the next chapter, and I shall not dwell on it here, beyond what is minimally required to support the present argument. Essentially, Pettigrew's point is that individuals may offer organizationally rational public statements, argue for particular policies, and engage in visible actions, which are in line with generally accepted organiza-tional norms and goals. But their real, hidden, motives refer to the personal advantage that will accrue from the adoption of such policies and activities. For example, a claim to expertise, and the assertion that this is essential for organizational survival, may be used as a defensive strategy by specialist staff striving to advance their status (Burns and Stalker, [1961] 1966: Chapter 9) or to protect their jobs (Pettigrew, 1973). Another arena for such action is in the hiring of external consultants, whose advocacy lends legitimacy to con-tentious organizational decisions (Maclagan and Evans-de Souza, 1995; Pfeffer, 1981: 142–6).

The significance of such situations is that one cannot clearly discern whether, in the terms I defined earlier, such action would be classed as orga-nizational as opposed to individual, even though we can speculate on the underlying motives. The problem is heightened by the ambiguity of goals. Precise objectives and courses of action may be varied within the parameters of more broadly defined missions and strategies, thus allowing personal inter-ests to inform putatively organizational decisions.

If one extends the definition of organizational action to include the culture as well as formal bureaucracy, then further arguments may be brought for-ward. Culbert and McDonough (1980) maintained that organizations by their nature encourage people to pursue their personal self-interest, but that at the same time it is unacceptable for such individuals to publicize these motives. The result is a damaging cycle of politics. Jonathan Klein (1988) dis-cusses the 'myth of the corporate political jungle', according to which people assume that everyone else is playing politics anyway, so that it becomes part of the culture of the organization, thus legitimizing such behaviour. It is a self-perpetuating phenomenon. However, despite the popular view that organizational politics reflects self-interest, it must be stressed that there can often be a sincerely held moral conviction behind such action. This will also be discussed in the next chapter. Meanwhile it leads into the question of overtly 'non-legitimate' action.

Non-legitimate action

Here I use the expression 'non-legitimate' action to denote any sort of overt behaviour which is inconsistent with managerially sanctioned values and norms. All of the possibilities outlined above refer to situations where people can hide behind the rules, or disguise their real motives, and to that extent such action may appear to be organizational rather than individual. But where one is dealing with instances of rule-breaking, or other irregular action, this seems to be more obviously personal, indicative of private motives and concerns.

However, just as with organizational politics, overt, irregular, non-legitimate action may be sincerely motivated by individual moral concern. Various cases of principled dissent would fall into this category (see Chapter 9). Whistleblowing is the most widely debated of these, but there are other forms, including outright insubordination. The issues raised are encapsulated in William H. Whyte's celebrated work *The Organization Man* (1956: Chapter 19) where he outlined and discussed the essence of Herman Wouk's 1951 war novel *The Caine Mutiny*. The minesweeper *Caine* is heading for trouble in a typhoon; the captain, Queeg, is manifestly incompetent and refuses to take advice from Lieutenant Maryk on how to save the ship; Maryk decides to relieve Queeg of his command, and is subsequently court-martialled for mutiny when they return safely to port. Maryk was acquitted thanks to a skilful defence, but afterwards his lawyer tells him that he, Maryk, had nevertheless acted improperly. Whyte construed this episode in the cultural context of postwar America, hence the title of his chapter: 'Love that system'.

Less dramatic instances arise continually in organizations. Irregular conduct inspired by a conviction that it is ethically justified in the circumstances: infractions of rules, circumvention of procedures, whistleblowing, or straightforward refusal to obey. Within the organizations in question this is often viewed unfavourably, although by questioning the legitimacy of the system it can provoke important changes.

Amoral conformity or moral conflict?

This theme, organizational pressures to conform, and the popular reaction, is elegantly summarized by Sampson (1995). As Sampson observes, in the 1960s a wave of protest – the youth culture and the emergent Green movement –

challenged corporations' domination of employees and consumers (Reich, 1970; Roszak, 1969); indeed many graduates at the time would not seek work in industry or business. It appears that a legacy of that era remains, in a continuing tendency towards employee dissent and whistleblowing, although, interestingly, Jos et al. (1989: 557) note that in the USA many whistleblowers are of an older and more conservative generation. In the UK such activity, provided it is responsibly conducted, has growing legitimacy in the eyes of the public and public bodies. The Institute of Management shows an active interest (Scarff, 1996) while the organization Public Concern at Work was set up as a designated legal advice centre, backed by the Joseph Rowntree Charitable Trust, and with support from several major UK corporations, to help those who might be contemplating blowing the whistle on their employers (see Dehn, 1994). In the USA, for a number of years, several states have provided legal protection for whistleblowers, and similar developments are on the agenda in the UK (Bright, 1996) although the Public Interest Disclosure Bill failed to win Parliamentary support in July 1996.

Conformity and obedience

Given the generality and ambiguity of formal rules and codes, it is entirely likely that informal, interpersonal, influences are the prime source of guidance for individuals faced with moral dilemmas at work (Falkenberg and Herremans, 1995). Insecurity of employment reinforces pressures towards conformity and compliance at work, but these pressures in turn have their roots in the culture of organizations; and on closer examination, they are seen to be held in place by the force of group dynamics and the psychology of obedience to authority.

Processes of group conformity and consensus are important here: specifically 'risky shift' (Wallach et al., 1962, 1964), 'group polarization' (Moscovici and Doise, 1994) and 'groupthink' (Janis, 1972). According to the risky shift theory, a group tends to take greater risks than its members would as individuals, if faced with the same decision. This is explained in terms of diffused responsibility, an explanation which is popular in relation to organizational ethics (Treviño and Nelson, 1995: 161–4). Polarization refers to the tendency for a group's collective decisions to 'converge towards the dominant pole of their scale of values' as individuals (Moscovici and Doise, 1994: 106). This is an advance on the earlier argument for risky shift, inasmuch as it allows for a 'cautious shift' also. These different social psychological theories are relevant to understanding groupthink. This is the tendency towards unanimity in group decision-making, and stems from various factors, notably collective arrogance, unwillingness to reconsider or reflect on the group's assumptions and decisions, and suppression of dissent (Janis, 1972; Sims, 1992).

Another important theme is the tendency for people to obey authority, irrespective of the consequences for others (Milgram, 1974). I shall not dwell long on this, as it is so well documented. In essence, Milgram engaged unsuspecting members of the public to take part in experiments, where they would be ordered by a 'scientist' interested in memory and recall, to administer what they believed to be increasingly severe electric shocks to a 'learner'. In fact there was no live current and the learner was a stooge. The research revealed the extent to which people would obey orders despite the moral implications of their compliant actions.

Milgram's explanations for why people tend to obey orders in such circumstances have important implications for organizational behaviour. The subjective meaning of social and organizational situations inclines many people to define themselves as open to regulation by higher-status individuals. Any moral sense which they might have is then shifted to the proper fulfilment of their bureaucratic duties. Milgram calls this the 'agentic shift'. But the extent to which this happens is affected by various things. A key variable is persons' distance, literally or psychologically, from the actual implications of their work. The closer that individuals feel to the consequences of action – especially if these have a direct negative impact on humans – the less likely they are to obey the order in question. Milgram also acknowledged the theory of cognitive dissonance reduction (Festinger, 1957), explaining obedience in terms of persons' gradual implication in activity which is at odds with their underlying values. His argument was that as people continue to engage in what is initially distressing activity, so their negative feelings are 'neutralized' by the pressure to justify such continuation to self and others.

Assumed processes of dissonance reduction underlie much of the explanation in this area. One manifestation of this is the possibility of diffused responsibility which I mentioned earlier. Another is seen in the idea of forced compliance. The combination of a formal role, authority, and often the felt need to retain one's job for economic reasons, may incline people to believe that they have no option but to conform, which thus relieves them from feeling responsible (Collins and Hoyt, 1972). Thus management may spare those who could have prevented untoward events from the burden of worrying about these, by telling them that it isn't their responsibility. (Recall, in Chapter 6, the discussion on responsibility, which alluded to this same possibility.)

A critique

It is suggested that these social psychological influences can serve as excusing conditions, exempting individuals from moral responsibility for outcomes in which they are implicated (Phillips, 1995). But if we consider Milgram's research, which is normally (and justifiably) cited as evidence for the tendency to obey authority, we find that a significant minority of his subjects defied authority (35–70 per cent, depending on the experimental conditions) (Milgram, 1974: 35). This equivocal nature of Milgram's findings prompts one to ask why it is that some people are able to resist such pressures.

Milgram himself observed that those who defied authority in his experiments were also more likely to take responsibility for the consequences of their own actions (1974: Appendix II). Apart from anything else, this has a bearing on the difference which may arise between what people say they would do when faced with hypothetical decisions or dilemmas, and what they would actually do in the real situation. This is clearly important when considering the praxis of moral development. Is it reasonable, because some people can, to expect everyone to be able to act according to their own subjectively defined sense of moral responsibility? There are numerous actual cases, apart from Milgram's very real experimental situation, where individuals' better judgment has been deflected or overridden by a shift in emphasis onto the formal authority system – for example, see Boisjoly et al. (1989) on the *Challenger* space shuttle disaster in 1986.

In a comprehensive analysis of factors influencing ethical decision-making in organizations, Treviño (1986) identified three variables, indicative of individuals' personal characteristics, which act as moderators between their moral judgments and organizational features such as culture, authority structures and group pressures. These variables are: ego strength, field dependence and locus of control, and they are presumed to affect individuals' capacity to maintain a consistent value-position and pursue actions in line with this.

Ego strength, or strength of personal conviction, has a bearing on one's ability to stand up for one's beliefs, to maintain consistency between values and action. Field dependence refers to the extent, when confronted with ambiguous situations, to which an individual depends on prevailing definitions of the situation, and seeks guidance from others such as superiors and colleagues. Locus of control refers to the extent to which people feel that they can control events in their life. Those who possess an internal locus of control are more likely to accept responsibility for their actions and for the consequences of these actions. They will therefore feel pressure to maintain consistency between such action and their stated values, since they cannot deny that it was their choice. By contrast, external locus of control entails a denial of responsibility and a belief (or claim) that one has no option. Jos et al. (1989: 557) report findings on whistleblowers which are consistent with Treviño's view.

Conclusion

Treviño (1986) did note that for some people there will be a personal cost attached to ethical conduct. Most obviously, should such action incur the wrath of management, it may result in job loss. What this highlights is the wider array of prima facie duties confronting individuals in such situations; the expectations of dependants, in particular, will weigh heavily. Thus it may be unrealistic to argue the strictly logical case that no one can hide behind their formal role prescription, that they chose to take it on, and can renegotiate it or redefine it as their conscience dictates (Flores and Johnson, 1983: 542–3).

In essence, we may hold individuals morally responsible for something if they acted freely, without compulsion, and in full knowledge of the situation and the probable outcomes of their actions (Downie, 1971). Where there is either compulsion or a lack of knowledge, we would regard these as excusing conditions. 'Compulsion' ranges from pathological medical conditions, through the threat of physical duress, to the kind of pressure most likely in organizations, namely threat of transfer, demotion or dismissal. But of course there is a question of degree here, and a choice; one might refuse to obey orders despite a warning that one will lose one's job. On the other hand many people will choose to avoid that outcome; so as Downie puts it, we do not blame people in such situations if we feel that they did the best thing in the circumstances.

In organizational situations, many of the undesirable things discussed in this chapter stem from deficiencies in the availability of knowledge and information. As Downie notes, we might blame people if they made no effort to obtain knowledge when they could have done. But often what appears to be an organizational outcome is the result of many people acting responsibly, in the bureaucratic sense, in their formal roles, suggesting that the overall structure or system is in some sense defective.

In so far as both compulsion and lack of knowledge are prevalent in organizations, individuals are often relatively blameless. But managers do have a responsibility to put things right after having had due warning, such as an initial untoward episode. Indeed, they have a responsibility to remain alert to possible problems even without such signals. Management must also attend to the proper conduct of related human resource or personnel issues: the evaluation of employees' contribution to events, their conduct generally, and consequent disciplinary action when called for.

Finally, to return to the central theme of this book, we can also talk of people having a sense of moral responsibility, unfettered by bureaucratic or even group definitions of the role (Downie, 1971; Maclagan, 1983). This lies behind the conviction felt by the internal dissenter or whistleblower. But short of that, and within the official machinery of organization, it can be stimulated by means of dialectical and devil's advocacy methods designed to overcome groupthink and similar phenomena (Janis, 1972; Schwenk, 1984; Sims, 1992). People in organizations have a duty to be aware of the potential implications of their actions and those of the organization, and to take appropriate action. But what that action should be will depend on the circumstances, which lend 'shape' to the dilemma faced by the individual: whether to remain loyal; to voice a dissenting opinion; to sink into apathetic unconcern; to blow the whistle; or to resign.

9 Moral Dissent, Loyalty and Politics

The discussion in the previous chapter culminated with reference to one of the most important types of moral dilemma encountered by people in organizations. Faced with what they judge to be unacceptable conduct by colleagues, or organizational behaviour which conflicts with their own moral standpoint, they must, first, arrive at a clear idea as to the locus of responsibility for the offending activity, and, second, they must decide on one of several possible courses of action. Prominent among these is the possibility of whistleblowing and other forms of 'voice' or moral dissent.

Following an initial overview, I shall locate this theme in relation to conceptions of loyalty in organizations, and then in relation to organizational politics. In each of these contexts I shall question some of the conventional wisdom regarding the morality of such behaviour. I shall then return to the ethics of whistleblowing, in terms of individuals' prima facie moral duties and the judgmental approach to handling dilemmas encountered.

Options for the moral dissenter

It has been said that

> perhaps the most singularly important result of the emergence of business ethics in the public forum has been to highlight such individuals [whistleblowers] and give renewed respectability to what their employers wrongly perceive as nothing but a breach of loyalty. (Solomon, 1993b: 364)

But whistleblowing is only one of a number of options open to the concerned employee. Nielsen has suggested several responses that managers, administrators and, by implication, most other concerned members of organizations, can adopt when confronted with what they view as ethically unacceptable behaviour by their organization or its members. These include:

> (1) not think about it; (2) go along and get along; (3) protest; (4) conscientiously object; (5) leave; (6) secretly blow the whistle; (7) publicly blow the whistle; (8) secretly threaten to blow the whistle; (9) sabotage; and (10) negotiate and build consensus for a change in the unethical behavior. (1987: 309)

Another, more coherent if less comprehensive, perspective is derived from Albert Hirschman's *Exit, Voice and Loyalty* (1970), which addresses the logic of these three types of response by dissatisfied participants in organizations. A fourth response, Neglect, was added by Farrell (1983), and, citing that source, Gorden offers the following definitions:

Loyalty		Consistent private and public support for the employing organization;
Voice		Suggesting improvements, discussing problems in the work setting, seeking outside help, whistleblowing, and some forms of union activity;
Neglect		Chronic absenteeism or lateness, reduced effort, increased error rate, obstructionism;
Exit		Looking for a new position, planning to quit, and turnover. (Gorden, 1988: 284)

Neither neglect nor exit is normally discussed in relation to the ethics of moral dissent, and I shall not dwell on them for long. However it is important to bear in mind that both of these types of response raise ethical issues. For example, neglect, in the form of apathy and demotivation, can be considered in relation to obligations to colleagues and to the employer. Perhaps it is also unconstructive by comparison with voicing an opinion on the original issue; unless one includes judicious sabotage aimed at obstructing the unethical behaviour (Nielsen, 1987). Exit may be an easy option, depending on the protester's circumstances; and its manner and timing can raise moral issues with regard to those colleagues or clients left behind. However it can also be a genuine statement, as in principled resignation, provided this isn't just an excuse to justify an unconnected and premeditated move.

Gorden suggests that voice may be located in various theoretical traditions each of which provides an ethical argument for the employee's right to speak out. In moral philosophy we see voice in a concern for one of the basic human rights of a person, namely the right to express oneself. In political theory we see very much the same concern in the right to participate in policy-making and government. Gorden refers to the human relations ideology (Bendix, 1956) and criticisms of this, in that human relations approaches were aimed at the integration of employees into a unitary system, and, by implication, the suppression of dissent. From a psychological perspective voice may be seen as a self-actualizing activity, as part of individuals' attempts to integrate themselves with their work environments.

Thus it is apparent that voice can be closely aligned with political action in organizations. There is a partial overlap between these concepts, and this helps to integrate some otherwise unconnected ideas, which I shall introduce later: not least, recalling points made in the previous chapter, the possibility that political action may be inspired by moral concern to a greater extent than is recognized in popular discussion on the matter. Such action need not be self-interested or unacceptably disloyal, so much as a pragmatic means to a justifiable end.

Dissent as loyalty

The four behavioural options listed by Gorden are, in practice, closely related. In particular, the definition of loyalty above fails to do justice to the full implications of the relationship between that concept and voice. Loyalty is significant, not just because it is one possible response to employee dissatisfaction, but because managers may regard dissent as unacceptably disloyal. Yet constructive criticism, and even some instances of whistleblowing where external parties are alerted to contentious activity, may in fact be functional for the organization. By arresting undesirable activity, voice may protect the organization from excessive retaliation by its public. Thus it may be construed as loyalty (Larmer, 1992).

This leads into the question of theorists' different positions or paradigms when discussing such matters. Fundamentally, those discussing employee dissent, especially whistleblowing, are engaging in disputation over the rights, wrongs and practical merits of alternative functions performed by such action. Is voice seen as a vital source of protection for the public? Or as a means to help the organization take corrective action? Or is it seen as nothing more than mischief-making; perhaps a form of catharsis for individuals? These different emphases carry quite different ethical meanings, according to which dissent may be condemned or lauded.

Citing Farrell (1983) and Rusbult and Lowery (1985) as his sources, Gorden identifies two dimensions on which to locate the four response-types: Active – Passive; and Constructive – Destructive. The neat solution to this mapping exercise, which is adopted by Rusbult and Lowery, would be to classify the four types of response as follows:

Loyalty: passive/constructive
Voice: active/constructive
Neglect: passive/destructive
Exit: active/destructive

As Gorden observes, this is inadequate, since it fails to make explicit the underlying values in the terms 'constructive' and 'destructive', so that 'when whistleblowing is categorized as constructive one must ask: Constructive for whom? The organization? The employee? The society? If whistleblowing is constructive, perhaps loyalty should be destructive because too much loyalty tends to cover up company mistakes' (Gorden, 1988: 284).

In his own refinement of this typology, Gorden locates whistleblowing on the boundary between constructive and destructive, since while it may alleviate a problem for society, equally it may damage the organization. As he observes, comparable arguments could be adduced for loyalty. Indeed, exit could be constructive for the organization in some situations, and perhaps for the individual; as could neglect, if it performs a personal stress-reduction function. So we return to the question of the theorist's perspective. Specifically, it is useful to ask what assumptions are being made about individuals' motivations. This comes to the surface when we look more closely at Hirschman's ideas.

The motivation for loyalty

Hirschman (1970) was writing as an economist, but drew on the decision-theory of March and Simon (1958) and Cyert and March (1963). His starting point was a model of the rational consumer, dissatisfied with the product, choosing whether or not to remain as a customer. But he extrapolated from this model to consider the parallels with employees in relation to their organizations, and citizens in relation to states. In essence, Hirschman's analysis moves through three or four possibilities. In the first, following the traditional economic model, it is assumed that individuals will leave, or exit, when they become dissatisfied. Or, more accurately, they will start to search for a better alternative, and leave once they have found it (March and Simon, 1958). The second possibility is where people try to change the organization from the inside, and only leave once they feel that their remonstrations will not be effective. Then Hirschman introduced the concept of loyalty to explain situations where people remain and articulate their concerns, despite the availability of alternative opportunities. (He observed that the concept of loyalty makes no sense unless individuals are aware of such alternatives.) Noting the incomprehensibility with which economists might view such behaviour, Hirschman arrived at the conclusion that in some situations, where organizations generate 'public goods' (or, more appropriately for this argument, 'bads') one cannot escape from the effects of these even by leaving the organization. So one stays, and exercises one's voice. And according to Hirschman:

> The only rational basis for such behavior is a situation in which the output or quality of the organization *matters to one even after exit*. In other words, *full exit is impossible*; in some sense, one remains a . . . member of the organization in spite of formal exit. (1970: 100)

For example, consider the motivation of parents who decide to keep their children in the state school system, even when they feel that a better education could be provided privately. According to Hirschman, they would take this decision 'for reasons of general welfare or even as a result of a private cost-benefit calculation' (1970: 100–1). In the latter case, this would be because they have a vested interest in the quality of the state education system; they must live in the society to which that system contributes. In the case of the general welfare, it is more complex, ambiguous and indicative of an altruistic impulse; the reference appears to be to the wider public interest, but it could include concern for the organization itself.

A model of organizations as locations for economic exchange relationships is also at the heart of Duska's (1988) argument that loyalty is not even a relevant concept in such essentially instrumental arrangements. However Larmer (1992) in his critique of Duska makes the point that loyalty may well entail acting according to what *you* believe to be in the organization's best interests. This is consistent with the general case for 'dissent as loyalty'. Larmer suggests that 'the argument can be made that the employee who blows the whistle may be demonstrating greater loyalty than the employee who simply ignores the immoral conduct, inasmuch as she is attempting to prevent her employer from engaging in self-destructive behaviour' (1992: 127). This reference to such individuals' motivation is indicative of a degree of moral concern, not just regarding the original issue, but for the fate of the organization. Thus it perhaps gets closer to the essence of loyalty than does the analysis of Hirschman, for whom, on an extreme interpretation, loyalty may be no more than a matter of staying rather than leaving; something objectively observable, rather than subjectively understood.

Loyalty: a critical note

Fletcher (1993) credits Hirschman with offering an alternative model to that populated by fickle individuals who trade up in their relationships. He maintains that voice is the 'medium used by those who stay and fight' (1993: 4). But what are they fighting for? Reinhold Niebuhr in his discussion on the plight of morally sensitive individuals within unethical collectivities, asserted that while at times such people might feel they must leave, this has its dangers; it leaves others in the organization to pursue their evil unchallenged from within (1932: 273). So people might decide to stay, and exercise voice, not because they envisage personal costs through their own continued exposure to public evils generated within the community, but because even if they could escape completely, they have an ethical concern for those who cannot.

For Fletcher, what matters in the relationships which constitute the focus for our loyalties is that they inform our sense of identity. Such relationships are 'logically prior to the individual' (1993: 15), whereas under the impartial ethical theories of Kant and the utilitarians, individuals choose their relationships. In other words, the institutions of family, community and those organizations of which we have been members long enough for them to contribute to what Fletcher calls 'the historical self', evoke in us a sense of loyalty. While the moral theories of Kant and the utilitarians assume a 'universal self . . . [which] entails obligations, the historical self generates duties of loyalty toward the families, groups, and nations that enter into our self-definition' (Fletcher, 1993: 16). This distinction may help to clarify Duska's argument to which I referred earlier. What it suggests is that loyalty towards any organization, business or otherwise, is possible; but this will depend on the individual's sense of identification with it.

There is, however, the question of parameters to the sources of our sense of identity. The possibility of cosmopolitan altruism, which I introduced in Chapter 3, and the idea of the organization as a moral community (in Chapter 11) are both implied when Fletcher says that loyalties 'circumscribe communitarian circles, all the members of which take others within the circle to be the objects of their concern' (1993: 20). This Fletcher contrasts with an ideal of extending our loyalty to the whole human race, something he feels may distract us from more immediate concerns on the doorstep.

Fletcher's definition of loyalty is persuasive, but where behaviour in organizations is concerned, some loose ends remain. If loyalty is owed to formative institutions and ideals in the life of the self, then these need not be coterminous with the organizations which are their embodiment. Take the case of higher education. A university professor, according to Fletcher's argument, is loyal to a particular conception of academic life: teaching, its contribution to society, and so forth. She identifies with this; it has contributed to the development of her 'self' over many years. But does that guarantee loyalty to the particular organization in which she is currently employed? Is it not entirely possible that her relationship to the employer in such a situation is more of an instrumental one, compared with the 'commitment to the cause' which the occupational identification harbours? So to say that in fighting for the maintenance of standards in its degree programmes, the professor is demonstrating loyalty to the university, is problematic. Much may depend on her length of tenure to date in that organization. If she has been there for many years, or is perhaps one of its graduates, then there is a basis for identification and loyalty. That organization, the university, has, one might say, become institutionalized in the life of the individual. But this is not always so, and will vary from one person to another within the same organization.

The virtue of loyalty is undoubtedly an important counter to the 'private self-seeking that dominates our consumer society' (Fletcher, 1993: 21). Loyalty is 'more than a habit of attachment; it is based on a recognition of duty' (1993: 77). But as a basis for morally significant conduct, we certainly cannot say that it is an *absolute* duty. As both Pfeiffer (1992) and Ewin (1993) have observed, there is a distinction between being disloyal and lack of loyalty. One can be disloyal only if one is already in a relationship of loyalty. This may apply to some employees and not to others. So Pfeiffer maintains that employees are not under an obligation to demonstrate loyalty to their employer (as opposed to just performing well in their work). Most obviously, there is clearly the danger of blind loyalty, where identification with the institution or organization can dull the sense of responsibility regarding other issues. The professor may well feel that she has specific moral obligations to her university, or at least to colleagues, which may or may not qualify as expressions of loyalty. And she may face conflicts between these and other such responsibilities, as prima facie duties, in which case, as Fletcher himself observes (1993: Chapter 8), she would have to fall back on judgment to guide her action.

The ethics of organizational politics

'[L]oyalty is the beginning of political life, a life in which interaction with others becomes the primary means of solving problems' (Fletcher, 1993: 5). Furthermore the moral conflicts which people in organizations may experience can give rise to various forms of voice, suggesting that there is a close relationship between voice and political behaviour in organizations. For example, Mintzberg used the term '*influencer* . . . for those who wish to affect the behaviour of the organization through what Hirschman [1970] has called "voice"' (1985: 139); while Dahl has pointed out that 'influence-terms', such as control and persuasion, are central to political analysis ([1963] 1970: 15).

Defining organizational politics

As Dahl ([1963] 1970) explained, such factors as the scope of X's influence over Y (that is, what aspects of Y's behaviour are affected?) its reliability, strength, and cost to the influencer, are useful analytical concepts common to all such political situations. The role of authority structures, access to and filtering of information, control over formal and informal agendas, and personal influence over potential sponsors among senior management, can all be discussed in such terms. But one also needs to understand what is going on under the surface: what are the motives behind such actions? This is where attempts at defining organizational politics run into difficulty.

Perhaps indicative of this is the fact that the entry on organizational politics in the glossary to Culbert and McDonough (1985) is longer than that for any other concept:

> The actions, machinations, and dynamics that take place as people strive to create acceptance either for themselves or for a point of view to which they are committed. The objective is to implant a view of reality that elicits a favorable response for one's views and actions. In organizations people are often unaware of their political behavior. However, they are unusually aware of how someone else's framing of reality is making it more difficult for them to get value and acceptance for their behavior and 'organizationally constructive' point of view. In response they experience the need to assert another view (of reality) and the resulting dynamics constitute organization politics. (Culbert and McDonough, 1985: 222)

Yet even this, despite its encapsulation of so much that other definitions miss, seems insufficiently explicit. There are several significant distinctions within what is broadly defined as 'political' which could be overlooked as a result. For example, the sheer variety of political means adopted, such as 'impression management' (Goffman, 1959), control over information (Pettigrew, 1973) or over financial resources (Salancik and Pfeffer, 1974), and building alliances (Pfeffer, 1981). The distinction between formal and informal aspects of the organization as a political system is also important in understanding particular cases (Burns, 1961, 1966). And, could we discern them, the underlying values in political actors' motivation, which may range from self-interest to a moral concern for one or more of many other considerations, is critical to any ethical evaluation of such behaviour (Maclagan and Evans-de Souza, 1995). This last point was intimated in Chapter 2, with reference to Rescher (1969).

Classifications, not definitions?

Distinctions such as these matter because on closer analysis one finds that different political strategies raise their own unique issues. Thus it is practically impossible to arrive at a general theory of organizational politics; and this undoubtedly applies also to the ethical dimension to such behaviour.

A definition of organizational politics, is, then, something of a will o' the wisp. Instead of seeking it, it is better to look for typologies, classifications or frameworks that help us to make sense of particular situations from a specific angle. Mintzberg (1985) offers an extensive list of thirteen 'political games played in organizations', which he subjects to systematic classification. I shall not detail these games, or strategies, in their entirety, but consider, in Mintzberg's terms, their function for the leading participants. Mintzberg confines that aspect of his typology to five possibilities:

1   to resist authority (the 'insurgency' game);
2   to counter resistance to authority (the 'counter insurgency' game);
3   to build a power base (games here include 'alliance building' and control over 'expertise');
4   to defeat rivals (for example what Mintzberg calls 'line *vs.* staff' games);
5   to effect organizational change (this category includes 'whistle blowing').

But even this focus on purposes leaves us with a problem of means and ends; for example, strategies aimed at building on a power base may be pursued with a longer-term aim of effecting change in organizational policy. There is ambiguity, also, concerning the assumed underlying motives of participants in such situations.

A possible alternative approach is to develop a conceptual framework, or checklist, which might provide guidance for those trying to make sense of politics in organizations. As a starting point, I suggest the following four distinctions:

1   a distinction between formal, structural aspects of organizations (including corporate governance) and the informal action typical of political behaviour in organizations;
2   a distinction between political means and substantive ends;
3   a distinction between self-interest and concern for others as political motives;
4   a distinction between individual and collective action.

The first of these distinctions, between formal and informal aspects of organizational behaviour, pervades discussion on the other points, and does not require further elaboration here (although I return to the question of governance in the next chapter).

Means and ends

Political means can be used to further what the participants view as ethically desirable ends. At least some of the strategies suggested by Mintzberg (1985), such as insurgency, and building alliances, come to mind. Of course the public statements of those who play politics will refer to officially recognized, 'legitimate', organizational values, as indicated in Culbert and McDonough's definition above, and in Burns's observation that 'political pressure is rationalized in terms of organization' (Burns, 1961: 277). But while such generally accepted, organizationally uncontentious goals (ends) are involved (for example, the profitability of a company) the specific argument offered as a means to that end may reflect a particular ethical position which, in itself, would not be sufficient to sway influential opinions within the organization. Typically, for example, an appeal to the long-term interests of the organization may be made, even if the prime moral concern of the political actors is more immediate, such as protection of employment for particular staff.

Self-interest and concern for others

Typically, also, such causes are espoused with great passion. For this reason it is both misleading and damaging to assume uncritically that politics in organizations is invariably in some sense nasty: a manifestation of individual and group self-interest, distasteful attitudes and 'dirty tricks'. French et al. say that 'organizational politics can have a positive and a negative face. The negative face is characterized by *extreme* pursuit of self-interest . . . The positive face of politics is characterized by a *balanced* pursuit of self-interest' (1983: 373). Now it would be naive to imagine that in most situations people have no concern for their own fate, especially if that is rather imprecisely defined to include the interests of their families or other dependants. But, at a theoretical level, one must be careful regarding the connotations harboured in the language used. Uncritical adherence to the assumption that people are necessarily self-seeking serves only to reinforce a particular paradigm, of which that cynical view is a major component.

Jonathan Klein (1988) presents an argument to the effect that: (1) people engage in political games for selfish reasons; (2) the self-image thus engendered threatens their self-esteem and conflicts with their preferred altruistic self-image; so that (3) they reduce the consequent dissonance by convincing themselves that everyone plays politics anyway, which somehow justifies their own actions. 'The myth of the corporate political jungle,' as Klein calls it, is thus perpetuated. The point here is that Klein's argument rests on the assumption that political behaviour will conflict with the person's self-image. But were we to recognize that some political actions are motivated by genuine moral concern, and indeed may even entail a risk of altruistic self-sacrifice (as when a dissident individual risks dismissal from employment), then individual self-esteem, far from being damaged, could be enhanced.

The distinction between self-interest and concern for others remains ambiguous, however. Who are these others? Very often there is a genuinely felt concern for the effective conduct of an organization's tasks: for example, industrial scientists fighting political battles against other groups in the company, in the hope that they may be able to make a more valuable contribution to the research function (Burns and Stalker, [1961] 1966). No doubt cynics

will say that this is no more than self-interest, and it is probably true that serious self-sacrifice seldom enters into such situations; but as Burns and Stalker
have observed, it would be wrong to view managerial behaviour as

> a continuous melodrama of hypocrisy and intrigue. These do, of course, exist, but
> the real problem, here or elsewhere, is most often that to the parties themselves, their
> opinions and policies seem utterly sincere and disinterested and their manoeuvres
> aimed at serving what they see as the best interests of the firm. ([1961] 1966: 145)

Collective and individual action in the formal organizational setting

Individuals in organizations may sometimes be expected by colleagues to
sacrifice personal ambitions in the interests of their particular group. Such
solidarity is well documented in the literature on organizational politics, both
empirical (for example, Pettigrew, 1973: Chapter 7) and theoretical (notably
Burns, 1966; Burns and Stalker, [1961] 1966). Burns's analytical scheme is
particularly insightful. He defined three 'social systems' which constitute distinct referents for individual action. These are, first, the 'working
organization', which includes organizational goals and policies, the formal
structure, and the official selection and promotion criteria and procedures.
Second, the 'career structure', partly defined in the formal terms just indicated, which provides one context in which individuals seek to realize their
personal goals. And, third, the 'political system' consisting of interest groups
such as departments or occupational communities, to which individuals may
feel a degree of loyalty (Burns, 1966; Burns and Stalker, [1961] 1966: xi–xxi).

Burns noted that not infrequently people in organizations may face a moral
dilemma when their own interests conflict with those of a group or department to which they belong. They are implicated in two different systems of
action, or games; the career system (individual) and the political system (collective). In deciding on which game they are playing they must almost
certainly make a moral choice. For example, consider the high-performing
individual in a management services group which is threatened with redundancies. This individual may be able to advance his or her career by justifiably
claiming personal credit for some innovative work. But the group may have
previously agreed that such credit would be shared by all, in order to support
the strategically important argument (a myth, let us assume) that any cutback
in staff would render them ineffective; that they need the full complement of
staff to operate adequately. Thus the individual member appears to have a
moral obligation to share the credit for his or her work, unless one takes the
view that attempts to mislead management invalidate such an agreement's
moral basis. However, the argument that the full complement of staff is necessary may indeed be valid, in which case the individual's moral dilemma is
accentuated.

Burns maintained that, in contrast to such situations, an individual's behaviour *within* any one system of action may represent a purely technical, or

non-moral, ordering of values (Burns, 1966: 177). For example, how best to maximize one's career prospects, or, as a group member, which political strategy to support. But moral issues may be lurking behind the apparently technical or prudential façade of such choices, and these may have implications for third parties. For example an individual may disagree on moral grounds with the political action of the group, and such disagreement could even provoke an act of whistleblowing. Or the group's action may itself represent an attempt to further sincerely held beliefs concerning public service, or concerning some other ethically significant impact of the organization on its environment. Again, this could take the form of collective dissent or whistleblowing.

Whistleblowing and organizational politics

So we may include whistleblowing as a distinct *political* strategy, which is 'antagonistic to legitimate systems' and aimed at changing the organization (Mintzberg, 1985: 136). Rothschild and Miethe are quite explicit in their insistence that 'whistleblowing needs to be viewed as a political act' (1994: 255), while Vallance (1995) discusses whistleblowing under the general heading of corporate governance. Thus in different ways the connection is made with organizations as political systems.

I want to make one further observation regarding theoretical integration, before turning to the ethics of whistleblowing. My analysis of the ethics of principled dissent has to some extent been informed by the literature on organizational politics generally. It is possible, therefore, that the reverse can also be true: that ideas and concepts from the literature on whistleblowing can contribute to the ethical analysis of organizational politics. I shall suggest just two possibilities, although there may be others. First, there is the question of whether the whistleblower remains anonymous; second, there is the difference between going public, outside the organization, and confining communication to internal channels. I suggest that these can be relevant to political action generally and may therefore be added to the checklist offered earlier. They could be construed as follows:

5   a distinction between secretive, anonymous, communications and open, possibly confrontational, political argument;
6   a distinction between internal, organizational, sources of political support, and those resources which are external (in other organizations or among the public at large).

The ethics of whistleblowing

While commonly associated with individuals, whistleblowing could take the form of concerted action by a number of people, and indeed Winfield advises would-be whistleblowers to seek support from colleagues, and if possible to pursue the action collectively, on the grounds that this can have greater impact (1990: 43). Joint action may also result in greater motivation to pursue the issue, ensuring a degree of mutual support and protection. Normally, whistleblowing calls for considerable encouragement from others; as numerous cases have shown, the threat of retaliation against whistleblowers is very real, and support, moral and otherwise, is crucial. Apart from colleagues in the workplace, advice and support can come from various sources, such as specific external agencies like Public Concern at Work in the UK (Dehn, 1994), or legal advice, counselling services and the family (Jos et al., 1989). Other conditions which encourage people to blow the whistle have been suggested by Near and Miceli (1985): the offending activity must be seen to pose a serious threat; the whistleblower must be confident that this activity has actually occurred and that it is definitely wrong; clear channels should exist for the expression of dissent, and the climate in the organization should support such action; lastly, the individual(s) involved should have a reasonable expectation that their action will be effective.

Some initial normative assumptions

Before considering the ethics of whistleblowing in more detail, I would stress certain normative assumptions which should apply in all cases. Some of these assumptions may be challenged on rare occasions, but in general they refer to a prima facie obligation to avoid unjustifiable harm to the organization and its members, in situations where no real dilemma arises out of conflict between that requirement and the moral demand to protect the public interest.

First, alerting people outside the organization should be a last resort, once all internal channels have been exhausted. Evidence shows that the overwhelming majority of whistleblowers try everything, short of resignation, to get management to listen and to change the offending situation. This applies also to innumerable cases where whistleblowing might have prevented an untoward event, but was never enacted (for example, Vandivier, 1972). This rule could, however, be overridden, if it is felt that voicing an opinion internally would alert the perpetrators of the offending action so that they could take evasive action, or might result in serious harm to the dissenter.

Second, whistleblowers should reflect conscientiously on their own motives. Principled dissent does not include seeking revenge against the organization, or engaging in political action, such as trying to collapse another department, or even engaging in whistleblowing as an unthinking, emotionally impelled, act. However, in some cases one might be able to present a consequentialist argument in terms of political strategy, to support what might be better described as a form of sabotage, if this was the only realistic way of stopping a quite unacceptable activity.

Third, it is assumed that the whistleblower is as sure as possible of the facts of a situation. Spreading ill-founded rumours, even though this also might be seen as part of a political strategy with a consequentialist justification, would not have a place in the present discussion.

Prima facie obligations for the whistleblower

Three main areas of concern give rise to prima facie obligations for whistleblowers. In broad terms these refer to the interests of the organization and its members or stakeholders; the public at risk; and whistleblowers themselves and their dependants.

Concern for the organization is often expressed in terms of loyalty. In earlier discussion I have raised a number of problems with this idea. To what or whom is one being disloyal? Is loyalty an obligation for everyone, or only for particular people, and perhaps not even for them? Could whistleblowing actually be an act of loyalty, if it protects the organization from public retaliation? The first of these points provokes further questions concerning the precise nature of any prima facie duties for whistleblowers in relation to their employing organization. Ewin has suggested that if there is something organizational at stake, as opposed to specific concern for its members, then this may concern things which are 'beyond the company itself' (1993: 392) such as principles relating to the quality of its programmes, or their effectiveness, or its environmental stance. But such questions can only be answered in the light of concrete situations. The principle of loyalty, in itself, would seem to have a basis in virtue theory or perhaps deontology; but consequentialist thinking can enter into concern for more specific issues and interests, and this can only be articulated in real situations.

Concern for the public raises several points regarding the justification for whistleblowing in the first place. The issue must refer to a serious threat (life, health, or perhaps severe financial harm) if it is to override the obligation to avoid damage to the organization and its members. Moreover, one must ask whether whistleblowing will make any difference anyway. There is a questionable justification for blowing the whistle if the threat has already receded, or the damage has been done, except in so far as one is talking of the provision of information as part of a subsequent enquiry.

The general prima facie duty to protect the public at risk also affects the detailed approach to be adopted. Where the threat is very serious, then there is a stronger case for overriding other obligations, to the organization or to one's own dependants. For example detailed confidential corporate information might be released if this was felt to be the only way to convince influential outside parties that action was needed. Similarly, one might reveal one's own identity, even in the face of threats to oneself or to dependants, if this would add credibility to the communication. The nature of the risk to the public, in its technical detail, would also influence the choice of recipient for one's information. There is a vast difference, sometimes overlooked in the whistleblowing literature, between judicious communication with, for example, specialist public agencies concerned with health or safety, and indiscriminate revelations to the media.

Then there is the question of whistleblowers' obligations to themselves. In particular, it is dependants' interests which are at stake here. The perceived degree of threat to them and to oneself is therefore another factor to take into account, and will affect the course of action to be adopted. Here the question of anonymity is a crucial issue, which deserves brief consideration.

Anonymity and the whistleblower

The arguments against anonymity are both deontological and consequentialist (Elliston, 1982). As a matter of principle, it can be said that concealing one's identity while revealing information about others' activities is, prima facie, offensive, and suggests an unwillingness or inability to defend one's position. This is especially the case when the accused is a person to whom one is close. It is also unfair to deprive the accused of the right to confront the accuser. From a consequentialist position anonymity may frustrate adequate enquiry into the case, may reduce the credibility of the message and, if widespread, could undermine the potency of whistleblowing in general.

The arguments in favour of anonymity are mostly consequentialist. Protection for whistleblowers and their dependants, when they face a threat to economic security or life, is the most obvious point here. Elliston argued that for this reason one cannot regard openness as an absolute duty. As a derivative from this, he felt that a general norm of permissible anonymity might encourage such action where otherwise people would be afraid to speak out; in other words this would be a rule-utilitarian justification.

Reasons and defeated reasons

The three areas of concern outlined above, interpreted in actual contexts, provide reasons for acting one way rather than another. Obligations to colleagues, and to dependants, might suggest that the concerned individual remain silent. But much depends here on the details of the actual case. What sort of public reaction will result from whistleblowing? Who in the organization could suffer from this? Or, conversely, what will be the effect, for the organization, of ignoring the issue so that the harm to the public is realized or amplified? Meanwhile, an obligation to the public dictates that one alert a responsible external party. These different obligations conflict, so that some give rise to 'defeated reasons' (Dancy, 1993a) which serve as constraints on the chosen course of action.

At this stage the concerned employee must be able to discern the 'shape' of the situation. What are the salient features, the things that make a difference in that particular case? For example, what is the detailed nature and seriousness of the threat to the public? Will whistleblowing change anything anyway?

How vulnerable is the organization, especially in relation to the release of confidential information? What are the risks to oneself, and do these matter? Who else would be affected if one suffered retaliation by the organization? What dependants does one have? What alternative employment is available should one need this?

The relative salience of such features will inform the whistleblower's judgment. They provide reasons, not only why one should or should not blow the whistle in the first place, but, as defeated reasons, for doing this in one way rather than another. A serious threat to the public will dictate that one should indeed alert someone. This may mean revealing confidential information to that external party, yet there are principled ethical reasons for not doing this. Another reason for keeping silent concerns the possible dangers for colleagues who may be implicated. Furthermore, an assessment of one's own situation and that of one's dependants may suggest that self-protection, remaining anonymous, is called for. Let us assume, however, that all of these reasons for doing nothing are overridden by the seriousness of the threat to the public. (We also assume that all appropriate internal channels have been exhausted.) These prima facie duties to keep sensitive organizational information confidential, to protect colleagues, and to look after oneself in the interests of those for whom this matters, still play a part in the choice of action. For example, they will probably influence the choice of person with whom one communicates, what one says to that person, what safeguards one seeks, and so forth. The case for anonymity may be defeated by the feeling, in the particular circumstances, that only by revealing one's identity can one really have an influence on events. However, the moral duty to one's dependants remains, so that here again special care may be taken with regard to whom it is that one is dealing with, and what one says to them.

Conclusion

Concerned individuals who wish to act in the face of unethical conduct have a variety of options from which to choose. In the previous section I concentrated on whistleblowing, but of course this is just one of several possibilities (Nielsen, 1987). An initial choice, between staying and leaving the organization and, assuming that one does stay, a secondary choice between passivity and active voice, are ethically laden. As Niebuhr (1932) observed, leaving the organization could be less than responsible if it results in continuing harm by those who remain. From another angle, exit may in effect leave one's colleagues or clients in the lurch. Thus one could raise issues concerning such matters as the timing of one's departure.

Meanwhile, for those who stay, a passive stance, or 'neglect', is also ethically questionable. Should one be more active in expressing one's voice? Is the unenthusiastic, demotivated response, which follows a loss of commitment to the organization, acceptable? The answers will depend on circumstances, on the ethical shape of the situation. Some of the salient features affecting this will be the same as with whistleblowing: one's own circumstances, the degree of loyalty one might feel, the nature of the original issue, who is responsible for it, and the harm to others which might follow from one's dissenting action.

The concept of loyalty is problematic, as I have indicated. Despite employers' desire to instil loyalty among members of organizations, the strongest arguments tend to support the view that loyalty reflects some sort of bonding indicative of an emotional orientation towards something: the organization as a whole, or its programmes, or particular colleagues. And this raises a point which I have held over until now, which is that the apparent trend in many societies towards employment insecurity, short-term contracts, the 'marketing character' (Fromm, [1976] 1979) or simply the 'cosmopolitan' orientation resulting from individuals' occupational rather than organizational identification (Gouldner, 1957–8), poses a question regarding the future of organizational loyalty (O'Sullivan, 1996b). Of course this will vary from one type of organization to another, and across cultures. The expectation of loyalty in Japanese corporations, for example, is still strong enough to overcome other ideas imported by those employees who have spent time working in Western societies, a factor of considerable importance regarding the possibility of any form of principled dissent in such organizations. However, much of the basic conceptualization which I have offered in this chapter can still be applied.

Even in Western societies it takes considerable courage to blow the whistle, or even to express verbal dissent from unethical organizational activity. Yet such activity is always a possibility, given certain almost invariant characteristics of organizations, such as economic pressures, communications blockages and individual ambitions. Hence the need for innovations such as legislative support for whistleblowers (to which I alluded in Chapter 8) and specific provision for internal communications channels for the expression of dissent (which I will note again in Chapter 11).

PART THREE
A DEVELOPMENTAL PERSPECTIVE

10 Developing Institutions: The Organization in Society

Walton has suggested that because of difficulties in resolving the problem of corporate moral agency, which I discussed in Chapter 8, 'managers and scholars have moved away from the 1950 concept of corporate social *responsibility* to the 1980 idea of corporate social *responsiveness*' (1988: 197). Smith (1990: 47) has also noted a shift in emphasis away from how business ought to conduct itself, to how society might ensure that it does act properly; in other words, placing an emphasis on the consequences of corporate activity rather than on the motives behind it.

In this chapter I shall look at varieties of societal influence over organizations, and consider the moral status of organizational reactions to these. I shall then outline the manner in which theorists of organization and management have addressed this issue; how, especially in the three decades after World War II, they shifted their ground, from a basis in deterministic models of the organizational response, reflecting the assumption of narrowly defined commercial goals, to recognition of the fact that managers can exercise choice and can accommodate moral concerns.

This reminds us of the importance of personal moral judgment and responsibility. I shall assume that it makes no sense to regard organizations as moral agents; only people can act ethically or unethically. This argument enables us to make a further important distinction, which I shall present in terms of two 'ideal types'. On the one hand we have what I shall call the *ethically acceptable organization*, which is treated as a 'black box'. What is inside this, such as individuals' motives and actions, the flow of information or the attribution of responsibility, remains largely unknown or unexplored. On the other hand, if one does examine these inner workings, we may have what I shall term the organization as a *moral community*. Here one finds people with moral motives; the organizational system facilitates their ethical thinking and action, and encourages the rooting out of moral dysfunctions and the propagation of appropriate values, norms and administrative arrangements. Of course the moral community will, one hopes, contribute to an ethically acceptable organization also; but the reverse is not necessarily the case. The consequences of organizational activity may be viewed as acceptable or otherwise, but that in itself tells us nothing about individuals' motives, since what the onlooker regards as ethically acceptable corporate conduct may be due to chance, or deference to societal pressures.

Finally in this chapter I shall consider organizational governance and the involvement of stakeholders. This introduces a further perspective on the integration of organizations and society in the context of ethics. Moreover, the fact that I include such discussion in this chapter rather than in the next is itself indicative of the problematic epistemological status of any 'boundary' between organizations and their social environments.

Societal influences and the organizational response

Although my eventual concern is with the development of the organization as a moral community, the idea of ethical acceptability in the public eye is critical too. Plainly one cannot treat organizations in isolation, unaffected by wider values or public pressures. People import societal values into the organization, which is one of the reasons why they sometimes find themselves expressing dissent, blowing the whistle or leaving. But more than that, it would be an insufficient analysis that failed to address some of the other obvious modes in which social influences and community values impact on organizations in ethically significant ways. The public are affected by perceptions of particular organizations as ethically acceptable or unacceptable. Organizations react to such public opinion and pressure in different ways, and people should have some appreciation of these matters if they are, as individuals, to contribute to the improvement of their organizations and to their own personal moral development.

Varieties of external influence

I shall preface this section by referring back to the point made in Chapter 6, concerning the possible emergence of a post-materialist culture in some Western economies. Whenever there are radically changing values in any society, there can be instances where organizations such as religious and educational institutions, charities, pressure groups, and some commercial enterprises, represent emergent values and face difficulties in winning support or in surviving. Viewed from the position of such organizations it could be society that is ethically unacceptable, thus highlighting the relativity of values.

Much corporate action in relation to what some regard as ethical obligations to society appears to stem from external forces. Such influences may take the form of government legislation, threatened litigation by those harmed, or direct action by other organizations and pressure groups (see Smith, 1990). These include single-issue lobbies, employees' unions, investors, and concerned commercial partners such as suppliers and customers. In the late 1980s the animal rights organization Lynx effectively destroyed the fur trade, although it was subsequently sued for libel and bankrupted, while in 1995 Greenpeace succeeded in getting Shell to abandon plans to sink the redundant oil platform *Brent Spar* in the Atlantic. There is also action by more directly involved stakeholders. This includes: the ethical consumer and investment movements (Adams et al., 1991; Cooper and Schlegelmilch, 1993; Sparkes, 1995; Vogel, 1978), and workers' movements such as the Lucas Aerospace Shop Stewards' campaign concerning UK arms manufacture, and the Australian construction unions' 'green bans' on urban desecration, both in the 1970s (Coates, 1978; Elliot, 1977).

The pursuit of such initiatives raises ethical issues analogous to those facing the whistleblower, in that other stakeholders, such as shareholders, employees and local communities, may be adversely affected by the action taken. But these possibilities are seldom experienced as cause for a dilemma by the pressure group involved, whereas they often do present the management of targeted organizations with moral conflicts. The position of Shell's local management in the *Brent Spar* episode was an example of this.

Meanwhile there is also a growing interest in ethics among bodies such as the Institute of Management in the UK, business schools worldwide, numerous features in the business press and, increasingly, conferences for senior managers, often involving consultancies that offer programmes and advice on these matters. However, whether all such initiatives should be defined as external to the corporate sector is open to question; are they a form of social pressure, or a strategy adopted by business in response to, or in anticipation of, adverse public opinion?

The moral status of the organizational response

Such external influences may be effective in changing a particular corporate decision, or even in altering the organization's more general stance on specific issues, but one may question whether this in itself turns it into a moral community. For example, in many countries the tobacco industry has been under pressure by the anti-smoking lobby and to some extent from governments. In 1995 Massachusetts became the fifth US state to take action against the industry, filing a lawsuit against six companies on the grounds that they had misled the public regarding health and the dangers of smoking. At the time, Scott Harshbarger, the state Attorney-General, was quoted as saying: 'It is time to snuff out this deadly and deceptive conspiracy. It is time for the industry to be forced to tell the truth. It is time for cigarette companies to pay for the damage they have done' (*The Independent*, 21 December 1995: 17). But would forcing people to tell the truth, even if that were possible, make them any more ethical? Legal action is more likely to evoke a prudential response than to change the inherent moral conduct of those involved.

If these influences are viewed by organizational management as constraints then the underlying rationale for their response would appear to be corporate self-interest. With explicit, direct, pressure, as is seen in, for example, consumer boycotts, self-preservation is an immediate concern for the organization. This can be contrasted with the longer-term view adopted by organizations which perceive changing values in society and act in anticipation of these changes, but for prudential reasons.

The concerned public tends towards an ambivalence regarding the moral status of such responses. There is relief and satisfaction when an offending organization changes its posture; yet there is widespread cynicism concerning the underlying motive. It is hard for managers to defend their actions against this when almost any form of community involvement or comparable activity can be seen as being in the organization's long-term interest through the enhancement of its image (Moore, 1995). Organizational management may well, and understandably, question whether this matters. What is the problem if good ethics is also good business? Well, the point is that although there may be an ethically acceptable outcome, that doesn't necessarily indicate a moral organization populated by morally motivated managers. If the ethical policy is a means to a commercial end, and the business situation subsequently demands a rethink, what price ethics then? The riposte to this is that if circumstances change, so the appropriate ethical response from the organization may also have to change. If an organization which has prided itself on avoiding employee redundancies, as an ethical principle, can no longer hold to this policy absolutely without risking a far larger number of jobs, what is it to do? The answer is that it depends on the ethical shape of the situation.

One other observation is called for here. This concerns the distinction between corporate social responsibility (CSR) and management/business ethics. CSR is about 'companies acting in ways that enhance quality of life for all their stakeholders. Ethics on the other hand is a process of decision-making in reality' (Clutterbuck, 1992: 35). These decision situations, as I suggest later, tend to entail concrete, probably inescapable, moral dilemmas (at least for those who apprehend them as such). CSR is relatively discretionary, less difficult, although it still involves some ethical decision-making, as I note later (and see Jones, 1980).

Some insights from organizational and management theory

In earlier chapters I have stressed the importance of countering the view that managers are necessarily caught up in a deterministic, profit-maximizing organizational situation. To reinforce this, one can identify a number of related ideas in organization and management theory which support this voluntaristic position in the context of the organization–environment relationship. What follows is a very partial summary, since the volume of literature from which one could draw is immense, and it would be easy to digress. It will suffice, therefore, to identify some key issues and connections which emerged between the 1940s and the 1970s, by which time recognition of anti-determinist and axiologically richer models of organization was becoming established. If nothing else, this may help readers with further exploration of their own.

The literature on organization and management theory in the latter half of the twentieth century is replete with concern for the relationship between organizations and their social and economic environments. Yet when reading texts for managers on the evolution of such thought, one is left with the impression that much of this work has been associated with the search for effectiveness and profitability, rather than with any moral concern about the impact, positive or negative, of organizations on their host communities or on the world at large.

The tendency alluded to reflects a more general propensity for late twentieth-century management theory to follow a scientific model which allows little or no room for ethical concerns, and which assumes, at least where business organizations are concerned, the normative validity of a free-market model and an unquestioned ethos of economic self-interest.

Functionalism

One of the earlier positions in organization theory was that of the functionalist sociologists such as Parsons (1951) and Selznick (1948, 1949). This school of thought was heavily influenced by the organic, or biological, analogy, and by the Social Darwinism and individualistic utilitarianism of the nineteenth-century sociologist Herbert Spencer. According to this tradition, organizations are seen as adapting to a set of norms in the social environment, and gaining legitimacy from the production of an output which meets the needs of (is 'functional' for) the larger social system. Parsons's theory assumed a normative integration of organizations into this larger social system (and of individuals into the organization) reflecting acceptance by each sub-system of central values at the supra-system level. This perspective is relevant to the function of organizational codes of ethics, to which I return in Chapter 11. (In that context it is worth noting that Parsons developed his ideas in relation to Durkheim's social theory and Hobbes's political philosophy, although space prevents amplification of those connections.)

Thus functionalism in social explanation entails an appeal to the contribution of a phenomenon, or system-element, to the maintenance of the status quo; and correlatively the legitimation of such a phenomenon or activity by the social system. Such explanation cannot easily accommodate conflict except when this is itself functional for the system, contained within normative parameters such as the legitimacy of the free market and profit as a goal for business. It seeks an explanation for social stability in terms of an accepted central (and well integrated) value system, ignoring the effect of power in either social scientific explanation or as a possible source of social change.

If we take the case of the tobacco industry, mentioned earlier, a functionalist perspective would suggest that such organizations' contribution to society was economic: the generation of wealth. This would, of course, entail a degree of consumer satisfaction, but so far as wealth creation and the provision of employment is concerned, cigarettes are a means to an end. If smoking causes health problems then this is defined as a 'dysfunction', which is assumed either to be of insufficient importance, or else it may, over time, elicit a corrective response from the sub-system, the industry, but all within the smooth operation of a harmonious set of societal values.

Power and conflict

The functionalist perspective was compatible with a rising tide of thought in the field of academic management science (and, not least in the years after World War II, much practical management thought also). Such management thinking took organizational goals, and a rationalistic conception of the management process, as unproblematic. In one, managerial, sense that may indeed have been justifiable, as we shall see below when the question of organizational goals is considered. Yet, to return to my example, both the persistence of the tobacco industry in the face of opposition, and that opposition itself (as with other instances of pressure group activity) highlights the reality of both corporate power and ethical conflicts in society. Parsons did recognize the possibility of limited moral conflicts facing top executives *within* organizations (here the influence of his industrialist friend Chester Barnard was conspicuous) but the idea that such managers might face responsibility for handling ethical dilemmas reflecting those at the societal level (such as employment versus public health) was not accommodated.

Yet, unless they are resolved at the societal level, such value-conflicts provoke 'legitimation crises' for those institutions which support some interests to the exclusion of others. Sutton (1993), for example, maintains that corporations maintain their legitimacy only in so far as their activities are compatible with the values of society, and, furthermore, that:

> Transitions and recalibrations in the values and needs of many societies, coupled with (or, in some cases, caused by) global crises on a number of levels, have highlighted the contrasts between the justifications of corporate power and the 'volonté générale'. (1993: 5)

Examples are widespread. They are seen in the tension between people as producers and (the same) people as consumers (Fox, 1971) including such issues as the demand for fair treatment and equal opportunities at work, and the possible economic costs of this. They are also seen in conflicts between the economic interests of business organizations (including their employees) and moral concern for the local, national and global community; between industrialism generally and radical social and environmental concerns.

Determinism and pessimism

Recognition of the arbitrary nature of power, politics and social choice formed the basis of a major intellectual attack on functionalism in the 1950s.

Prominent in the critique of functionalist organizational theory, although he had started off in that camp, was Alvin Gouldner, who, together with Philip Selznick and others, was engaged in what Albrow (1970) called the 'debate with Weber' on the question of bureaucratic rationality.

Selznick's major study had concerned the failure of what most people would see as an ethically laudable effort by the American government to contribute to social improvement in the Tennessee valley states, part of President Roosevelt's 'New Deal' in the 1930s. This involved the creation of the Tennessee Valley Authority (TVA) and its failure was explained by Selznick in terms of 'the things . . . which bind the hands of good men' (1949: 266). In essence, Selznick argued that it was inevitable that such a radical social programme would fail in the southern states at that time, given the TVA's dependence on political support by local congressmen and senators, whose most influential constituents were opposed to the policy. Through what Selznick saw as a necessary process of co-optation into the TVA's administration (since otherwise it would have lost political support in Washington) these powerful members of the local community gained a say in the policy-making process and diverted the organization's resources from intended recipients among the poorer sectors of the community, and towards their own interests.

Despite a contrary interpretation which could be derived from the detailed evidence in his book, Selznick's functionalist theoretical stance inclined him to define what happened at the TVA in determinist terms: as inevitable goal-displacement, a system responding to its environment, rather than as a failure of the TVA's administrative leadership in the face of political opposition. The organization survived in name; but the nature of its programmes changed.

Then, in an important paper, Gouldner singled out Selznick for criticism, accusing him of engaging in 'the pathos of pessimism, rather than the compulsions of rigorous analysis' (1955: 505–6). More generally, he attacked both technological determinism and the pessimistic assumption that oligarchic tendencies would prevail in all organizations, which he saw in many functionalist writers' work. Thus Gouldner sowed one of the seeds for a subsequent crop of writing which emphasized the possibility of choice, rather than constraint, in social affairs.

Organizational goals and objectives

Perrow observed, with reference to Selznick's TVA case, that more often than not 'there is no "community" value, there is only the conflict of group interests' ([1972] 1979: 190). In the case of the tobacco industry, we may all agree that the effects of passive smoking are unacceptable, and this inclines a large sector of the population (at least in some societies) to condemn the manufacture and sale of cigarettes; to regard the firms involved as ethically unacceptable. But management have other stakeholders to consider, such as employees. Similarly, in the *Brent Spar* case, it emerged that while popular opinion, influenced by an emotive campaign, supported Greenpeace in their pursuit of a single ethical issue, Shell's management faced dilemmas that raised additional moral concerns, which they were entirely justified in considering.

The various stakeholders' interests can be understood in the ambiguous terminology of organizational goals and objectives (Frost, 1995). As noted earlier, at first such rationalistic concepts seemed unproblematic. Then came analyses such as Etzioni's (1964) discussion in terms of two models of organizations, a goal model and a system model, where the system model refers to the organization solving problems 'other than those directly involved in the achievement of the goal', and where 'excessive concern with the latter may result in insufficient attention to other necessary organizational activities' (1964: 17). These other activities may be understood in terms of system maintenance; thus while pursuit of the 'goal' may suggest short-term self-interest, support for the organizational system suggests a longer-term strategy, or enlightened self-interest.

However, the complexity of the organization–environment relationship posed major problems for theorists. The goal concept was nebulous. All sorts of attempts at clarifying the matter appeared (Abrahamsson, 1977; Eldridge and Crombie, 1974). Not least with business organizations, the functionalist assumption that one could identify a particular primary goal for the organization was now threatened, and with it the assumption that one is able to talk of goal-displacement except in a very partial or short-term sense. The expression goal-displacement is value-laden, as Perrow ([1972] 1979: 189–90) pointed out. Referring to the 'moral ambiguity of functionalism', Perrow observed that a reading of Selznick's dispiriting earlier work and his later (1957) statement on the importance of good leadership in preventing institutional drift suggested that 'when we get results we approve of, this is leadership; when we do not, it is a process of goal displacement' ([1972] 1979: 190).

All of this reminds us that the ethically acceptable organization is, in all but the most obvious cases, vulnerable to contrary interpretations by different people. In the case of universities, for example, consider the tension, given resource constraints, between the call for wider student access and the demand to maintain traditional educational standards. Both are goals, but which does one choose? Giving priority to one may well work against the other. Goal-displacement; or an ethically laudable policy?

Organizational systems, environments and responsibility

This ambiguity of goals is in part a consequence of the corresponding ambiguity and complexity of organizational environments. In the 1960s, various developments in management theory indicated that more attention was being paid to this subject. In the field of socio-technical systems theory, Emery and Trist (1965) built on Selznick's (1957) concern for 'institutionalization' in their argument that, to survive in the progressively more 'turbulent' social environments which were becoming the norm, organizations would need to adopt and act according to values that would align them with the expectations of society. When contemporary business ethics writers talk of organizations acting out of enlightened self-interest, they are describing much the same sort of action as Emery and Trist advocated. But more than that, Emery and Trist asserted that beyond a certain level of environmental complexity and uncertainty, it would be necessary for interconnected organizations to contribute to the creation of shared value-systems 'that have overriding significance for all members of the field'. They continued:

> Unable to trace out the consequences of their actions as these are amplified and resonated through their extended social fields, men in all societies have sought rules, sometimes categorical, such as the ten commandments, to provide them with a guide and ready calculus. (1965: 28)

And in a later paper, Trist offered the concept of 'domain formation', which referred to a situation whereby organizations would collaborate in the context of a 'set of problems, or societal problem area, which constitutes a domain of common concern for its members' (1983: 270).

The resolution of complex policy matters such as environmental despoliation, or crime, as well as commercial problems, would require this sort of approach. Crucial to our understanding here is the subjective nature of the organizational environment. This became a vital element in much organizational theorizing, and one could pick out Karl Weick's idea of the 'enacted' environment, '*constituted by* the actions of interdependent human actors . . . a phenomenon tied to processes of attention' (1969: 27–8) and Geoffrey Vickers's (1968, 1970, 1980) notion of 'appreciation awareness' as key theoretical contributions here. For Vickers, an 'appreciated world' refers to that which we are aware of, which we notice because of our interests. It is 'given form by our expectations . . . given meaning by our standards of judgement, ethical, aesthetic, political and other' (1970: 98). Our experiences, communications and actions are structured and guided accordingly, and personal responsibility assumes critical importance (Vickers, 1980).

The possibility of managerial choice

Explicit attention to the possibility of managerial choice, both in organizational design and in more fundamental strategy, surfaced periodically from the late 1940s onwards. In management theory the work of the socio-technical school at the Tavistock Institute in London gave additional impetus to this movement, by demonstrating that there were economically feasible alternatives to centralized bureaucratic forms (Rice, 1958; Trist and Bamforth, 1951; Trist et al., 1963). During these same decades there was also the emergence of what came to be known as contingency theory, where the appropriate organizational arrangements were seen to reflect factors such as technology

(Woodward, 1965), or conditions in the commercial environment (Burns and Stalker, [1961] 1966; Lawrence and Lorsch, 1967; and for a summary, see Hales, 1993: 148–55). Compared with the Tavistock research, however, much of this writing indicated an apparently more deterministic position, implying that administrative systems had perforce to fit extant contingencies if performance was to be maximized.

Certainly the interpretation placed on contingency theory by many management teachers, and in their texts, often ensures that discussion of such ideas has remained largely within the constraints of the functionalist position. In the case of Burns's work, students are usually taught about 'mechanistic' and 'organic' management systems and about their appropriateness for stable and changing circumstances respectively. This matching is sometimes assumed to 'just happen', the result of some sort of deterministic force, while at other times it is supposed that there is a deliberate and organizationally rational managerial choice. Attention is less often drawn to why it was that, for political reasons, senior executives in some firms prevented the emergence of organic systems when this was called for, and why, in other instances, junior and middle managers played, or were caught up in, political games (Burns, 1961, 1966; Burns and Stalker, [1961] 1966; and see my discussion in the previous chapter). Recognition of these factors is crucial if we are to appreciate further possibilities.

Students of management and organization were presented with a more explicit escape route from the constraints of narrowly defined contingency theory in a paper by Child (1972), who highlighted the arbitrary nature of managerial decisions and organizational strategy. Citing Gouldner (1955), Burns (1966) and Weick (1969), Child observed that not only are managers frequently able to select the environments in which their organizations will operate, but this selection may be part of an overall strategy including a chosen level of performance. By settling for a lower profit margin, or resisting the temptation to expand, for example, one can avoid particular complications or risks. Furthermore, like Burns, Child stressed that much managerial decision-making reflects individuals' personal concerns and the internal politics of the organization. And once we recognize this, we can also introduce the idea of choice based on ethical grounds. This Child did in a subsequent paper (1973). There, both explicitly and by implication, he drew attention to the possibility that different interested parties could share in corporate decisions, which could be made on moral grounds, as when a company decides for such reasons to avoid a particular market, product, technology or commercial practice.

Stakeholder theory and organizational governance

We can see, therefore, that organizations are not so constrained by unquestionable goals or external forces that management has no choice. And we can add to that the possibility that such choices may take account of various ethical considerations. Moving closer to the practical implications of this, we find corporate social responsibility (CSR) as a distinct label attached to theories of the business–society relationship. Two decades ago Hay et al. (1976) pointed to a historical trend in managerial orientations, from a purely profit-maximizing position, through concern for directly involved stakeholders, to an additional concern for the solution of major problems in society. The trends in organization theory outlined above seem to approximate to this. While undoubtedly the general issue of CSR remains very salient, it is unwise to over-generalize. In particular, variations between national cultures, types of industry, organizations' differing experiences of public concern and protest, the diversity of managerial characteristics and their functional locations (such as human resources, engineering, finance) are all likely sources of variation in attitudes to social policy and business ethics.

I shall turn now to 'stakeholder' theory (Abrahamsson, 1977; Freeman, 1984; Rhenman, 1968). A great deal has been written on this topic, and in keeping with my developmental emphasis I shall identify a tension between what Goodpaster (1991) called a 'strategic' interpretation and a 'multi-fiduciary' model of stakeholder management. In the former, stakeholder theory is employed in the organizational interest, so as to manage its environment. Here the contributions of stakeholders are viewed as a means to the end, which is to benefit the owners; shareholders, in the case of business organizations. In the multi-fiduciary model, on the other hand, management is seen as having comparable obligations to all stakeholders; shareholders, as owners of a firm, have no special privileges. I shall support the argument from the multi-fiduciary model, because it is becoming clear that the concept of organizational ownership, as with that of organizational survival, is sufficiently problematic that one must exercise great caution in identifying any one group that, from a *moral* point of view, would have a primary claim to some conception of organizational 'self-interest'. Furthermore, even if such a group could be identified, one would question the ethical justification for ignoring the interests of (or 'using') the other stakeholders. In short, a developmental model calls for a move away from self-interested behaviour, and towards a wider and more responsible concern for all affected parties.

Corporate social responsibility may be viewed as a process in which managers take responsibility for identifying and accommodating the interests of those affected by the organization's actions (Jones, 1980). This entails the exercise of moral judgment, which in turn benefits from a conceptual framework to make sense of the organizational context and to help people identify their responsibilities. Such a framework could be derived from the following very general questions:

1 What sort of organization are we dealing with in any particular case? Discussion ought not to be confined to business organizations.
2 Who are the stakeholders? To whom does management have moral obligations? In what respects?

3   What motives lie behind concern for the stakeholders identified in (2)?
4   What provision is there for consultation with, or participation by, these
    stakeholders? I address this under the heading of governance.

Varieties of organization

For the most part, stakeholder theory has been developed in the context of
private sector business, but it is equally applicable to any organizational type
(Rhenman, 1968; Stewart, 1991). One of the effects of a preoccupation with
private sector companies is that much intellectual energy has been spent on
the question of the relationship between shareholders, management, and the
other stakeholders. Yet the public–private distinction may not be very meaningful, and questions of ownership and accountability may be problematic,
when, for example, publicly funded universities increasingly have support
from other, private, sources also, and some industrial firms rely heavily on
government contracts to stay in business. Also relevant to this problem is
Abrahamsson's useful concept of a mandator: 'those who have established the
organization as a means for achieving certain goals' (Abrahamsson, 1977:
26). This reminds us that those to whom management are accountable in the
legal or bureaucratic sense may not be the intended beneficiaries, as in the
case of charitable institutions. As there are various organizational types,
therefore, and different cultural contexts, it is impossible to generalize except
in very bland terms. Some cases may be more clear-cut than others; but as
often as not a situation will call for *ad hoc* analysis and judgment.

Who are the stakeholders?

It helps in identifying stakeholders if one draws a distinction between (a) the
strategic view, that stakeholders are resources, to be managed in the interests
of the 'prime beneficiaries' (Blau and Scott, 1963) and (b) a multi-fiduciary
view (Goodpaster, 1991) in which management have a prima facie moral
obligation to all stakeholders.

The use here of Blau and Scott's term 'prime beneficiary' is deliberate,
because their 1963 work owed something to a tradition in organization
theory, not confined to business, originating with Barnard (1938) and pro-
ceeding through Simon ([1947] 1957) and March and Simon (1958), sources
also acknowledged by Rhenman (1968) and other writers on stakeholder
theory. It connects with the earlier discussion on goals; yet as we noted, the
goal-concept is problematic, often ambiguous, and from an ethical standpoint
other functions of an organization's activity, such as the provision of employment, service to dependent customers or pollution control, may be just as
significant as return on investment for shareholders or benefits for local taxpayers in the case of a county council. Thus Keeley has referred to 'presently
powerful, but morally arbitrary, beneficiaries – for instance a *prime
beneficiary*, as defined by Blau and Scott' (Keeley, 1978: 285).

With regard to the private sector, a significant part of the debate has concerned Friedman's ([1970] 1990) claim that 'the social responsibility of business is to increase its profits'; that shareholders are the only claimants on managerial concern and to suggest anything else is subversive. One response to this owes its origins to the famous statement by Berle and Means (1932) concerning the separation of ownership from managerial control, and the questioning of property rights in modern capitalism. Hence now we find papers such as Boatright (1994) and Freeman (1994) in which shareholders' special status is questioned, and other stakeholders' claims can assume greater salience. The implied ethical dilemmas faced by management would be inescapable: no longer could they refer solely to shareholders' financial interests to inform decisions. In particular, there is the point that shareholders (Freeman would redesignate them 'financiers') in a company may be able to sell, but other stakeholders such as employees or the customers of a monopoly cannot always disengage themselves so easily. This specific argument connects with that in the previous chapter concerning the cost of 'exit' (Keeley and Graham, 1991: 353). It also gains strength from the fact that so much corporate shareholding is part of large, institutional portfolios, where some losses from share dealings can be absorbed by gains made elsewhere. This whole debate is particularly relevant given the active role increasingly advocated for shareholders and other stakeholders, an aspect of governance to which I return shortly (see Mahoney, 1994, who suggests 'trusteeship' rather than 'ownership' as a preferable status for shareholders). In the case of non-profit organizations the problems are often even more complex.

In extreme cases of the strategic model, the stakeholder concept is understood purely as means to thinking about companies' economic self-interest. Once we adopt a concern for social responsibility and ethics, we require different types of conceptualization. Programmes of corporate social responsibility would reflect genuine moral concern rather than prudential reasons. L'Etang (1995) for example, invokes a Kantian perspective in which motive is all-important. As did Jones (1980), L'Etang views corporate responsibility as a process through which management works on a constantly changing situation, in which one cannot specify in advance which stakeholders are more deserving. However, as a starting point, she subdivides responsibilities into those which arise out of the direct relationship stakeholders have with the organization (as with employees, customers or the local community); and those (indirect) which may be identified in the potential of an organization to influence opinions and events through actions such as political lobbying, by example, and other forms of communication.

Comparable analytical schemes have been offered by other writers; for example Carroll (1989). It is more obvious that management must take account of those with whom they are immediately involved or affect directly, than that they should get involved in the concerns of more remote or diffuse interests, not that these are unimportant. Here it might also be useful to reflect on the differences, such as they are, between philanthropy, ethics and responsibility, although there is no space to explore this fully. Philanthropic actions, and probably most cases of what L'Etang calls indirect responsibilities, are discretionary, and it is questionable whether any sin of omission is perpetrated by organizations that avoid them. Direct responsibilities, on the other hand, do seem more critical, and indeed it is probably in respect of these relationships that business ethics, concerned with moral dilemmas rather than just issues of social responsibility, applies.

Motives

So we turn to the question of motives. This is a particularly elusive concept in the present context, since while one frequently finds reference to organizational 'self-interest', given my earlier analysis in Chapter 8 and the denial of corporate moral agency, how can one say that an *organization* has a 'self-interest'?

It is probably fair to say that if one adheres to the strategic model, with a clear assumption of a particular prime beneficiary, then that interest can be favoured or sacrificed. Conversely, if one adopts a multi-fiduciary viewpoint, where no one stakeholder has a prior claim, then one would have to fall back on some conception of organizational survival (for whom?) as the referent for self-interest. Etzioni's (1964) notion of a 'system model' referred to earlier would be relevant here (see p. 144). Organizational morality would then entail some sort of corporate sacrifice, where there was no obvious benefit to any existing stakeholders, even in the long term. This form of analysis is, however, rendered tautological if one assumes an extreme multi-fiduciary model in which any potentially affected party becomes a stakeholder. One point to be made regarding quoted private sector companies is that there is a necessary deference to shareholder interests in so far as poor financial performance and prospects leaves the business vulnerable to takeover, perhaps to be followed by relocation or plant closure. Another complication is encountered in the objection that even what appears as socially responsible, or, in some other sense, ethical, action, is really no more than enlightened self-interest. In terms of motive it is generally maintained that this is less creditable than purely moral, even altruistic, concern. However it is common among those who are trying to influence managers (such as some writers and consultants) to use the 'good ethics is good business' argument to 'sell' (perhaps literally) the idea of ethics and responsibility.

To return to the claim first forwarded in Chapter 8, what I would suggest is that rather than focusing on *organizational* self-interest or sacrifice, one should consider the motivation and moral choice of individual managers acting for the organization. Now this is far from straightforward, for we have to face up to the complex interaction of organizational role enactment and individual motive. For present purposes I shall assume a 'black box' here, but if, in any actual situation, one was to open it up, one would find managerial values and orientations, trust and distrust, politics, situationally specific motivations; all matters addressed in earlier chapters. And as a normative proposition, I shall suggest that responsible action is grounded in concern for others, in a sense of service, in a 'being' mode of existence which carries with it a capacity for critical reflection on moral issues (Fromm, [1976] 1979).

Having reintroduced the individual moral agent, I suggest that managers and directors can be the conscience of the corporation, or of specific mandators or owners. Here we may find a clue to the puzzle: what is the ethically acceptable or responsible organization? A number of writers have explored ways of conceptualizing organizations and organizational motives in terms of Kohlberg's stage-theory of moral development, introduced in Chapter 2. I shall look at that in the next chapter; but first we need to consider, briefly, the question of stakeholder involvement through corporate governance, consultation and participation.

Governance, participation and consultation

In the aftermath of successive business and public sector scandals in the UK (including the question of executive salaries referred to in Chapter 7) practical concern with corporate governance has emerged in recent years as a distinct focus of attention. It has been closely associated with the Cadbury Committee's 1992 report into financial management and accountability in listed companies (Cadbury, 1992). But governance has both a wider relevance than that, and a much longer history. In the mid-1990s Lord Nolan's Committee on Standards in Public Life examined the governance of publicly funded bodies (Nolan, 1995); and twenty years earlier the Bullock Committee (1977) reported on the then equally topical issue of industrial democracy, recommending that employees and shareholders should have equal directorial representation on company boards and that these directors should then appoint additional, independent, members. (These recommendations did not take effect due to opposition from the Confederation of British Industry and the fall of the Labour Government in 1979.)

In general, such initiatives share a concern for two things. First, the monitoring and control of managerial decisions and actions, so that particular stakeholder groups' interests should not be harmed; and second, the representation of those stakeholders' views. To say this leaves open, of course, which stakeholders are included, and how and to what extent they are involved. Thus for the purposes of my overall argument I define governance broadly, as a process of interaction between stakeholders, involving the articulation of their views and, give or take variations in practice, their contribution to decisions. This involves modes of enablement; structures and procedures, which may be formal or otherwise. Thus participation and consultation can be part of the governance process, and so also, from an extreme perspective, can whistleblowing (Vallance, 1995). More generally, this topic provides a link between this chapter so far, and, in the next, a more practical concern with codes, administrative mechanisms, leadership, and the relationship between all of these and individuals' moral thought and action.

One of the more fundamental issues raised concerns the reasons for such initiatives. Most commentators seem to agree that the practical aim of such attention to governance in the 1990s has been to ensure self-regulation by organizations, rather than have them face external legislation following concern by the public generally as well as those with a direct financial stake such as shareholders and members of pension funds. More bluntly, however, a concern for corporate governance may be viewed as 'damage limitation' (Jackson and Carter, 1995: 878).

Ideally, from a moral standpoint, governance should not have to be viewed thus. In Chapter 6 I referred to Dachler and Wilpert's (1978) four paradigms for the analysis of employee participation in organizations. These were: 'socialist', 'democratic', 'human growth and development', and 'productivity and efficiency'. The 'socialist' view refers to the ideal of employee control over the production process (Abrahamsson, 1977; Vanek, 1975). A contemporary expression of this is employee ownership of companies through shareholding; this is how the airline TWA, for example, became employee owned in 1993 (Hugill, 1994b). The argument from democratic theory concerns the political maturity of society as a whole; in this view, individuals' experience of participation (in unions, the workplace, and elsewhere) contributes to political efficacy more generally (Pateman, 1970; and see Chapter 6 above). For recent overviews of this whole area internationally see Széll (1992) and Knudsen (1995).

By extension from this predominant but limited context of *employee* participation, one can arrive at the question of stakeholder responsibilities generally (Mahoney, 1994; Monks and Minow, 1995). Shareholders, more specifically institutional investors, are subject to an increasing expectation that they should participate actively in the governance of their companies. They 'cannot abdicate their moral responsibilities to management as they have tended to do in the past' (Mahoney, 1994: 214), and recent events involving shareholders in Shell bear witness to this (Caulkin, 1997). To pursue this in detail would be a digression from my present argument, but it does take me back to earlier points on the subject of consumer pressures, the moral concerns of trade unions and whistleblowers. Thus while one tends to think of organizations being managed (governed?) by a small number of people, most of whom have executive responsibilities, governance is not just about *their* responsibilities, but can be construed in terms of the mutual obligations of all stakeholders.

This is in some respects reminiscent of Trist's (1983) idea of domain formation, mentioned earlier, where several organizations would respond collaboratively to societal problems, forming a 'referent organization'. In Trist's view, both the referent organization, and its constituent parts, should be so organized as to facilitate wide access to policy decisions, enabling the articulation of a variety of viewpoints. A decade later Freeman (1994) seems to pursue a similar line, but with explicit emphasis on moral concern for a wider range of stakeholders rather than the mutual self-interest of a limited coalition apparent in Trist's model. Freeman's avant-garde argument would require, for its practical expression, legislative changes so that organizations were managed in the interests of all stakeholders (as indeed would the not unrelated idea of a 'stakeholder economy' about which there has been considerable discussion in political circles at the time of writing).

Corporate governance is a matter of global interest, but there are obvious variations between social and economic systems, reflecting differences in history and culture (see Demb and Neubauer, 1992; Monks and Minow, 1995), between types of institution (for example, Peck, 1995, on UK National Health Service Trust boards) and in ideological perspectives (Sutton, ed., 1993). However, as Cannon observes, there are equally obvious commonalities:

> Transparency is a central plank of reform across the world. It is the best defence for the high-quality, capable and responsible management that exists in the vast majority of firms and the finest reassurance for shareholders against those who do not meet these standards. (Cannon, 1994: 172)

That apart, variation exists in terms of the formalization of arrangements, and the nature of participation and access to actual decisions. Various modes of informal consultation, whether with employees or with external parties, may appear to preclude the need for structural provision such as board representation. For employees, the communicative facet of participation is usually by consultation, either directly or through employee or union representatives, who, in turn, may or may not have a seat on the board. Access to actual decision-making can also be understood in terms of degrees of influence, one extreme being formal participation in the final resolution. (See for example Knudsen, 1995, regarding employee participation in Europe.) Allied to this is the likelihood that different occupational categories, groups and individuals will in practice have differential influence depending on such factors as the type of industry, technology, their strategic importance in the eyes of management, cultural and other factors affecting affinity between those involved, and internal organizational politics. As Cannon (1994: 172) points out, where there are trading communities such as in Europe, the desire to ensure a 'level playing field' exerts pressure for a uniform system of governance. But to what extent this will actually happen remains to be seen, not least because of the gap between the letter and the spirit of directives, and the latitude which this permits for cultural variations such as those alluded to above.

Conclusion

In many ways, the most significant themes in this chapter have concerned a disintegration in modern society as manifest in lack of responsibility (and sometimes of responsiveness) by organizations *vis-à-vis* their environments. Social issues, *ethical* issues, may be understood in these terms. For more than thirty years there has been a discernible trend in management theory which has been informed by some awareness of these matters. The work of those such as Trist, Emery and Vickers recognized the need for organizations, in their own and society's interests, to collaborate with others in the same problematic domain. Child's statement offered the insight that not only was organizational and strategic choice seldom determined by absolute commercial imperatives, but that it was arbitrary, perhaps reflecting the personal interests and whims of individual managers, and that therefore other, ethical, criteria could equally well be brought to bear on decision-making. And then there was the growth of writing on business ethics and corporate responsibility, and the broadening out of the debate on stakeholders. Who are they? What are their rights? How should they be accommodated in policy-making?

Theorists are now seriously questioning the idea of corporate ownership, and such questioning is not constrained by the assumed immutability of prevailing legal systems. Of course, there is a wide gap between these views and the taken-for-granted world inhabited by many who are directly involved in organizational life, but that is understandable. Some of the underlying intellectual issues have been simmering for some time: apart from the theoretical developments adduced above, consider the argument that if all organizational research is value-laden anyway then it is better to point one's theorizing explicitly in the direction of social improvement, as one conceives this, than to confine analysis within the parameters of some assumed and reluctantly accepted reality.

Recent writers on the subject of postmodern organization have a lot to say on these matters (Clegg, 1990; Gergen, 1992; Hassard, 1994). The present discussion is not consciously written from that perspective, however, and it is not the intention to say much on it except that there is a common concern, and probably some disagreement also. Gergen's is a particularly readable statement which supports my overall argument. He calls for a realization of the potential of our theorizing, which will be all the greater once we are freed from the shackles of (in)essential empirical verification. In contrast to theoretical perspectives which emphasize a differentiation of organizations from society (and managers from stakeholders) Gergen observes that organizations cannot survive mutual misunderstandings with society, where one party's solution is another's problem, and neither recognizes the other's position, not least because of the absence of a shared language. Such misunderstandings must be overcome; realities must be shared, criticism and the dissent of minority voices encouraged, hegemonic tendencies (not least of top management) held in check, so that 'as organizations join with their surrounding cultures for purposes of mutual empowerment, and the circle of interdependence is ever widened, we may become aware of the world as a total system' (Gergen, 1992: 224). Hence the justification for those who would increase the range of stakeholders and their level of participation. However one interprets it, one may situate the contemporary 'governance' debate in this context.

All of this points to the idea of the organization as a 'moral community'. That is the context in which people engage in their ethical discourse, grapple with dilemmas collectively as well as individually, and exercise personal moral judgment. In the next chapter I will take this further, stressing a distinction between that paradigm and the alternative emphasis on managerial control as a means to ensuring the (merely) ethically acceptable organization.

11 Developing Organizations: Towards the Moral Community

The idea of a boundary between organizations and society is problematic. Nevertheless, in so far as formal administration is the locus of bureaucratic authority, with all that this implies in terms of hierarchy and management control, such organizational systems clearly call for separate attention in the context of ethical improvement.

The possibility that they might display varieties of response to societal influences, ranging from the avoidance of sanctions, strict compliance with the law, and enlightened self-interest, to genuine concern for their stakeholders, has led a number of writers to conceptualize *organizations* in terms comparable to Kohlberg's levels and stages of personal moral development (Lavoie and Culbert, 1978; Reidenbach and Robin, 1991; Snell, 1993; Sridhar and Camburn, 1993; Victor and Cullen, 1988), although any implication that one can assign moral agency to the organization as a whole would be to misrepresent these authors. While we may indeed worry about organizational outcomes, I would reassert the view that what really concerns us are the moral responsibilities of *individuals*, including managerial responsibilities regarding systems (in the widest sense) which may cause unintentional and undesirable outcomes. Hence my distinction between the ethically acceptable organization and the organization as a moral community.

That distinction is paralleled in this chapter by contrasting, respectively, a *control paradigm* and an *autonomy paradigm* from which to view organizational characteristics and artefacts such as culture, leadership style, formal procedures and codes of ethics. From within the control paradigm, such characteristics and artefacts can be 'engineered' or used as part of a managerial strategy to elicit desired behaviour from the members of an organization, with the aim of ensuring its ethical acceptability. But under the autonomy paradigm, while culture, leadership, and even codes of ethics, can still play a part, emphasis shifts to their emancipatory function for individuals acting within a moral community. In short, in so far as one can apply the language of moral development to organizations, this is because they possess features which influence *individuals'* moral conduct: sanctioning self-interest, demanding conformity or encouraging personal moral judgment. Among such features, concepts of culture and bureaucracy are especially important, and I shall attend to these separately before discussing the control and autonomy paradigms. First, however, the significance of the latter must be explained more fully.

Organizational control or individual moral judgment?

The acceptable organization is a construct of the public imagination; it is grounded on perceptions of the observed social, economic or environmental impact of organizational activity, irrespective of how this comes to pass. Thus the pursuit of such ethical acceptability by management is frequently understood in terms of the control paradigm. The moral community on the other hand is populated by individuals who have a sense of personal responsibility and of service (as suggested in Chapter 6), who can think for themselves and act in self-consciously ethical terms.

While the acceptable organization is justified in terms of consequentialist ethics, the moral community reflects a concern for the moral motive; it is closer to a Kantian position. When writers such as Goodpaster and Matthews (1982), Reidenbach and Robin (1991) or Sridhar and Camburn (1993) talk of *organizations* as having a conscience or as being at a high level of moral development, this does not necessarily mean that their members possess such qualities. The fact that management systems, and organizational codes or cultures, incline people to act in a particular way may simply mean that their members are complying with rules, deferring to various pressures, or following the herd. Indeed it is indicative of this point that the essence of Sridhar and Camburn's research into the stages of corporations' moral development was the content analysis of public statements made by company representatives. These statements were made in response to situations where the organizations faced adverse publicity following episodes such as Union Carbide's Bhopal chemical plant explosion in India, the *Exxon Valdez* oil spill in Alaska, and Ford's launch of the Pinto with its fuel tank safety problems. The scope here for *ex post facto* ethical rationalization is considerable, and I am not sure that it really tells us very much about moral development.

Of course we should be concerned with the development of the organization as a whole, and this includes the elimination and prevention of those unintended outcomes or side effects of corporate action which are ethically unacceptable. But if there is no underlying moral concern for such matters, other than making sure that the organization is protected from public condemnation and adverse publicity, then we have not made much progress. Yet much of the literature on business ethics, especially in so far as it is intended to assuage the concerns of practising managers or their mentors, seems to assume that if one can ensure acceptable organizational outcomes then that is sufficient. Moreover, in adopting this view, it often seems to be assumed that employees should conform to a particular organizational culture, towards which leadership, codes of ethics and other management devices are instrumental. As critical writers have observed, this is morally problematic; for example Moore (1993) highlights the tension between corporate effectiveness in implementing ethical policies, and individual autonomy, asserting that the latter is essential if business ethics is to have any significance. (For a contrary view, see Vallance, 1995: 178.)

A key distinction is, therefore, that between conformity and autonomy as understood in terms derived from my earlier discussion in Chapters 2 and 3. Individual development entails a progression from mere conformity towards greater independence of thought and capacity for moral judgment. While not disputing the importance of creating an ethically acceptable organization, that in itself is inadequate; we need a moral community also.

A note on organizational culture

Since it is clearly central to the theme of this chapter, the concept of organizational culture demands attention. We are confronted here with a poorly defined field, and a plurality of terms and definitions which tend to reflect the disciplinary backgrounds or practical interests of their authors. It is not my intention, nor is it within my particular compass at present, to explore this comprehensively, but it is necessary to introduce some ideas which will inform subsequent discussion.

There is a strong argument to the effect that one cannot appreciate organizational cultures without reference to the more inclusive cultures which impinge on them. Morgan points out that '[national] culture, whether Japanese, Arabian, British, Canadian, Chinese, French, or American, shapes the character of organization' (1986: 117). There is a long tradition of research here: Crozier (1964) on France, Dore (1973) on Japan, Hofstede (1980, 1990) on comparative analysis and Fukuyama (1995) on the specific question of trust between people in the business context.

Over the years, objections have been raised against this view, principally understood in terms of the argument that similarities are appearing in both economic and industrial development across societies, and in terms of the methods applied to the management of organizations (Kerr et al., [1960] 1973). But one must be careful not to misrepresent the authors of that thesis, which applied more to economic development than to the minutiae of management practice in organizations. As Hofstede (1990) points out, 'ethnocentric' (usually American) management methods, applied in different cultures, ultimately either fail or are adapted in response to local values and norms.

Following Smircich (1983), cultural environments may be viewed as external variables affecting organizations. This can be distinguished from a view of culture as internal to the organization, as a variable to be manipulated by managers and consultants in the interests of corporate performance (Deal and Kennedy, 1982; Peters and Waterman, 1982; and with explicit reference to ethics, Waters and Bird, 1987). Smircich then suggests that rather than viewing organizational culture as something that an organization *has* (such as a bureaucratic culture, or a culture of public service), one may conceptualize it as a 'root metaphor'; as something that the organization *is*. In this use, organization is 'a particular form of human expression' in which the organized social world has 'much less concrete status . . . [existing] only as a pattern of symbolic relationships and meanings sustained through the continued processes of human interaction' (Smircich, 1983: 353). According to this second view, everything contributes to, and is an expression of, the culture; including formal administration, ethical codes and other devices. These are often, but not necessarily, indicative of attempts at managerial control, as is apparent if one considers various writers' different paradigmatic perspectives on organizational culture as delineated by Meyerson and Martin (1987).

Many managers, and those who write for them, represent an 'integration' paradigm. They assume the possibility of a uniform organization-wide culture, which can be deliberately changed as an internal variable. Other writers assume a 'differentiation' paradigm in which organizations are viewed as pluralist and political, reflecting the interests and subcultures of different departments and groups based on occupational, ethnic, gender and other identifications. But there is still, in this paradigm, a belief in the feasibility of planned change and development at the sub-unit level and the possible reintegration of the whole organization. Finally, there is the paradigm in which 'ambiguity' is tolerated. Here cultural change is accepted as a continual and relatively uncontrollable process, relating to specific issues and reflecting often irreconcilable disparities in values, norms, meanings and significations.

The views from Meyerson and Martin's integration and differentiation paradigms are paralleled in Sinclair's (1993) exposition of unitary and subcultural approaches to 'improving ethics in organisations'. But even subcultures threaten individuals' moral autonomy. Those whose conception of moral development in organizations supports the facilitation of such autonomy, would be uncomfortable with such emphases on unitary cultures, or even differentiated subcultures, despite the dissensus implied. More probably they would assume constant experimentation, flux and ambiguity. Thus I shall shortly elaborate on my overall theme, of organizational control versus individual autonomy, by exploring what approximates to a conceptual continuum regarding the development of organizations. In this, I locate the views both from unitary integration and from subcultural differentiation at the control end of the spectrum, while it seems that the possibility of individual moral autonomy implies something closer to ambiguity, as Meyerson and Martin suggest (1987: 640). But before that, a further note, this time on the more specific, often formalized, systems of rules, procedures and codes in organizations.

Formalized means to ethical ends

There are various types of bureaucratic mechanism which one could discuss in relation to ethics in organizations. Contrary to a popular view, such arrangements are not necessarily tools of managerial control; they can perform an emancipatory function or contribute to an egalitarian organization, for example by providing formal protection for those who wish to express dissent. Thus formalization in general is compatible with both the control and autonomy paradigms.

The issues raised may be divided into two categories: first, where ethical dysfunctions are liable to arise; second, where a contribution to the development of the organization as a moral community can be made. In the latter case it may be argued that both governance (discussed in Chapter 10) and codes of ethics (discussed below) should be included. Both governance and codes are formal arrangements designed, respectively, to facilitate the articulation of concerns and interests in organizational policy, and to guide action. I chose to include explicit treatment of governance in the earlier chapter because it is mainly about the incorporation into organizations of so-called external parties (the public, the community, specific interests) although there is no clear boundary between that topic and the wide spectrum of subject matter and theory concerning employee participation. Moreover, Brooks (1989) sees codes as a contribution to corporate governance, but I deal with them in this chapter since they relate more closely to other topics discussed here.

Moral dysfunctions in administrative systems

The first aspect of administrative systems to consider is also the most diffuse, and I shall try to confine discussion to some underlying conceptualizations and general implications. The rules and procedures alluded to here are authorized by management and serve to guide and control action. They are usually, but not always, written (Mills and Murgatroyd, 1991). Their phraseology frequently requires *ad hoc* interpretation whereby broad principles are translated into concrete terms for application in specific contexts (Selznick, 1949). Through such interpretation, unwritten knowledge about what to do in particular circumstances is informally 'scripted' (Gioia, 1992) and 'institutionalized' (Selznick, 1948). But while this is an important point, it remains the case that written, formal statements and directives have a peculiar significance in the eyes of management: protecting those who benefit from them; justifying sanctions against those who ignore them; and conferring legitimacy on the actions of those who follow them, even when adverse consequences have arisen (Gouldner, 1954a). In Chapter 8, when discussing responsibility in organizations, I outlined the problem of bureaucratic dysfunctions, which can have ethical implications. This type of problem has been recognized for decades (for example, Ridgway, 1956); yet it constantly recurs.

It is a managerial responsibility, then, to install and amend such bureaucratic arrangements as appropriate. Action to counter such weaknesses is nowadays discussed in terms of systems, reliability, total quality management, organizational learning and related concepts. Husted (1993) extends arguments from reliability in relation to disaster prevention and control, to include concern for lesser issues. For example the inclusion of new perspectives representing different ethnic, gender or professional groups can increase the 'requisite variety' on boards and committees, and so anticipate issues affecting stakeholders. Duplication and overlap in monitoring and decision-making units ('redundancy') also provide safeguards (see for example Waxman, 1990, on provisions for the prevention and alleviation of sexual harassment).

Codes of ethics

The idea of a code is often the first thing that comes to the mind of managers if one raises the subject of ethical development. This is especially true if one broadens the proposition to include mission statements and declarations of company philosophy. The greatest incidence of such codes is in the USA (Center for Business Ethics, 1986, 1992; Murphy, 1995) and while a trend is now apparent in the UK (Pearson, 1995; Webley, 1992) it is debatable whether the same will happen in other parts of the world (Langlois and Schlegelmilch, 1990).

The distinction between codes and other types of pronouncement is problematic. Codes usually include precisely worded proscriptions, whereas mission statements tend to be worded more vaguely, spelling out objectives and responsibilities in positive terms. Thus the statement of 'our endeavour' in the John Menzies Group *Annual Report 1992* included (among other articles):

To carry out our business with the highest standards of integrity.

To contribute wherever possible to the welfare and quality of life of the community.

To maintain real growth in earnings per share, at a better than average sector rate, in the long-term interest of our staff and shareholders.

There are also higher-level or universal codes such as those recommended in the Cadbury Report (Cadbury, 1992), the (British) Institute of Management's Code of Conduct (British Institute of Management, 1991), or the Interfaith Declaration (Webley, 1996). These do not fit easily into either category: they are not mission statements, but nor are they specific to particular organizations.

There is an extensive literature on company codes of ethics, including a spate of articles in the *Journal of Business Ethics* in the late 1980s and 1990s. Some sources are specifically about codes, while in others codes are considered in the context of wider-ranging studies concerned with the introduction of ethics policies in organizations. Among relatively more recent sources in the first category are Manley (1992), Webley (1992), and Warren (1993) all from the UK; Kaye (1992) in Australia; Benson (1989), Hyman et al. (1990) and Weaver (1995) from the USA; and Langlois and Schlegelmilch (1990) on international comparisons. As part of more comprehensive discussions one could cite Donaldson (1989, 1992) in the UK, Brooks (1989) from Canada and Weber (1993) in the USA. These contributions range from purely descriptive (Webley, 1992) to highly critical (Hyman et al., 1990; Warren, 1993), but most sources contain a mixture of exposition and critique.

On the whole, codes are similar in their content, referring to relations with different stakeholder groups (including shareholders, employees, customers, the community and the environment) and also to the conduct of employees, and of representatives of the company in relation to international business and other matters (see Benson, 1989; Brooks, 1989; Manley, 1992; Webley, 1992). More important, however, is a number of recurring topics which are of particular interest in relation to my overall argument. These pertain to the relationship between organizational control and individuals' moral judgment:

1 The *procedure* by which a code is arrived at: who decides on its content, and on associated procedures for implementation and enforcement? (Donaldson, 1989; L'Etang, 1992; Manley, 1992).
2 The *communication* to employees of a rationale for clauses within the code (Benson, 1989; Manley, 1992; Weaver, 1995);
3 The question of *enforcement* is particularly significant and is discussed by most commentators (for example Benson, 1989; Brooks, 1989; Donaldson, 1992; Manley, 1992; Weaver, 1995).
4 The actual corporate *rationale* for introducing a code is also raised (Manley, 1992). Here in particular one faces the problem of separating rhetoric from reality. In general, one can detect the following reasons for introducing codes:
   (a) ensuring that the organization is a 'good citizen' (an 'acceptable organization') and does not offend public opinion or the law;
   (b) contributing to corporate performance in various ways which are assumed to contribute to good public image and high employee morale;
   (c) unifying the organization in the context of a strategic mission;
   (d) inculcating and reinforcing company values and culture.

What one can infer from this is that, apart from the more general statements of corporate values and missions, it may be felt that something else is needed, something more specific, which can direct managers and employees in a manner *which is enforceable*. Thus, in relation to such value-statements and credos, Murphy views codes as 'more detailed discussions of a firm's ethical policies' (1995: 728), while Donaldson suggests that 'codes, codes of practice, codes of ethics, sets of working rules, model procedures and procedure agreements are all variants on the same theme' (1992: 61). Indeed in some cases the clauses of codes approximate to bureaucratic rules, and insights concerning the latter may apply here also.

The work of Selznick (1948, 1949) has considerable relevance to an understanding of codes. His often underrated contribution has for long been associated with the theory of co-optation and his 1957 work on leadership. But the significance of leadership, for Selznick, was that no formal system of rules could ever fully control people, whose various idiosyncrasies and personal goals incline them to interpret formal, but often abstract, administrative directives in ways not intended by those seeking to shape organizational behaviour in a bureaucratic mould. Thus Selznick's infrequently acknowledged concepts of 'unanalyzed abstractions' and 'administrative discretion' are hugely important in appreciating his thinking (Selznick, 1949: Chapter 2). They raise precisely the same issues as I discussed in Chapter 4 concerning the need for further, contextualized, interpretation of ethical principles. Only, for Selznick, such interpretation would be guided by institutionalized values in a culture created by leadership (Selznick, 1957).

The Caterpillar Tractor Company's 'Code of Worldwide Business Conduct and Operating Principles' (revised May 1985) (reproduced in Webley, 1992: 29–35) contains many examples of this unavoidable ambiguity of abstract language. To take just one, on the question of privacy of information on employees, we find:

> Personal data will contain only such individually identifiable information as is necessary for business purposes and compliance with law.

I leave it to the reader to consider what, depending on the circumstances, might be deemed 'individually identifiable' or 'necessary for business purposes'. Thus discretion resides with those who must interpret such wording, and this discretion can be affected by all sorts of matters.

Such ambiguity makes it hard to enforce a code, something widely assumed to be essential. In so far as enforcement is possible, it is indicative of the tension between control and individual autonomy. This raises a moral critique of codes, to which I return shortly. As an effective contribution to the ethically acceptable organization, there are many situations where the most that a code can achieve is to draw attention to what may be seen as organizationally defined principles or prima facie duties, leaving further judgment to individuals. Goodpaster and Matthews's (1982) 'corporation with a conscience' would then need, in addition, institutionalized structures and procedures to monitor activity against these principles. Thus we find corporate ethics audits and committees, and various forms of reporting mechanism including provision for the expression of dissent by employees.

Audits and committees

In the UK, discussion on such innovations has tended to be general in nature (for example, Clutterbuck et al., 1992; Manley, 1992; Pearson, 1995; Vallance, 1995; Winfield, 1990) whereas in the USA attention has been paid to specific arrangements such as ethics audits, committees, ombudsmen and internal reporting, and whistleblowing; for example Murphy (1988) on the McDonnell Douglas ethics implementation project, and Ostapski and Isaacs (1992) and Ostapski and Pressley (1992) on corporate moral audit systems.

Ostapski and Pressley describe the setting up of an independent Moral

Audit Committee (MAC) at the Diabco Corporation, a US multinational. The MAC was appointed by the board, and comprises one of the directors as chairman, two upper managers, and three external experts in technical areas relevant to the Corporation's activities. The MAC's task is to identify and make recommendations concerning matters such as working conditions, environmental impact, customer relations and international operations, where the company's activities might raise issues of ethical concern. One of the three external members has responsibility for liaison with employees, and can be contacted at an office within the company. Those experiencing moral dilemmas are encouraged to contact this person for advice. After discussion, the liaison member may give an immediate answer based on company policy, or may refer the matter to the MAC, which then convenes to consider it.

This approach can perform either an additional or an alternative function to a code of ethics. Were company policy enshrined in a code (and the MAC at Diabco recommended the adoption of a corporate code) there would still be ambiguity and a need for judgment. However, the relationship between codes and committees is reciprocal, since an MAC would refer to a code or mission statement for its guiding principles. The overall process operates confidentially, guaranteeing anonymity for the employee, and its decisions are 'non-binding'. 'The objective of this procedure is to assist individuals in making ethical decisions and not to dictate results' (Ostapski and Pressley, 1992: 73). Clearly, however, this may be questioned, since companies vary in the extent and manner of the encouragement they give to employees to refer issues and dilemmas to a higher authority.

Internal reporting

The principle of internal whistleblowing as a first step for employees wishing to report wrongdoing in, or by, the organization, was raised in Chapter 9. The MAC at Diabco aimed at eventually developing an organizational culture which would encourage employees to report such matters, and a system of internal mailboxes was provided for this purpose. Barnett et al. (1993) discuss policies which can be incorporated into company codes concerning employees' duty to inform on wrongdoing, and clarifying the appropriate reporting procedure. These channels include hot-lines, ethics committees and ombudsmen. Such policies would also detail procedures for the investigation of cases and would guarantee protection for such internal whistleblowers provided the latter had acted in good faith.

This last point is problematic; the risks for all employees are very real, both for those who may be falsely accused of acting maliciously, and for those who may be fearful of taking justifiable risks in their work lest they are reported for improper conduct (Dunfee, 1990). Doubtless the response to all of this is that with the appropriate balance of confidentiality, openness and trust, all will be well; in principle, there need not be incompatibility between these formal mechanisms, the application of personal ethical judgment, and responsible dialogue. There may be parallels here with survey-based approaches to organization development (OD) (Nadler, 1977), which, in turn, connect with OD methods based on dialogue and the creation of an ethos in which such issues can be discussed openly and without threat. But such methods have had their share of criticism, being seen as potentially manipulative and not at all conducive to the encouragement of individuals' moral autonomy.

The control paradigm: leadership, codes and cultures

Referring back to the earlier discussion on culture, the control paradigm in organizational change and development assumes the possibility of integration (Meyerson and Martin, 1987). In the context of ethics, this is informed by the search for public acceptability, or the ethically acceptable organization. By contrast, a concern for personal moral autonomy would reflect Meyerson and Martin's ambiguity paradigm. Leadership and codes, also, are often associated with control, integration and the unitary approach (Sinclair, 1993). Certainly there is justification for that view, but I suggest that the concepts of culture, leadership and even codes of ethics can also feature in the autonomy paradigm. This assertion rests on a distinction between *content-as-content* and *process-as-content* in the treatment of ethics in organizations; a distinction which seems to get insufficient explicit attention in the literature. An emphasis on *content* as the content of organizational codes and proclamations refers to the particular substantive goals and values towards which people are expected to strive; for example, product characteristics such as quality, patient care in hospitals or educational standards in universities. By contrast, if leaders' pronouncements, ethical codes or cultural norms emphasize the importance of moral thought, decision-processes, judgment, dialogue with and respect for others in that context, then this is what I mean by *process*-as-content, which will assume salience later when I look at the organization as a moral community. First, however, I shall set out the position of the control paradigm, and the moral critique of that stance.

Leadership and 'strong' cultures

Leadership, like motivation, is a hugely researched subject and there is no space to dwell extensively on it here. But two major themes should be identified. First, the characteristics, traits or qualities of successful leaders and, second, the search for the best style. While the first of these can be related to the ethical virtues, the question of effective styles, almost axiomatically, has reflected the control paradigm, assuming that leadership is about influencing others into making greater contributions to organizational goal-attainment.

This raises the question of manipulation, which I have already discussed in

Chapter 6. As Ciulla observes in a recent overview, while people seem to agree that leadership is a process of influence, leadership theories differ considerably in the degree to which they represent democratic values, advocating recognition of others' ethical autonomy, or conversely, 'appear to be coercive, manipulative and disregard the input of followers' (1995: 12). It is the old autocratic–democratic leadership distinction, but expressed in terms of the moral acceptability of such positions, rather than their functional efficacy.

For decades, writers and managers concerned with the institutionalization of values in organizations have stressed the role of leadership. An oft-quoted seminal source on the connection between leadership and culture is Selznick: 'Leadership creates and molds an organization embodying – in thought and feeling and habit – the value premises of policy' (1957: 62). But usually this has referred to strategic values and goals of prudential concern; it is fundamentally indicative of organizational self-interest. Schein stressed the particular importance of the organization's founder in shaping 'basic assumptions and beliefs' (1985: 6). This would ensure a high degree of consensus, which 'makes it possible for people to function comfortably with each other and to concentrate on their primary task' (1985: 82). Earlier, James MacGregor Burns was credited with the term 'transforming leadership' which, while apparently 'engaging the full person of the follower' (1978: 4), was premised on the hope that 'whatever the separate interests people might hold, they are presently or potentially united in the pursuit of "higher" goals' (1978: 425). Then, later, Peters and Waterman drew on Burns's thinking, calling for 'leadership that builds on man's need for meaning, leadership that creates institutional purpose' (1982: 82).

Many other writers have referred to the connection between leadership and the creation of 'strong' organizational cultures (for example, Deal and Kennedy, 1982). The idea of a strong culture refers to consistent adherence to beliefs and norms across the organization, presumed to facilitate a relatively smooth operation and high level of motivation. Regarding ethics, Walton says that: 'Disciplined organizations reflect disciplined leaders whose honed abilities lead them to behave consistently, almost instinctively, in moral ways' (1988: 178), while Treviño and Nelson report that for 'most of the executives we talked with, leadership was the most important ingredient in a solid ethical culture' (1995: 297).

Codes of ethics: a critical comment

As I observed earlier, codes are typically introduced to help ensure that an ethically acceptable organization has a good public image. It is widely believed, among both managers and academics, that codes must be enforced if they are to be of any value (see Manley, 1992; Weber, 1993). For this reason (and bearing in mind my earlier discussion on the abstract language of most codes) some writers have been forthright in their calls for greater precision. Murphy notes that 'Ford and GM stipulate that employees cannot give or receive gifts exceeding $25' (1988: 909). Compare this with United Biscuits's much vaguer prohibition of 'gratuities or gifts of money or any consideration of significant value which could be perceived as having been offered because of the business relationship or to gain a business advantage' (Webley, 1992: 26). Clearly here there is room for dispute over what counts as 'significant'.

As an organization moves towards greater specificity in its code, allied to enforcement through various reporting mechanisms and sanctions (ranging, for example, from reprimand, through suspension or demotion to dismissal), it moves closer to the purely bureaucratic mode of control. Here insights could be drawn from research into the effects of rules, such as Gouldner (1954a) and Fox (1974b). Are rules imposed unilaterally? To what extent is their rationale agreed by everyone affected, as in most rules about safety? To what extent does anyone pay attention to them anyway? And do rules suggest, as Fox claimed, management's lack of trust in employees? This emphasis on control and enforcement raises profound issues for those interested in moral development. The position outlined so far is that a deliberately contrived culture and enforceable codes can contribute to the ethically acceptable organization; more cynically, these mechanisms can help the organization avoid trouble with public opinion or the law. Doubtless this may be true, but in terms of *individuals'* moral development the imposition of enforceable rules is liable to evoke punishment-avoidance behaviour; in Kohlberg's terms, the preconventional level, or, at best, role conformity.

There is an argument that if codes put ethics on the agenda, then this can be a step on the road to more independent thinking, a precursor to the emergence of individuals' autonomous moral reasoning (Benson, 1989). But there are many who subscribe to the view presented in the previous paragraph. Donaldson stresses that 'the contents of a code . . . are not sufficient: they must have been put there by due process, amendable by due process, and drawn up, operated and discussed by efficiently autonomous participants' (1989: 131). L'Etang (1992) adopts an explicitly Kantian position in observing that the unilateral imposition of codes may infringe individuals' moral autonomy. Warren says that 'ethical codes of conduct are superficial and distracting answers to the question of how to promote ethical behaviour in corporate life' (1993: 186). Hyman et al. suggest that 'well-intentioned companies may actually hinder the development of management's moral character by too much attention to rules and too little attention to questions' (1990: 15). Pastin asserts that the 'scarce resource in ethics is independent thinking – not rule compliance. Codes constrict thinking and reinforce the myth that the heart of ethics is compliance' (1986: 124).

However, these objections assume traditional codes, the content of which refers largely to the *content* of decisions and conduct. Now it is possible to design codes which emphasize the *processes* by which one might arrive at such decisions or which guide one's conduct (Hyman et al., 1990; Munro, 1996). The McDonnell Douglas 'Ethical Decision Making Checklist' (in Murphy, 1988: 913) is one example. It comprises fifteen questions which employees should ask *of themselves*, requiring analysis of situations based on various ethical positions, and reminding the decision-maker to consider all 'creative solutions', to treat everyone implicated fairly, to consult as appropriate, and so on. Not only does this approach offer greater encouragement for the exercise of judgment in ambiguous situations, but if codes are to have any place in contributing to individual moral development, then this seems the most fruitful way forward.

Pluralism, professions and 'weak' organizational cultures

A genuinely unitary culture may be found in some organizations, enabled by the social environment and the 'technology' (Perrow, 1970) and a consequent occupational homogeneity among employees. But normally there will be differentiation by functional area and by employees' personal characteristics, derived from professional subcultures and other differences such as gender, ethnicity, age or education (Lawrence and Lorsch, 1967, 1969). Thus organizations can be viewed as multiple subcultures, as in Meyerson and Martin's 'differentiation paradigm' (1987).

Such differentiation does not mean that people have individual moral autonomy, however, given the hold that organizational and occupational subcultures can have. But in recognizing pluralism, conflict and politics among groups, this paradigm does suggest a 'weak' overall organizational culture which cannot ensure commitment to centrally sanctioned values and norms. What this indicates is a political metaphor for organizations (Morgan, 1986). A synthesis of this political metaphor with the cultural, in the context of ethics, brings a number of themes into the picture. Most obviously, the organization is now seen as a shifting configuration of alliances between different groups, each with its own values and norms, to which individuals subscribe with varying degrees of moral fervour. One such type of group is that based on occupation or function within the organization, where the literature on professional and specialist employees provides useful insight: on the nature of professional orientations, cultures and codes, and the tensions these may generate between host employers and such professional employees in bureaucratic organizations (Armstrong, 1989; Child et al., 1983; Hall, 1968); and on the role of organizational management in all of this (Reed and Anthony, 1992).

One could also turn to those who have considered organizations in the language of political philosophy. Rejecting the organismic model of organizations, characterized by overall goal-consensus, Keeley (1980: 355) observed that Selznick's (1957) view of leadership failure reflects the managerial assumption that the organization ought to have a clear mission. Rather, Keeley suggested, we should not assume such consensus on end-values, so much as on means. But the relationships involved, even if they are often described as political and negotiated, do have a fundamental moral content (Reed and Anthony, 1992). This is especially the case when the values in question implicate the (professional) ethical concerns of employees. These may well concern what Mohr called 'transitive' goals for the organization, concerned with its intended impact on the state of its environment, as with service occupations or people with a service orientation (Mohr, 1973: 476). Such relationships ought (morally and, for researchers whose concepts inform their findings, epistemologically) to be associated with an overall organizational culture in which concepts of justice, the acceptance of others' rights and interests, and integrity, are emphasized (Keeley, 1978, 1980).

Pastin maintains that organizations, need 'weak cultures and strong ethics' (1986: Chapter 7). While agreeing with Pastin's underlying sentiment, this overlooks the distinction between process and content *as the content* of cultural norms. Could one have a strong culture of concern for individuals' own moral viewpoints? To quote Pastin (who himself draws on Keeley's thinking), a culture of 'organizational social contracts' emphasizing 'voluntariness and fairness' (Pastin, 1986: 138)?

Pastin maintains that the way to change organizational culture is to talk about ethics (1986: 132). This leads to shifts in 'the underlying social contract of the organization' (Pastin, 1986: 135). Now if the culture is in large part the 'language, symbols, myths, stories, and rituals' (Smircich, 1983: 353) then what Pastin is, in effect, saying, is that changing the culture is about changing what is acceptable in organizational discourse. As a result, one can envisage changes in patterns of power and status as discussions are opened up in a more participative forum. Indeed, in such conditions culture would not be a controllable variable, but would define the organization.

The differences between such images of organizations, consensual on the one hand and discordant on the other, compare with those indicated towards the conclusion to Chapter 4, where the need for dialogic approaches to handling ethics was suggested. In that earlier discussion I anticipated a reconsideration of Kohlberg's work, with greater emphasis on the role of social interaction in persons' moral development. This takes us to the idea of the moral community, a form of organization which I defined earlier as being 'populated by individuals who have a moral concern, a sense of personal responsibility and of service . . . and who can think for themselves and act in ethical terms'.

The autonomy paradigm and the moral community

If the control paradigm is fundamentally concerned with the ethically acceptable *organization*, the autonomy paradigm is underpinned by a concern for *individual* moral development. In Chapter 3 various interpretations of autonomy were suggested. I noted that as well as the Kantian basis to Kohlberg's post-conventional level, there was an implied need for autonomy in the sense of resistance to social pressures. I also noted Meyers's (1987) idea of 'responsibility reasoning', with its emphasis on self-image and self-respect, as an alternative to the Kantian position. Now, as I have said before, in my advocacy of an approach based on a theory of prima facie duties, I am not unduly concerned with where people get their moral beliefs from, but relaxing the interpretation of autonomy suggests that one could be guided by norms and principles critically considered, but ultimately derived from society, and nevertheless interpret these, in their actual application, on the basis of personal judgment.

Durkheim, Kohlberg and the 'Just Community'

Despite his emphasis on consensus in society, Durkheim's theory of moral development indicated a concept of autonomy which is relevant to this discussion (Durkheim, [1925] 1961). Durkheim's view was that individuals willingly submit to the 'discipline', in terms of norms and values, of social groups to which they belong. Now while in a simple society this would entail unthinking conformity, in more complex societies, where novel situations are encountered, individuals have to reflect on, and choose, their actions. According to Durkheim's theory, therefore, such choices are made within socially defined, and personally accepted, moral constraints, by people who are nevertheless aware of the reasons for their own actions. This is paralleled in the way that even a code of ethics does not eliminate the need for personal judgment in novel organizational situations, and in the argument that employees should understand the reasons for specific articles within corporate codes (see Barnard, 1938: Chapter 17; and Weaver, 1995, for a related argument).

Kohlberg drew selectively upon Durkheim's thinking in his Just Community approach to moral education (Power et al., 1989). He recognized that young people learn how to think morally through interaction and cooperation with each other, employing ethical concepts at the conventional level, in the real setting of their school as an institution. 'The autonomous self is in a sense created and sustained through dialogue with other autonomous selves' (Power et al., 1989: 28). So, contrary to the view presented by many in the field of business ethics who have drawn on Kohlberg's ideas, these ideas cannot be taken as eulogizing Kantian moral autonomy to the exclusion of all else (but see Snell, 1993: 17–27, for a critical commentary).

Incremental moral development

What this means is that initiation into Kohlberg's conventional level can be seen as a first step in the moral development of individuals who are not yet at that point. This is not inconsistent with a more distant goal: that of persons' subsequently attaining a capacity for some sort of autonomous moral reasoning. This seems to be the same kind of argument as that employed by those who claim that organizational codes can be a stage in the advancement of employees' moral development. Significantly, the general form of this argument is also seen in the work of some organization development writers who have noted the need to select intervention strategies which match the extant level of their clients' (moral) development, rather than assume that everyone is equally able to handle ethical concepts, tolerate others' conflicting positions, and so forth (Harrison, 1970; Lavoie and Culbert, 1978).

In the Just Community projects, Kohlberg sought to counter the more extreme features of the Durkheimian position (societal indoctrination) by ensuring a democratic basis to the groups' structures. Here he was influenced by Dewey (1916) and by observations of kibbutz education in 1969. This exemplifies (admittedly in schools rather than in fully adult work contexts) the political dimension which I have adduced on several occasions already (Pastin, 1986; Pateman, 1970). Indeed those authors' views gain support from the discussions of moral issues which took place among students in the schools, where dialogue increasingly focused on the nature of their own organization, as a community: 'The norms which emerged [in the Just Community schools] concerned power relations between individuals and between the community and the wider world, and the maintenance of the community as a functioning unit' (Weinreich-Haste, 1986: 350).

Etzioni's 'Responsive Community'

Amitai Etzioni is another who is associated with the idea of community, providing a number of connections between various strands in my overall argument. His recent well-publicized advocacy of 'communitarianism' as a political ideal has inspired the idea of 'stakeholder capitalism', indicated in the previous chapter. This is a product of Etzioni's earlier thinking on paradigms for economic and social relations (Etzioni, 1988). There he describes (a) an 'undersocialized' view of unfettered, self-interested action in the laisserfaire market, (b) an 'oversocialized' view epitomized by Durkheim's work, and (c) a third perspective which, following Martin Buber, he calls the 'I and We' view. For Etzioni, this third paradigm emerges out of the struggle between the oversocialized and undersocialized views. Individuals are seen as acting out of rational self-interest, but constrained by moral commitments to their 'responsive community' (the 'We'). Here the separation of self from other is what distinguishes it from the 'I am We' dialogic approach offered by Nielsen (1991), discussed in Chapter 4.

As with the problem of defining who are one's stakeholders, there are critical questions to be raised concerning the delineation of boundaries around any such community. This is much the same issue as I raised in Chapter 9 concerning identity and loyalty. If, as Etzioni argues, the community is defined in terms of mutual trust and cooperation, how does one make sense of intensely pluralist systems? Labour relations conflicts, or South Africa under apartheid, for example (see Swanson, 1992). It also raises a conceptual problem regarding the category of altruism into which such I/We relations might fall: are they 'communal' or 'cosmopolitan' (Galston, 1993; and see Chapter 3 above)? My normative conclusion is that whereas in human relations theory (representing the control paradigm) 'We' is the organization in the narrow sense, for members of the 'responsive community' 'We' would be all stakeholders, in the widest sense. Thus the powerful, in a pluralist situation, would be expected to take account of the concerns and interests of others, and not define the 'community' interest simply in terms of their own values and aspirations.

Conclusion

I have argued for a widening of discussions about organizational moral development, from primary concern with the ethically acceptable organization (control-oriented, stressing *content* in codes and directives, purportedly integrated) to an emphasis on the community of morally responsible individuals (emancipatory, supporting *processes* of democratic ethical management rather than the imposition of particular behavioural norms, and with a concern for individuals' moral education and learning). A similar standpoint is adopted by many others, including, in the UK, Donaldson (1989) and Warren (1996).

In the processes characteristic of the moral community, responsible individuals can follow judgmental, dialogic and dialectical modes in their ethical (self-) management (Janis, 1972; Nielsen, 1990; Schwenk, 1984; Sims, 1992). The culture and formal systems of organization, including codes of ethics, can encourage values and conduct which support these processes. There is mutual respect and concern for others, capacity to exercise personal judgment, moral discourse rather than 'moral muteness' (Bird and Waters, 1989). Leaders have an important role in encouraging such 'good conversation' (Bird and Waters, 1989: 86; Bird et al., 1989); although as Treviño and Nelson (1995: 212) observe, explicit use of terms such as 'moral' and 'ethical' is not always well received, reminding us of the need to make allowance for persons' current level of comfort with such language.

A caveat

There is an objection that, by strict definition, no prescriptions for ethical conduct and decision-making, be they Kant's categorical imperative or something more prosaic, such as the judgmental approach which I introduced in Chapter 4, can facilitate individuals' moral autonomy. Especially if taken too literally as some sort of algorithm for 'solving' ethical problems, these do no more than spell out organizational definitions of responsible role performance (Broughton, 1986: 375–8). I see this not as a reason for giving up the quest, but as a warning to guard against mere conformity with such guidelines. Kohlberg himself was aware of the dangers (1973: 194–5). The answer resides somewhere in the region of the weak/strong cultures distinction, the leadership function, and management education. Cultures and codes, if any, should be the product of, and emphasize, participative processes, rather than being a means to top-down control over employees. In such contexts, disagreement would be tolerated, as the natural outcome of individuals' thoughtful, critical contributions to organizational dialogue.

12 Developing People: Moral Learning for Organizational Life

In the previous chapter I reiterated a central theme of this book: that, at root, ethics in organizations is a matter of individual responsibility. It is possible to assert this once one recognizes a managerial requirement to correct, or make allowance for, systemic factors which affect people's lives and actions. Individuals in organizations, especially those in positions of authority, require what I shall call 'moral attributes': a balance of relevant knowledge, understanding, intellectual and social skills, and other personal qualities. They should be able to appreciate ethical issues, understand the organizational context in which these arise, apprehend prima facie moral duties, think intelligently about the dilemmas which confront them, and use their judgment, individually and collectively, when searching for ways forward in such situations. Thus without some attention being paid to the development of individuals' critical capacities and personal qualities, through education, training and, increasingly, workplace-based (and often self-managed) learning, there will be a major gap in any systematic approach to the institutionalization of ethics in organizations (Maclagan, 1990a; Weber, 1993).

However, the provision of education and development programmes relating to management ethics can take various forms, reflecting different underlying purposes. Very often, organizational management adopts a control-oriented approach, placing considerable reliance on codes, the promotion of 'strong' ethical cultures, and other forms of regulation. In such contexts any educational and training programmes in ethics have as their rationale the function of reinforcing the corporate ethos. At best, they may help to provide individuals with the additional intellectual resources with which to handle those issues and dilemmas not covered by the necessarily vague wording of formal policies and pronouncements. But in so far as they emphasize conformity at the expense of critical thinking, such programmes do little to help change situations where the moral ethos of the organization fails to support what the public generally would regard as ethically good practice. In short, they are really just programmes of organizational socialization (Snell, 1993: 172–5).

Snell stresses another vital point also. Much of the work on ethics education for managers and other employees is concerned with narrowly defined personal development. It confines attention to the moral issues and dilemmas which people face as individuals, and fails to attend sufficiently to their potential as members of the community that is an organization. Many situations which individuals may be inclined to view as personal problems are in fact in some sense shared with others. Snell sees the cultivation of moral leadership qualities and the development of political skills as important factors in such circumstances. Thus what he calls 'critical pragmatism and social transformation' emerges as another rationale for ethics programmes, not incompatible with personal development, and indeed dependent on this, in so far as the requisite leadership training is indicated (Snell, 1993: 176–80).

Personal moral attributes and the concept of competence

Interest in management education and development has grown enormously in recent decades. Programmes, courses and approaches to the subject range over a variety of academic and more practically oriented possibilities, and are addressed to the needs of various different types of participant, from university undergraduates to experienced middle and senior managers. Two particular trends are worth a mention so far as the UK context is concerned. First, the excitement in the late 1980s with the idea of managerial competencies as something to be cultivated through training and education. Second, a more recent expansion in the provision of Masters of Business Administration (MBA) programmes, about which I shall say little more (although such programmes are implied in later discussion on the teaching of ethics to business and management students).

The competency debate was part of the Management Charter Initiative (MCI) to 'professionalize' the practice of management in Britain (Silver, 1991). In this, there seemed to be very little concern with moral aspects of management. Despite some brief references to ethics, the overall emphasis was on managerial effectiveness in limited and seemingly unrelated functional contexts. Burgoyne (1989) remarked at the time that there was in this debate an overemphasis on the technical at the expense of the ethical, very largely due to the reductionist nature of the perspective adopted when trying to make sense of what it might mean to be a competent manager. As he observed: 'Being competent is different from having competencies' (Burgoyne, 1989: 60). In short, much work on the identification of essential managerial competencies lacked a sound theoretical basis. But a basis was in fact available, since Boyatzis (1982) had developed an integrated model of competence based on the same generic management process to which I referred in Chapter 1 (namely: planning, organizing, controlling, motivating and coordinating).

Maturity and moral development

One interesting point which is hidden in Boyatzis's text concerns managers' maturity, as something which they acquire through life experiences, and a somewhat elliptical reference in that context to Kohlberg's theory of moral development (Boyatzis, 1982: 159–60). This is significant because a number of writers outside the field of management have identified individual characteristics associated with personal maturity and competence in life generally. This seems to be connected with moral development in a holistic sense. Heath (1977) listed several attributes, indicative of personal maturity, which focus our attention on the need to be able to understand and manage oneself: being a well-integrated person with a stable set of values; being flexible enough to be able to adjust to changing circumstances, something of particular importance in complex roles such as those occupied by managers; being able to think rationally even in emotionally charged situations; and having sufficient integrity and inner strength to follow one's personal moral convictions, overriding narrow self-interest where required. Subsequently Raven (1984) drew attention to the point that competence is not an end in itself, but refers to the capacity to realize particular values. In that context, Raven included a number of attributes relevant to the relationship between self and others in organizations: a willingness to trust others and to delegate; being prepared to challenge those in authority; an ability to understand value-conflicts and their behavioural manifestations.

This takes us back to Kohlberg's thinking. It is important to note here the distinction between four elements in the overall process of moral development. First of all there is the *cognitive* component, with which Kohlberg is popularly associated. But this cognitive element in itself is insufficient. Based on a synthesis of his own work and that of Erikson (1964) on ego-stage development, Kohlberg (1973) recognized the need for significant personal experiences before people could acquire *commitment to particular moral values*. These would have an emotional dimension. Take the question of equal opportunities. A student in the seminar room may be quite able to engage in abstract moral reasoning about discrimination, but it will make a great deal of difference if she has actually experienced this personally; the concept of fairness will take on a new significance. As Treviño (1986: 606–7) observes, such experiences stimulate continuing moral development among adults, and could arise at almost any point in one's life. Thus moral development is an ongoing, lifelong, process.

Furthermore, even after this commitment has been acquired, *personal and interpersonal qualities* such as assertiveness are often called for. Indeed, this is true whatever the basis of one's ethical position, whether it reflects conformity with societal norms or independent reasoning, since even in the former case one may be confronted with others who oppose the prevailing moral position which one supports. Such conflicts may force individuals to confront identity crises in which, for moral development to take place, they must resolve contradictions between the ideals arising out of their moral thinking, and the reality of organizational norms and other pressures, including other interests of their own, such as family responsibilities. Is one really prepared to face hostility from others for campaigning to end dishonest working practices? Are potential whistleblowers really prepared to sacrifice their careers? Individuals faced with such situations must make a *choice of personal identity*, or 'self'.

Personal moral attributes in organizations

Note that I did not call these four elements 'stages'. Even though the impression may be that development follows a sequential pattern, it is not clear that the elements do follow in progression. For example, the cognitive element, involving thinking about a situation and perhaps gleaning further information, may follow an initial emotional reaction, or may be bound up with an interpersonal aspect involving others who are party to the same moral dilemma. In other words a holistic perspective is called for, just as with the judgmental mode of dealing with moral issues and problems, described in Chapter 4. This developmental process could, of course, take place naturally; that is, people might gradually acquire, over a period of years, knowledge and understanding, commitment to values and princi- ples, personal and interpersonal skills, and self-knowledge. And of course this is what does tend to happen. But, in comparable fashion to the work done on competencies, it is possible to construe such elements in the moral development process as 'domains of learning behaviour' (Huczynski, 1983: 8) which can then be conceptualized in terms of training or educational objectives and the provision of appropriate programmes to facilitate their attainment.

Following Pedler (1978) and others, Huczynski identified five such domains or areas of managerial learning in general: psychomotor, cognitive, affective, interpersonal and self-knowledge. Again, as with so much else, a holistic approach is required, and it is recognized that 'when one considers a typical managerial behaviour, a number of these separate learning areas come together' (Huczynski, 1983: 8).

Ignoring psychomotor aspects (mainly manual skills), if one looks at the other four areas for management learning in this list, then a close parallel with the four elements of the moral development process is apparent. I shall now expand on this similarity, and this will lead into a more specific consid- eration of the provision of management ethics programmes. My discussion will for the most part follow an evolution of ideas which can be found in Maclagan (1990a; 1991a), Maclagan and Snell (1992) and Snell (1993), start- ing with a comment on the four areas – cognitive, affective, interpersonal and self-knowledge – in terms of the moral attributes required by individuals in organizations (Maclagan, 1990a).

The cognitive area can be subdivided into two: tools for ethical analysis; and all the other subject matter which is germane to the conceptualization of actual moral issues and dilemmas. Ethical analysis includes the meta-ethical question of recognizing a moral issue in the first place, the apprehension of prima facie duties, appreciating different moral standpoints, establishing the 'shape' of situations, ethical reasoning, and also the judgmental element, all of which was addressed in Chapters 3 and 4. The balance of the cognitive area covers almost any knowledge that might be deemed relevant to an apprecia- tion, understanding and contextualization of ethically significant situations faced by people in organizations. The importance of this should not be ignored; presumably it includes most of the other components of business and management programmes, and doubtless much else besides.

The affective area, initially, can be understood in terms of the acquisition of those attitudes and feelings which reinforce individuals' commitment to particular moral values. Construed thus, and as implied in my outline of the developmental process, such attributes are at least as likely to be the product of life experiences generally, as they are to result from programmes of education and development.

The interpersonal attributes required in relation to the moral development process are little different from those usually recognized in training and development programmes. However, as qualities which can contribute to personal effectiveness in the context of ethics, assertiveness, the ability to listen to and appreciate others' viewpoints, and the choice of ethically appropriate, tactful, modes of communication (for example, when and when not to use written, telephonic, or face-to-face contact) are particularly important. The capacity to handle one's own emotional reactions to ethically charged episodes may also, at least in some situations, be viewed as an interpersonal attribute, although I shall qualify that suggestion later in this discussion.

Finally there is the important and often overlooked matter of self-knowledge and the acquisition of a stable self-concept. There is a danger that without a clear and well integrated set of values and sense of direction, one can drift into work or career 'traps' where, too late, one becomes committed (for example, through economic dependence on that particular employment combined with obligations to one's dependants) to activity which explicitly or implicitly runs counter to one's own moral position. Processes of dissonance reduction and other social pressures can have an impact here, in that such entrapment may have the effect of 'enforcing' a change in personal beliefs and values to align with the new reality in which the individual is enmeshed. People should be able to make their own 'moral career choices' (Leary and Leary, 1988: 165) rather than allow themselves to fall victim to the designs of others, which often happens in organizational settings. Of course it isn't always possible to avoid such situations, and indeed they may provide learning opportunities if they confront one with a quandary to be resolved, as I noted earlier with reference to identity crises in the moral development process. However, having a personal strategic sense, and being able to face up to choices before it is too late, should help forestall problems of this sort.

Towards a programme for development

An attempt at identifying managers' need for such moral attributes, and then relating these to different types of management education and development programme, was offered in Maclagan and Snell (1992). This was based on Snell's interviews with people who were in mid-career (also reported in Snell, 1993: especially Chapter 8). The interview transcripts provided rich descriptions of dilemmas and other ethically significant situations faced by these individuals, and these were then analysed in terms of a set of moral attributes very similar to that which I have just outlined. But there was one significant difference, which was that in this analysis very little explicit attention was paid to the affective or emotional dimension to individuals' behaviour, other than to the self-control needed in heated situations. The reason for dropping the affective area as a distinct category was that, construed as it was in Maclagan (1990a; and as I have described it above) this had not seemed amenable to cultivation through formally instituted management development programmes.

Subsequently, Snell (1993: 180–5) has produced a much more sophisticated 'template curriculum' for education and development in management ethics. In this, three broad areas are identified:

1 cognitive: defined as previously;
2 performative: comparable to the personal and interpersonal skills area in Maclagan and Snell (1992);
3 affective: broadly defined so as to include, for example, a 'sense of responsibility' and 'moral courage'.

Snell then identifies four further areas where the three broad areas overlap:

4 core ethical qualities: a combination of cognitive, performative and affective, relevant to the handling of ethical conflicts and dilemmas;
5 strategic skills: combining cognitive and performative, relevant to working out what to do from an ethical and 'critically pragmatic', perhaps political, standpoint, as in moral leadership;
6 self-insight: combining cognitive and affective, and comparable to self-knowledge as defined previously;
7 emotional management: combining performative and affective, and covering areas previously included in the personal and interpersonal area concerned with emotional self-control.

A significant aspect of Snell's contribution is the way in which the pervasiveness of the affective element is accommodated by explicit recognition of the overlap between the different areas. In particular, emotional management can be distinguished from other performative skills, and proper recognition can also be given to emotion and concern for values in the processes leading to self-insight and the emergence of a stable self-concept.

Management education and development

It appears that that little had been published on teaching and learning in managerial and business ethics prior to the mid-1980s (Kohls et al., 1989; Maclagan, 1990a). Since then, there has been a great increase in published work on this aspect of the subject; so much so, that a new journal, *Teaching Business Ethics*, was launched in 1997.

For the most part, such writing emphasizes the cognitive domain and relatively traditional teaching and learning situations, rather than the non-cognitive areas, which depend more on experiential learning. However, to adhere to too crude a dichotomy here would be an oversimplification, as a moment's reflection on the moral development process, and on Snell's (1993) analysis of the requisite curriculum, will confirm. Theoretical learning may be reinforced by additional practical or emotional experience; and, conversely, an appreciation of the relevant knowledge and theory assists in the acquisition of social and behavioural skills.

Implicit in this is a distinction between conventional academic programmes and company-based or other in-service courses. The latter offer different types of learning context, in terms of aims, participants' expectations and pedagogical methods. A number of sources have referred to in-company contexts for ethics programmes as part of more comprehensive efforts to institutionalize ethics in organizations (for example, Center for Business Ethics, 1986, 1992; Weber, 1993). Fewer contributors have examined, in detail, the specific question of ethics training within companies (but see Kohls et al., 1989).

An awareness of these different contexts is one factor which is important in making sense of debates over such matters as whether or not one can teach business ethics, what the purposes of this should be anyway, and how to go about it. A pure academic grounding in philosophy might be one purpose, as Snell (1993) notes, but this is a function associated with traditional university education, especially at bachelor's level. As such, it may quite properly demand a thorough exposure to rigorous theoretical analysis. But it performs a different function, in a different context, using different methods, to that which one encounters in the training facilities of a large corporation. Nevertheless, even where company-based programmes are under discussion, the focus has tended to be on cognitive, theoretical or decision-making skills (Kohls et al., 1989). This should be no surprise. Following the moral development model outlined earlier, whatever else is required by way of moral attributes, an awareness of ethical issues and a capacity to engage with these (reasoning, judgment) is required.

In the numerous articles (and to a lesser extent, books) which have recently addressed the teaching of business and management ethics, the issues raised fall, for the most part, into the following areas:

- the incidence and content of ethics components in academic or company training programmes (for example, Center for Business Ethics, 1986; Cowton and Dunfee, 1995; Kohls et al., 1989; Mahoney, 1990);
- the aims and relevance of ethics programmes (for example, Cooke and Ryan, 1988; Cowton and Dunfee, 1995; Dunfee and Robertson, 1988; Kohls et al., 1989; McDonald and Donleavy, 1995; Mahoney, 1990; Snell, 1993; Treviño and McCabe, 1994; Treviño and Nelson, 1995);
- the integration of ethics components into management education and training as a whole (for example, Dunfee and Robertson, 1988; Kohls et al., 1989; McDonald and Donleavy, 1995; Mahoney, 1990; Pamental, 1989: Snell, 1993; Treviño and McCabe, 1994; Weber, 1993);

- pedagogical issues; the detail of teaching and learning methods (for example, Bain, 1994; Binns, 1994; Cowton and Dunfee, 1995; Dunfee and Robertson, 1988; McDonald and Donleavy, 1995; Mahoney, 1990; Pamental, 1989; Snell, 1993).

The incidence of ethics provision

The general descriptive evidence strongly suggests that the incidence of ethics inputs, especially in educational programmes such as MBA degrees, has risen during the 1980s and 1990s. This is particularly true of the UK and elsewhere in Europe. It is relevant to add, however, that critical perspectives on management and management theory (as epitomized in books such as Burrell and Morgan, 1979; and Perrow, [1972] 1979) have been included in some university programmes for many years, even if the label 'ethics' was seldom attached, and a movement in support of such teaching appears to be gaining renewed impetus (French and Grey, 1996). In many respects, such as the faculty involved, this is distinct from the business ethics community, and the relationship between the two is interesting and, I feel, poorly understood. Critical management education can undoubtedly prepare the ground for teaching in business and managerial ethics by raising students' awareness of underlying issues (such as value-biases) in management theory and practice. Following that, ethics programmes can provide the intellectual resources with which to appreciate and perhaps resolve moral dilemmas that arise in practice.

The aims and relevance of ethics programmes

A common impression is that ethics programmes for managers and management students are intended to make them 'more moral'. In the view of many of those involved in the provision of such programmes this is mistaken. Such courses usually have a twofold aim: first, to raise awareness of moral issues that can arise in and around organizations; second, to provide the intellectual (cognitive) and, to a limited extent, other resources required to handle the dilemmas which frequently result. Such aims presuppose that people in organizations, if not possessing a conscious predisposition to seek out the morally right action (the 'moral orientation'; see Chapter 2), are, at any rate, well-meaning citizens who may nevertheless not previously have thought seriously about ethics in the workplace.

There are of course those who are doubtless incorrigible; for whom no amount of exposure to ethical theory – *particularly* theory – will make any difference. Here I note Cooke and Ryan's (1988) observation that programmes in business ethics should not be viewed as a process of 'moral conversion'. Suggesting that 'there is no reason to believe Ivan Boesky would have acted differently if he had taken a dozen seminars in business ethics' (1988: 31) Cooke and Ryan stress that many of the misunderstandings about the potential, and the limitations, of this whole area as an applied field rest on a failure to appreciate this point. (See also Kohls et al., 1989: 56–8).

So far as the provision of intellectual resources is concerned, this refers to a combination of ethical theory and appreciation of its application. For the most part, I have addressed this area in Chapters 3 and 4. However some aspects of the actual teaching and learning involved need to be noted. The other, non-cognitive, resources alluded to above concern performative, interpersonal skills and other aspects of self-management as outlined earlier. Here again some comment on development in these respects is called for.

The institutional context

A number of questions are raised concerning the integration of ethics components into the wider academic or institutional context. For whom is the course designed? What is their background knowledge? How much philosophical theory is appropriate? Who should teach it? Should the course be compulsory? How does it relate to the rest of the educational programme – should ethics be a separate module, be integrated into other courses, or both?

Several of these questions apply to both academic and organization-based programmes. The amount of philosophical ethics which is appropriate depends on the background and expectations of the participants. This also has a bearing on who should do the teaching. Where one is working with managers on a part-time basis there will usually be restrictions on the amount of theory which is appropriate. Not only is time short, but such participants are unlikely to be enthusiastic unless they can engage with what they see as real problems. By contrast, the 'academic grounding' which Snell (1993) sees as one possible aim for management ethics education is more appropriate for full-time university students, and even then it probably depends on the rationale of the overall programme; on some MBAs, for example, comparable situations arise as those found with company-based workshops.

The judgmental mode I suggested in Chapter 4 does not require a vast amount of philosophical knowledge. What is required is an ability to identify moral issues, and, crucially, to appreciate the organizational context in which concrete instances arise. The case for this position is to some extent reinforced by the fact that in real situations managers can seldom spend much time pondering over the theoretical implications.

In formal educational settings a further cluster of issues pertains to such matters as overall programme structure and administration. One question concerns whether or not ethics should be addressed separately, or whether it should be included in the various other subjects such as marketing, human resource management and information technology. An objection to the former strategy, especially when the course is optional, is that it may give the impression that ethics is an unimportant appendage. An answer to this, which also helps where the other subject specialists are unfamiliar with ethical theory, is to have a separate module, and also to introduce ethics into other subjects as and when staff involved feel ready to do so. But whichever approach is adopted, it is essential to recognize that moral issues are pervasive and can be found in every area of management practice and organizational life.

One final but important observation concerns the institutional setting in a real sense. Both Snell (1993: Chapter 11) and Treviño and McCabe (1994) argue for collective responsibility, or Kohlberg's Just Community approach (which I mentioned in the previous chapter) in the management of business ethics programmes. In essence, this introduces a participative, experiential element, whereby students 'become part of an "honorable" business school community where real ethical issues are openly and regularly discussed' (Treviño and McCabe, 1994: 406).

Teaching and learning

Whatever the answer to the aforementioned questions, there is a general consensus that the teaching of management ethics requires the use of cases or comparable material. This is largely to do with the problem of relating ethical theory to practice. A grasp of ethical theory, even an ability to engage in ethical reasoning, is insufficient on its own. Students must also be able to appreciate the organizational context from the perspective of those who would in reality face the moral dilemmas indicated. This, of course, applies to their tutors also (Pamental, 1989). In short, and in the absence of the actual experience which may be available to participants on company-based programmes, students require material with which to practise the judgmental approach to handling moral dilemmas. Specifically, they need as much practice with conceptualization and contextualization as with the associated ethical thinking; these are all of a piece.

This is, in effect, a pedagogical inference from my exposition in Chapters 3 and 4. It is supported by Binns (1994) in a comparable argument. Such an explicit insistence on the need for contextualization is an indispensable advance on the baldly stated decision-models, and some simple checklists, which are provided in many texts. However, the process of contextualization, and why it is essential, must be made clear to participants on ethics courses. They must appreciate the need to discern the 'shape' of the situation as they see it; its salient features, 'the things that make a moral difference' (Dancy, 1993b: 221). This may, however, entail the dialogic mode where several people are involved. Thus, individually or collectively, a choice of 'duty proper' can be made; an ordering of prima facie obligations with an emphasis on some 'reasons' over 'defeated reasons', where the latter nevertheless remain as factors influencing the detail of one's ethical action.

I have been critical of checklists and decision-models, and I now wish to redress the balance. Some of these, if only in their accompanying narrative, invite us to examine situations in detail, gathering information, identifying affected parties, establishing reasons why one should act this way rather than that (for example, Treviño and Nelson, 1995: 71–5). Luijk (1994) stresses the importance of the institutional and cultural context. Why, for instance, should a company be responsible, rather than its host government, when it faces a dilemma as to whether or not to comply with environmental legislation if this means many redundancies at its factory? In what ways might local culture affect an issue faced by a pharmaceutical manufacturer marketing a contraceptive drug?

Apart from gaining practice with the judgmental approach, working on cases helps students to understand ethical theory better (Derry and Green, 1989) and generates new conceptualizations which themselves will have applicability beyond the immediate case in question. (Figure 7.1 in Chapter 7 was developed during a workshop with experienced managers, in the context of discussion on a real case introduced by one of the group.) One issue raised here concerns the nature of case material. While it is often assumed that cases should be comprehensive, often necessarily lengthy, so as to provide enough detail to enable the moral issues to be contextualized (for example, Harvey et al., 1994) there are alternatives. Short vignettes, sometimes no more than a few lines long (as with press cuttings) can be useful (Bain, 1994; Donaldson, 1992). These can catch the interest of tired or unenthusiastic participants. But of more direct relevance to the question of conceptualization and judgment is the point that such vignettes, precisely because they require amplification, enable one to ask 'what if . . . ?' questions. What if some aspects of the situation were different in respects which affect its 'ethical shape'? Furthermore, there are other types of material which can be useful. Literary sources are increasingly popular in both management education generally and in business ethics (for example, Coles, 1987). Blessed with the imaginative empathy which novelists have with their characters, these sources provide rich insight of value, especially, in the development of the affective and self-knowledge areas.

This takes us closer to the experiential approaches to learning which are associated with the development of individuals' non-cognitive moral attributes. I shall not say much on this. Perhaps it can be suggested that approaches such as action-learning (in relation to performative skills) or mentoring (as an aid to self-knowledge and self-development) do not, in their application to the cultivation of personal moral attributes, require much amendment from their normal usage in management development practice (further brief comment on this is found in Maclagan and Snell, 1992). However, as one final point here, I return to decision-models and checklists. Most of these address the cognitive dimension to handling moral issues and dilemmas. But it is also possible to use such lists to test projected action against one's own self-concept: 'could I live with the knowledge that I had taken this decision?'; or to assess one's performative skills or moral courage: 'do I have the skills and character to speak up for this course of action?' Such 'diagnostic instruments' (Snell and Maclagan, 1992) can be useful in a variety of experiential or self-management contexts.

Conclusion

The key to managerial ethics is the development of individuals so that, ideally, they will possess the moral attributes required for the apprehension, appreciation and handling of ethical issues and dilemmas. To say this is to emphasize a human potential for independent moral judgment, rather than any need for enforced organizational rules or codes. It also assumes that most people in organizations are well intentioned, and prepared to benefit from the opportunity to contribute to a 'moral community'. Yet some may be corrupted by organizational, business or other institutional arrangements, and if this is so, it is a further argument for educating those who can change the system, so that such ethically distorting and corrupting systemic forces can be removed. Of course, it may be objected that sometimes these more influential and powerful members of organizations are themselves unsympathetic to moral concerns. This brings back into focus the whole question of organizations' 'moral ethos' (Snell, 1993). It is undoubtedly a real issue for those involved in ethics training and consultancy, who need to appreciate the nature of power and politics in such institutional contexts (Maclagan, 1996), and who may themselves need to engage in ethically charged dialogue with organizational management – the 'dialogic mode'. Finally, it may also be argued that at least some people are inherently amoral or even unethical. If this is the case then it becomes a societal concern; for governments, parents and educational institutions as well as organizational leaders. Moral development is, after all, a lifelong process.

References

Abrahamsson, B. (1977) *Bureaucracy or Participation*. Beverly Hills, Calif.: Sage.

Adams, R., Carruthers, J. and Hamil, S. (1991) *Changing Corporate Values*. London: Kogan Page.

Agor, W. (1986) 'The logic of intuition: how top executives make important decisions', *Organizational Dynamics*, 14: 5–18.

Albrow, M. (1970) *Bureaucracy*. London: Macmillan.

Almond, B. (1990) 'Male or female ethics for corporations?', in G. Enderle, B. Almond and A. Argandoña (eds), *People in Corporations: Ethical Responsibilities and Corporate Effectiveness*. Dordrecht: Kluwer. pp. 155–9.

Alvesson, M. (1987) *Consensus, Control and Critique: Three Paradigms of Work Organization Research*. Aldershot: Gower.

Andrews, K.R. (1969) 'Towards professionalism in business management', *Harvard Business Review*, 47 (March–April): 49–59.

Anscombe, G.E.M. (1958) 'Modern moral philosophy', *Philosophy*, 33: 1–19.

Anthony, P.D. (1977) *The Ideology of Work*. London: Tavistock.

Anthony, P.D. (1986) *The Foundation of Management*. London: Tavistock.

Argyris, C. (1962) *Interpersonal Competence and Organizational Effectiveness*. Homewood, Ill.: The Dorsey Press.

Argyris, C. (1964) *Integrating the Individual and the Organization*. New York: John Wiley.

Armstrong, P. (1989) 'Limits and possibilities for HRM in an age of management accountancy', in J. Storey (ed.), *New Perspectives on Human Resource Management*. London: Routledge. pp. 154–66.

Baier, A. (1994) *Moral Prejudices*. Cambridge, Mass.: Harvard University Press.

Baier, K. (1993) 'Egoism', in P. Singer (ed.), *A Companion to Ethics*. Oxford: Blackwell. pp. 197–204.

Bain, W.A. (1994) 'Creating and using vignettes to teach business ethics', *Business Ethics: A European Review*, 3(3): 148–52.

Barclay, Sir Peter (1995) *Inquiry into Income and Wealth Chaired by Sir Peter Barclay* (2 volumes). York: Joseph Rowntree Foundation.

Baritz, L. (1960) *The Servants of Power: a History of the Use of Social Science in American Industry*. Middletown, Conn.: Wesleyan University Press.

Barnard, C. (1938) *The Functions of the Executive*. Cambridge, Mass.: Harvard University Press.

Barnett, T., Cochran, D.S. and Taylor, G.S. (1993) 'The internal disclosure policies of private-sector employers: an initial look at their relationship to employee whistleblowing', *Journal of Business Ethics*, 12(2): 127–36.

Bendix, R. (1956) *Work and Authority in Industry*. New York: John Wiley.

Bendix, R. (1960) *Max Weber: An Intellectual Portrait*. London: Heinemann.

Benn, S.I. and Peters, R.S. (1959) *Social Principles and the Democratic State*. London: Allen & Unwin.

Bennett, R. (1974) 'Orientation to work and some implications for management', *Journal of Management Studies*, 11(2): 149–62.

Bennis, W. and Nanus, B. (1985) *Leaders: The Strategies for Taking Charge*. New York: Harper & Row.

Benson, G.C.S. (1989) 'Codes of ethics', *Journal of Business Ethics*, 8(5): 305–19.

Berger, P. and Luckman, T. (1966) *The Social Construction of Reality*. New York: Doubleday.

Berle, A. and Means, G. (1932) *The Modern Corporation and Private Property*. New York: Macmillan.

Bernoux, P. (1994) 'Participation: a review of the literature', *European Participation Monitor*, 9: 6–11.

Binns, P. (1994) 'Ethical business: thinking thoughts and facilitating processes', *Business Ethics: A European Review*, 3(3): 174–9.

Bird, F. and Waters, J. (1989) 'The moral muteness of managers', *California Management Review*, 32(1): 73–88.

Bird, F., Westley, F. and Waters, J. (1989) 'The uses of moral talk: why do managers talk ethics?', *Journal of Business Ethics*, 8(1): 75–89.

Bishop, J.D. (1991) 'The moral responsibility of corporate executives for disasters', *Journal of Business Ethics*, 10(5): 377–83.

Blackhurst, C. (1995) 'Who lets pay run away?', *Management Today*, September: 36–40.

Blackler, F.H.M. and Brown, C.A. (1978) 'Organizational psychology: good intentions and false promises', *Human Relations*, 31(4): 333–51.

Blau, P.M. (1955) *The Dynamics of Bureaucracy*. Chicago: University of Chicago Press.

Blau, P.M. (1986) *Exchange and Power in Social Life*. New Brunswick, NJ: Transaction Publishers. (1st edn, 1964. John Wiley & Sons).

Blau, P.M. and Scott, W.R. (1963) *Formal Organizations: a Comparative Approach*. London: Routledge.

Blauner, R. (1964) *Alienation and Freedom: the Factory Worker and his Industry*. Chicago: University of Chicago Press.

Blum, L. (1980) *Friendship, Altruism and Morality*. London: Routledge & Kegan Paul.

Blum, L. (1982) 'Kant's and Hegel's moral rationalism: a feminist perspective', *Canadian Journal of Philosophy*, 12(2): 287–302.

Blumberg, P. (1968) *Industrial Democracy: The Sociology of Participation*. London: Constable.

Boatright, J.R. (1994) 'Fiduciary duties and the shareholder – management relation: or, what's so special about shareholders?', *Business Ethics Quarterly*, 4(4): 393–407.

Boden, M. (1994) *The Business of Talk*. Cambridge: Polity Press.

Boisjoly, R.P., Curtis, E.F. and Mellican, E. (1989) 'Roger Boisjoly and the Challenger disaster: the ethical dimension', *Journal of Business Ethics*, 8(4): 217–30.

Boyatzis, R. (1982) *The Competent Manager*. New York: John Wiley.

Boyd, C. (1990) 'The responsibility of individuals for a company disaster: the case of the Zeebrugge car ferry', in G. Enderle, B. Almond and A. Argandoña (eds), *People in Corporations: Ethical Responsibilities and Corporate Effectiveness*. Dordrecht: Kluwer. pp. 139–48.

Boyd, D.R. (1986) 'The oughts of is: Kohlberg at the interface between moral philosophy and developmental psychology', in S. Modgil and C. Modgil (eds), *Lawrence Kohlberg: Consensus and Controversy*. Lewes: The Falmer Press. pp. 43–63.

Braid, M. (1994) 'Overdrawn on goodwill', *The Independent* (Weekend Section), 13 August: 25.

Braverman, H. (1974) *Labor and Monopoly Capital: the Degradation of Work in the Twentieth Century*. New York: Monthly Review Press.

Bright, M. (1996) 'A change of tune from whistling in the dark', *The Guardian* (Part 2), 27 February: 13.

British Institute of Management (1991) *Code of Conduct and Guide to Professional Management Practice*. London: British Institute of Management.

Brooks, L.J. (1989) 'Corporate codes of ethics', *Journal of Business Ethics*, 8(2/3): 117–29.

Broughton, J. (1986) 'The genesis of moral domination', in S. Modgil and C. Modgil (eds), *Lawrence Kohlberg: Consensus and Controversy*. Lewes: The Falmer Press. pp. 363–85.

Brown, R.K. (1973) 'Sources of objectives in work and employment', in J. Child (ed.), *Man and Organization: The Search for Explanation and Social Relevance*. London: Allen & Unwin. pp. 17–38.

Brown, R.K. (1992) *Understanding Industrial Organisations: Theoretical Perspectives in Industrial Sociology*. London: Routledge.

Bryman, A. (1986) *Leadership and Organizations*. London: Routledge & Kegan Paul.

Buchholtz, R.A. (1983) 'The Protestant Ethic as an ideological justification of capitalism', *Journal of Business Ethics*, 2(1): 51–60.

Bullock, Lord (1977) *Report of the Committee of Inquiry on Industrial Democracy*. London: HMSO (Cmnd 6706).

Burgoyne, J. (1989) 'Creating the managerial portfolio: building on competency approaches to management', *Management Education and Development*, 20(1): 56–61.

Burns, J.M. (1978) *Leadership*. New York: Harper & Row.

Burns, T. (1961) 'Micropolitics: mechanisms of institutional change', *Administrative Science Quarterly*, 6: 257–81.

Burns, T. (1966) 'On the plurality of social systems', in J.R. Lawrence (ed.), *Operational Research and the Social Sciences*. London: Tavistock. pp. 165–77.

Burns, T. and Stalker, G.M. (1966) *The Management of Innovation*. 2nd edn. London: Tavistock. (1st edn, 1961).

Burrell, G. and Morgan, G. (1979) *Sociological Paradigms and Organisational Analysis*. London: Heinemann.

Cadbury, Sir Adrian (1992) *Report of the Committee on the Financial Aspects of Corporate Governance*. London: Gee and Co. Ltd.

Cannon, T. (1994) *Corporate Responsibility*. London: Pitman.

Carroll, A.B. (1989) *Business and Society: Ethics and Stakeholder Management*. Cincinnati, Ohio: South Western Publishing.

Carroll, L. (1947) *Alice's Adventures in Wonderland and Through the Looking Glass*. London: Pan Books. (1st edn of *Through the Looking Glass*, 1871. Macmillan).

Carter, P. and Jackson, N.V. (1993) 'Modernism, postmodernism and motivation, or why Expectancy Theory failed to come up to expectation', in J. Hassard and M. Parker (eds), *Postmodernism and Organizations*. London: Sage. pp. 83–100.

Caulkin, S. (1995) 'Private lessons for the public sector', *The Observer* (Business Section), 19 February: 10.

Caulkin, S. (1997) 'Amnesty and WWF take a crack at Shell', *The Observer* (Business Section), 11 May: 6.

Cederblom, J. and Dougherty, C.J. (1990) *Ethics at Work*. Belmont, Calif.: Wadsworth.

Center for Business Ethics (1986) 'Are corporations institutionalizing ethics?', *Journal of Business Ethics*, 5(2): 85–91.

Center for Business Ethics (1992) 'Instilling ethical values in large corporations', *Journal of Business Ethics*, 11(11): 863–7.

Child, J. (1972) 'Organizational structure, environment and performance: the role of strategic choice', *Sociology*, 6(1): 1–22.

Child, J. (1973) 'Organization: a choice for man', in J. Child (ed.), *Man and Organization: The Search for Explanation and Social Relevance*. London: Allen & Unwin. pp. 234–57.

Child, J., Fores, M., Glover, I. and Lawrence, P. (1983) 'A price to pay?: professionalism and work organization in Britain and West Germany', *Sociology*, 17(1): 63–78.

Chryssides, G.D. and Kaler, J.H. (1993) *An Introduction to Business Ethics*. London: Chapman & Hall.

Ciulla, J. (1995) 'Leadership ethics: mapping the territory', *Business Ethics Quarterly*, 5(1): 5–28.

Clegg, H.A. (1979) *The Changing System of Industrial Relations in Great Britain*. Oxford: Blackwell.

Clegg, S. (1990) *Modern Organizations: Organization Studies in the Postmodern World*. London: Sage.

Clutterbuck, D. (1992) 'Identifying and managing social responsibility', *Business Ethics: A European Review*, 1(1): 34–8.

Clutterbuck, D. (with Dearlove, D. and Snow, D.) (1992) *Actions Speak Louder: A Management Guide to Corporate Social Responsibility*. London: Kogan Page.

Coates, K. (ed.) (1978) *The Right to 'Useful' Work*. Nottingham: Institute for Workers' Control/Spokesman Books.

Coch, L. and French, J.R.P. (1948) 'Overcoming resistance to change', *Human Relations*, 1(4): 512–32.

Cohen, A.P. (1992) 'The personal right to identity: a polemic on the self in the enterprise culture', in P. Heelas and P. Morris (eds), *The Values of the Enterprise Culture: The Moral Debate*. London: Routledge. pp. 179–93.

Coles, R. (1987) 'Storytellers' ethics', *Harvard Business Review*, 65 (March–April): 8–14.

Collier, J. (1995) 'The virtuous organisation', *Business Ethics: A European Review*, 4(3): 143–9.

Collins, B.E and Hoyt, M.F. (1972) 'Personal responsibility for consequences: an integration and extension of the "forced compliance" literature', *Journal of Experimental Social Psychology*, 8: 558–93.

Cooke, R.A. and Ryan, L.V. (1988) 'The relevance of ethics to management education', *Journal of Management Development*, 7(2): 28–38.

Cooper, M. and Schlegelmilch, B. (1993) 'Key issues in ethical investment', *Business Ethics: A European Review*, 2(4): 213–27.

Cooper, N. (1970a) 'Morality and importance', in G. Wallace and A.D.M. Walker (eds), *The Definition of Morality*. London: Methuen. pp. 91–7.

Cooper, N. (1970b) 'Two concepts of morality', in G. Wallace and A.D.M. Walker (eds), *The Definition of Morality*. London: Methuen. pp. 72–90.

Coussey, M. and Jackson, H. (1991) *Making Equal Opportunities Work*. London: Pitman.

Cowton, C. and Dunfee, T.W. (1995) 'Internationalizing the business ethics curriculum: a survey', *Journal of Business Ethics*, 14 (5): 331–8.

Crozier, M. (1964) *The Bureaucratic Phenomenon*. Chicago: University of Chicago Press.

Culbert, S.A. and McDonough, J. (1980) *The Invisible War: Pursuing Self-Interest at Work*. New York. John Wiley.

Culbert, S.A. and McDonough, J. (1985) *Radical Management: Power, Politics and the Pursuit of Trust*. New York: The Free Press.

Cyert, R. and March. J. (1963) *A Behavioral Theory of the Firm*. New York: John Wiley.

Dachler, H.P. and Enderle, G. (1989) 'Epistemological and ethical considerations in conceptualizing and implementing human resource management', *Journal of Business Ethics*, 8(8): 597–606.

Dachler, H.P. and Wilpert, B. (1978) 'Conceptual dimensions and boundaries of participation in organizations: a critical evaluation', *Administrative Science Quarterly*, 23: 1–39.

Dahl, R.A. (1970) *Modern Political Analysis*. 2nd edn. Englewood Cliffs, NJ: Prentice-Hall. (1st edn, 1963).

Dahrendorf, R. (1959) *Class and Class Conflict in Industrial Society*. London: Routledge & Kegan Paul.

Dancy, J. (1993a) *Moral Reasons*. Oxford: Blackwell.

Dancy, J. (1993b) 'An ethic of prima facie duties', in P. Singer (ed.), *A Companion to Ethics*. Oxford: Blackwell. pp. 219–29.

Daniel, W.W. (1969) 'Industrial behaviour and orientation to work – a critique', *Journal of Management Studies*, 6(3): 366–75.

Daniel, W.W. (1973) 'Understanding employee behaviour in its context: illustrations from productivity bargaining', in J. Child (ed.), *Man and Organization: The Search for Explanation and Social Relevance*. London: Allen & Unwin. pp. 39–62.

Danley, J.R. (1990) 'Corporate moral agency: the case for anthropological bigotry', in W.M. Hoffman and J.M. Moore (eds), *Business Ethics: Readings and Cases in Corporate Morality*. 2nd edn. New York: McGraw-Hill. pp. 202–8. (Paper first published 1980, in *Action and Responsibility: Bowling Green Studies in Applied Philosophy*. Vol. II).

Davis, K. and Moore, W.E. (1945) 'Some principles of stratification', *American Sociological Review*, 10(2): 242–9.

Deal, T.E. and Kennedy, A.A. (1982) *Corporate Cultures: The Rites and Rituals of Corporate Life*. Reading, Mass.: Addison-Wesley.

Dehn, G. (1994) 'Who's who in business ethics: Public Concern at Work', *Business Ethics: A European Review*, 3(4): 233–6.

Demb, A. and Neubauer, F-F. (1992) *The Corporate Board: Confronting the Paradoxes*. Oxford: Oxford University Press.

Derry, R. and Green, R.M. (1989) 'Ethical theory in business ethics: a critical assessment', *Journal of Business Ethics*, 8(7): 521–33.

Deutch, M. (1962) 'Cooperation and trust: some theoretical notes', in M.R. Jones (ed.), *Nebraska Symposium on Motivation*. Lincoln: University of Nebraska Press. pp. 275–319.

Dewey, J. (1916) *Democracy and Education*. New York: Macmillan.

Dittmar, H. (1992) *The Social Psychology of Material Possessions: To Have is To Be*. Hemel Hempstead: Harvester/Wheatsheaf.

Donaldson, J. (1989) *Key Issues in Business Ethics*. London: Academic Press.

Donaldson, J. (1992) *Business Ethics: A European Casebook*. London: Academic Press.

Donaldson, T. (1982) *Corporations and Morality*. Englewood Cliffs, NJ: Prentice-Hall.

Dore, R. (1973) *British Factory – Japanese Factory*. London: Allen & Unwin.

Dowie, M. (1987) 'Pinto madness', in S.L. Hills (ed.), *Corporate Violence: Injury and Death for Profit*. Totowa, NJ: Rowman & Littlefield. pp. 13–29. (Article first published 1977, in *Mother Jones*, 2, September–October).

Downie, R.S. (1971) *Roles and Values: An Introduction to Social Ethics*. London: Methuen.

Doyle, W. (ed.) (1990) *Women in Management: Journal of Business Ethics*, 9(4–5)(Special Issue): 243–453.

Dunfee, T.W. (1990) 'To encourage or repress? Corporate policy and whistle-blowing', in G. Enderle, B. Almond and A. Argandoña (eds), *People in Corporations: Ethical Responsibilities and Corporate Effectiveness*. Dordrecht: Kluwer. pp. 129–38.

Dunfee, T.W. and Robertson, D.C. (1988) 'Integrating ethics into the business school curriculum', *Journal of Business Ethics*, 7(11): 847–59.

Durham, M. (1994) 'Short day, low pay, no prospects?', *The Observer*, 17 April: 20.

Durkheim, E. (1961) *Moral Education*. Tr. E.K. Wilson and H. Schurer. New York: Free Press. (1st edn, 1925. Felix Alcan).

Duska, R. (1988) 'Whistleblowing and employee loyalty', in T.L. Beauchamp and N.E. Bowie (eds), *Ethical Theory and Business*. 3rd edn. Englewood Cliffs, NJ: Prentice-Hall. pp. 299–303.

Duska, R. (1993) 'Aristotle: a pre-modern post-modern? Implications for business ethics', *Business Ethics Quarterly*, 3(3): 227–49.

Dyer, C. (1994) 'Long hair "no job bar for men"', *The Guardian*, 13 December: 2.

Eldridge, J.E.T. and Crombie, A.D. (1974) *A Sociology of Organisations*. London: Allen & Unwin.

Elliot, D. (1977) *The Lucas Aerospace Workers' Campaign* (Young Fabian Pamphlet 46). London: Fabian Society.

Elliston, F.A. (1982) 'Anonymity and whistleblowing', *Journal of Business Ethics*, 1(3): 167–77.

Emery, F.E. and Trist, E.L. (1965) 'The causal texture of organizational environments', *Human Relations*, 18(1): 21–32.

England, G.W. (1967) 'Personal value systems of American managers', *Academy of Management Journal*, 10(1): 53–68.

England, G.W. (1975) *The Manager and his Values: an International Perspective from the United States, Japan, Korea, India and Australia*. Cambridge, Mass.: Ballinger.

Erikson, E. (1964) *Insight and Responsibility*. New York: Norton.

Etzioni, A. (1961) *A Comparative Analysis of Complex Organizations*. New York: The Free Press.

Etzioni, A. (1964) *Modern Organizations*. Englewood Cliffs, NJ: Prentice-Hall.

Etzioni, A. (1988) *The Moral Dimension: Toward a New Economics*. New York: The Free Press.

Ewin, R.E. (1991) 'The moral status of the corporation', *Journal of Business Ethics*, 10(10): 749–56.

Ewin, R.E. (1993) 'Corporate loyalty: its objects and its grounds', *Journal of Business Ethics*, 12(5): 387–96.

Falkenberg, L. and Herremans, I. (1995) 'Ethical behaviors in organizations: directed by the formal or informal systems?', *Journal of Business Ethics*, 14(2): 133–43.

Farrell, D. (1983) 'Exit, voice, loyalty, and neglect as responses to job dissatisfaction: a multidimensional scaling study', *Academy of Management Journal*, 26: 596–606.

Fayol, H. (1949) *General and Industrial Management*. Tr. C. Storrs. London: Pitman. (First published 1916, in *Bulletin de la Société de l'Industrie Minérale*).

Festinger, L. (1957) *A Theory of Cognitive Dissonance*. Evanston, Ill.: Row, Peterson.

Filley, A.C. (1975) *Interpersonal Conflict Resolution*. Glenview, Ill.: Scott, Foresman.

Fineman, S. (1993), 'Organizations as emotional arenas', in S. Fineman (ed.), *Emotion in Organizations*. London: Sage. pp. 9–35.

Fineman, S. (ed.) (1993) *Emotion in Organizations*. London: Sage.

Flanders, A. (1964) *The Fawley Productivity Agreements*. London: Faber & Faber.

Fletcher, G.P. (1993) *Loyalty: An Essay on the Morality of Relationships*. New York: Oxford University Press.

Flood, R.L. and Jackson, M.C. (1991) *Creative Problem Solving: Total Systems Intervention*. Chichester: John Wiley.

Flores, A. and Johnson, D.G. (1983) 'Collective responsibility and professional roles', *Ethics*, 93(3): 537–45.

Follett, M.P. (1973) 'How must business management develop in order to possess the essentials of a profession?', in E.M. Fox and L. Urwick (eds), *Dynamic Administration: The Collected Papers of Mary Parker Follett*. 2nd edn. London: Pitman. pp. 103–116. (1st edn, 1941. H. Metcalf and L. Urwick, eds. Paper originally presented in 1925).

Fox, A. (1971) *A Sociology of Work in Industry*. London: Collier-Macmillan.

Fox, A. (1974a) *Man Mismanagement*. London: Hutchinson.

Fox, A. (1974b) *Beyond Contract: Work, Power and Trust Relations*. London: Faber & Faber.

Freeman, R.E. (1984) *Strategic Management: A Stakeholder Approach*. Marshfield, Mass.: Pitman.

Freeman, R.E. (1994) 'The politics of stakeholder theory: some future directions', *Business Ethics Quarterly*, 4(4): 409–21.

French, P.A. (1979) 'The corporation as a moral person', *American Philosophical Quarterly*, 3: 207–15.

French, P.A. (1984) *Collective and Corporate Responsibility*. New York: Columbia University Press.

French, P.A. (1992) *Responsibility Matters*. Lawrence, Kan.: University Press of Kansas.

French, R. and Grey, C. (eds) (1996) *Rethinking Management Education*. London: Sage.

French, W., Bell, C.H. and Zawacki, R. (1983) 'Power, politics and organization development', in W. French, C.H. Bell and R. Zawacki (eds), *Organization Development: Theory, Practice and Research*. 2nd edn. Plano, Texas: Business Publications. pp. 371–8.

Friedman, M. (1990) 'The social responsibility of business is to increase its profits', in W.M. Hoffman and J.M. Moore (eds), *Business Ethics: Readings and Cases in Corporate Morality*. 2nd edn. New York: McGraw-Hill. pp. 153–7. (Article first published 1970, in *The New York Times Magazine*, 13 September.).

Fromm, E. (1979) *To Have, or To Be?* Abacus edn. London: Sphere Books. (1st edn, 1976. Harper & Row).

Frost, F.A. (1995) 'The use of stakeholder analysis to understand ethical and moral issues in the primary resource sector', *Journal of Business Ethics*, 14(8): 653–61.

Fukuyama, F. (1995) *Trust: The Social Virtues and the Creation of Prosperity*. London: Hamish Hamilton.

Furnham, A. (1990) *The Protestant Work Ethic: The Psychology of Work-Related Beliefs and Behaviours*. London: Routledge.

Galston, W.A. (1993) 'Cosmopolitan altruism', in E.F. Paul, F.D. Miller and J. Paul (eds), *Altruism*. Cambridge: Cambridge University Press. pp. 118–34.

Gambetta, D. (1988) 'Can we trust trust?', in D. Gambetta (ed.), *Trust: Making and Breaking Cooperative Relations*. Oxford: Blackwell. pp. 213–37.

Gambetta, D. (ed.) (1988) *Trust: Making and Breaking Cooperative Relations*. Oxford: Blackwell.

Gandz, J. and Bird, F. (1996) 'The ethics of empowerment', *Journal of Business Ethics*, 15(4): 383–92.

Garrett, J.E. (1989) 'Unredistributable corporate moral responsibility', *Journal of Business Ethics*, 8(7): 535–45.

Gergen, K. (1992) 'Organization theory in the postmodern era', in M. Reed and M. Hughes (eds), *Rethinking Organization: New Directions in Organization Theory and Analysis*. London: Sage. pp. 207–26.

Gerth, H.H. and Mills, C.W. (eds) (1946) *From Max Weber: Essays in Sociology*. New York: Oxford.

Ghazi, P. (1996) 'The age of the downwardly mobile', *The Observer*, 4 February: 11.

Gilligan, C. (1982) *In a Different Voice: Psychological Theory and Women's Development*. Cambridge, Mass.: Harvard University Press.

Gini, A.R. and Sullivan, T. (1987) 'Work: the process and the person', *Journal of Business Ethics*, 6(8): 649–55.

Gioia, D.A. (1986) 'Symbols, scripts and sensemaking: creating meaning in the organizational experience', in H.P. Sims and D.A. Gioia (eds), *The Thinking Organization: Dynamics of Organizational Social Cognition*. San Francisco: Jossey-Bass. pp. 49–74.

Gioia, D.A. (1992) 'Pinto fires and personal ethics: a script analysis of missed opportunities', *Journal of Business Ethics*, 11(5/6): 379–89.

Glaser, B.G. and Strauss, A.L. (1967) *The Discovery of Grounded Theory: Strategies for Qualitative Research*. New York: Aldine.

Goffman, E. (1959) *The Presentation of Self in Everyday Life*. New York: Doubleday.

Goldsmith, E., Allen, R., Allaby, M., Davoll, J. and Lawrence, S. (1972) *A Blueprint for Survival*. Harmondsworth: Penguin Books. (First published 1972 as Vol. 2[1] *The Ecologist*).

Goldstein, K. (1939) *The Organism*. New York: American Book Company.

Goldthorpe, J., Lockwood, D., Bechhofer, F. and Platt, J. (1968) *The Affluent Worker: Industrial Attitudes and Behaviour*. London: Cambridge University Press.

Goodpaster, K.E. (1991) 'Business ethics and stakeholder analysis', *Business Ethics Quarterly*, 1(1): 53–73.

Goodpaster, K.E. and Matthews, J.B. (1982) 'Can a corporation have a conscience?', *Harvard Business Review*, 60 (January–February): 132–41.

Goodwin, S. (1995) 'Firm comes under fire for paying smokers less', *The Independent*, 8 September: 5.

Gorden, W. (1988) 'Range of employee voice', *Employee Responsibilities and Rights Journal*, 1(4): 283–99.

Gouldner, A.W. (1954a) *Patterns of Industrial Bureaucracy*. New York: The Free Press.

Gouldner, A.W. (1954b) *Wildcat Strike*. Yellow Springs, Ohio: Antioch Press.

Gouldner, A.W. (1955) 'Metaphysical pathos and the theory of bureaucracy', *American Political Science Review*, 49(2): 496–507.

Gouldner, A.W. (1957–8) 'Cosmopolitans and locals: toward an analysis of latent social roles', *Administrative Science Quarterly*, 2: 281–306 and 444–80.

Gouldner, A.W. (1959) 'Reciprocity and autonomy in functional theory', in L. Gross (ed.), *Symposium on Sociological Theory*. New York: Harper & Row. pp. 241–70.

Gouldner, A.W. (1960) 'The norm of reciprocity', *American Sociological Review*, 25(2): 161–78.

Gouldner, A.W. (1975a) 'The importance of something for nothing', in A.W. Gouldner, *For Sociology: Renewal and Critique in Sociology Today*. Pelican edn. Harmondsworth: Penguin Books. pp. 260–99. (1st edn, 1973. Allen Lane).

Gouldner, A.W. (1975b) 'The two Marxisms', in A.W. Gouldner, *For Sociology: Renewal and Critique in Sociology Today*. Pelican edn. Harmondsworth: Penguin Books. pp. 425–62. (1st edn, 1973. Allen Lane).

Green, M.K. (1986) 'A Kantian evaluation of Taylorism in the workplace', *Journal of Business Ethics*, 5(2): 165–9.

Green, R.M. (1994) *The Ethical Manager*. New York: Macmillan.

Greenbury, Sir Richard (1995) *Directors' Remuneration: Report of a Study Group Chaired by Sir Richard Greenbury*. London: Gee Publishing Ltd.

Greenleaf, R.K. (1977) *Servant Leadership*. New York: Paulist Press.

Grzeda, J. (1994) 'Disability and discrimination – a UK perspective', *Business Ethics: A European Review*, 3(3): 145–52.

Guest, R.H. (1962) *Organizational Change: The Effect of Successful Leadership*. London: Tavistock.

Gulick, L. (1937) 'Notes on the theory of organization', in L. Gulick and L. Urwick (eds), *Papers on the Science of Administration*. New York: Institute of Public Administration. pp. 1–45.

Hackman, J.R. and Oldham, G.R. (1980) *Work Redesign*. Reading, Mass.: Addison-Wesley.

Haddon, R. (1973) 'Foreword', in C. Kerr, J.T. Dunlop, F. Harbison and C. Myers, *Industrialism and Industrial Man*. Harmondsworth: Penguin Books. pp. 1–27.

Haire, M., Ghiselli, E.E. and Porter, L.W. (1966) *Managerial Thinking: an International Study*. New York: John Wiley.

Hales, C. (1993) *Managing through Organisation*. London: Routledge.

Hall, R.H. (1968) 'Professionalization and bureaucratization', *American Sociological Review*, 33(1): 92–104.

Halmos, P. (1970) *The Personal Service Society*. London: Constable.

Harrison, D. (1993) 'Banks foreclose on traditional manager', *The Observer*, 5 December: 10.

Harrison, E.F. (1975) *The Managerial Decision-Making Process*. Boston, Mass.: Houghton Mifflin.

Harrison, Roger (1970) 'Choosing the depth of organizational intervention', *Journal of Applied Behavioral Science*, 6(2): 182–202.

Harrison, Ronald G. and Pitt, D.C. (1984) 'Organizational development: a missing political dimension?', in A. Kakabadse and C. Parker (eds), *Power, Politics and Organizations: A Behavioural Science View*. Chichester: John Wiley. pp. 65–85.

Hart, D.K. (1988) 'Management and benevolence: the fatal flaw in Theory Y', in K. Kolenda (ed.), *Organizations and Ethical Individualism*. New York: Praeger. pp. 73–105.

Harvey, B., van Luijk, H. and Steinmann, H. (eds) (1994) *European Casebook on Business Ethics*. Hemel Hempstead: Prentice-Hall.

Hassard, J. (1994) 'Postmodern organizational analysis: toward a conceptual framework', *Journal of Management Studies*, 31(3): 303–24.

Haworth, L. (1959) 'Do organizations act?', *Ethics*, 70(1): 59–63.

Hay, R.D., Gray, E.R. and Gates, J.E. (eds) (1976) *Business and Society: Cases and Text*. Cincinnati, Ohio: South-Western Publishing.

Heath, D.H. (1977) *Maturity and Competence*. New York: Norton.

Heilbroner, R.L. (1974) *An Inquiry into The Human Prospect*. New York: Norton.

Herriot, P., Gibbons, P., Pemberton, C. and Jackson, P.R. (1994) 'An empirical model of managerial careers in organizations', *British Journal of Management*, 5(2): 113–21.

Herzberg, F. (1966) *Work and the Nature of Man*. Cleveland, Ohio: World Publishing.

Hill, T.E. (1993) 'Beneficence and self-love: a Kantian perspective', in E.F. Paul, F.D. Miller and J. Paul (eds), *Altruism*. Cambridge: Cambridge University Press. pp. 1–23.

Hirschman, A.E. (1970) *Exit, Voice and Loyalty: Responses to Decline in Firms, Organizations and States*. Cambridge, Mass.: Harvard University Press.

Hofstede, G. (1980) *Culture's Consequences: International Differences in Work-Related Values*. Beverly Hills, Calif.: Sage.

Hofstede, G. (1990) 'The cultural relativity of organizational practices and theories', in D.C. Wilson and R.H. Rosenfeld, *Managing Organizations: Text, Readings and Cases*. London: McGraw-Hill. pp. 392–405.

Hollis, M. (1994) *The Philosophy of Social Science: an Introduction*. Cambridge: Cambridge University Press.

Horsburgh, H. (1960) 'The ethics of trust', *Philosophical Quarterly*, 10: 343–54.

Hosmer, L.T. (1987) 'The institutionalization of unethical behavior', *Journal of Business Ethics*, 6(6): 439–47.

Huczynski, A.A. (1983) *Encyclopedia of Management Development Methods*. Aldershot: Gower.

Hugill, B. (1994a) 'A civil service on its last legs', *The Observer*, 29 May: 22.

Hugill, B. (1994b) 'Capitalism that gives power to the people', *The Observer*, 4 December: 12.

Husted, B.W. (1993) 'Reliability and the design of ethical organizations: a rational systems approach', *Journal of Business Ethics*, 12(10): 761–9.

Hyman, M.R., Skipper, R. and Tansey, R. (1990) 'Ethical codes are not enough', *Business Horizons*, March–April: 15–22.

Isenberg, D.J. (1984) 'How senior managers think', *Harvard Business Review*, 62 (November–December): 81–90.

Jackall, R. (1988) *Moral Mazes: the World of Corporate Managers*. New York: Oxford.

Jackson, J. (1996) *An Introduction to Business Ethics*. Oxford: Blackwell.

Jackson, N.V. and Carter, P. (1995) 'Organizational chiaroscuro: throwing light on the concept of corporate governance', *Human Relations*, 48(8): 875–89.

Jamieson, D. (1993) 'Method and moral theory', in P. Singer (ed.), *A Companion to Ethics*. Oxford: Blackwell. pp. 476–87.

Janis, I. (1972) *Victims of Groupthink*. Boston, Mass.: Houghton Mifflin.

Jebb, F. (1996) 'New bones for top dogs', *Management Today*, August: 56–7.

Jenkins, A. and Gibbs, G. (1995) 'Groves of academe', *The Guardian* (Part 2), 15 August: 15.

Johnson, T.J. (1972) *Professions and Power*. London: Macmillan.

Jones, M. (1988) 'Managerial thinking: an African perspective', *Journal of Management Studies*, 25(5): 481–505.

Jones, T.M. (1980) 'Corporate social responsibility revisited, redefined', *California Management Review*, 22(2): 59–67.

Jos, P.H., Tompkins, M.E. and Hays, S.W. (1989) 'In praise of difficult people: a portrait of the committed whistleblower', *Public Administration Review*, November–December: 552–61.

Katz, D. (1964) 'The motivational basis of organizational behavior', *Behavioral Science*, 9: 131–46.

Kaye, B.N. (1992) 'Codes of ethics in Australian business corporations', *Journal of Business Ethics*, 11(11): 857–62.

Keeley, M. (1978) 'A social-justice approach to organizational evaluation', *Administrative Science Quarterly*, 23: 272–92.

Keeley, M. (1980) 'Organizational analogy: a comparison of organismic and social contract models', *Administrative Science Quarterly*, 25: 337–62.

Keeley, M. and Graham, J.W. (1991) 'Exit, voice and ethics', *Journal of Business Ethics*, 10(5): 349–55.

Kelman, H.C. (1961) 'Processes of opinion change', *Public Opinion Quarterly*, 25: 57–78.

Kelman, H.C. (1965) 'Manipulation of human behavior: an ethical dilemma for the social scientist', *Journal of Social Issues*, 21(2): 31–46.

Kerr, C., Dunlop, J.T., Harbison, F. and Myers, C. (1973), *Industrialism and Industrial Man*. Pelican edn. Harmondsworth: Penguin Books. (1st edn, 1960. Harvard University Press).

Klein, J. (1988) 'The myth of the corporate political jungle: politicization as a political strategy', *Journal of Management Studies*, 25(1): 1–12.

Klein, L. (1963) *The Meaning of Work* (Fabian Tract 349). London: Fabian International Bureau.

Klein, S. (1988) 'Is a moral organization possible?', *Business and Professional Ethics Journal*, 7(1): 51–73.

Klein, S. (1989) 'Platonic virtue theory and business ethics', *Business and Professional Ethics Journal*, 8(4): 59–82.

Kluckhohn, C. (1951) 'Values and value-orientations in the theory of action: an exploration in definition and classification', in T. Parsons and E.A. Shils (eds), *Toward a General Theory of Action*. Cambridge, Mass.: Harvard University Press. pp. 388–433.

Knudsen, H. (1995) *Employee Participation in Europe*. London: Sage.

Kohlberg, L. (1969) 'Stage and sequence: the cognitive-developmental approach to socialization', in D.A. Goslin (ed.), *Handbook of Socialization Theory and Research*. Chicago: Rand McNally. pp. 347–480.

Kohlberg, L. (1973) 'Continuities in childhood and adult moral development revisited', in P.B. Baltes and K.W. Schaie (eds), *Life-Span Developmental Psychology: Personality and Socialization*. New York: Academic Press. pp. 179–431.

Kohlberg, L. (1981) *Essays on Moral Development: Vol. 1. The Philosophy of Moral Development*. San Francisco: Harper & Row.

Kohlberg, L. (1986) 'A current statement on some theoretical issues', in S. Modgil and C. Modgil (eds), *Lawrence Kohlberg: Consensus and Controversy*. Lewes: The Falmer Press. pp. 485–546.

Kohls, J., Chapman, C. and Mathieu, C. (1989) 'Ethics training programs in the Fortune 500', *Business and Professional Ethics Journal*, 8(2): 55–72.

Kohn, A. (1993) 'Why incentive plans cannot work', *Harvard Business Review*, 71 (September–October): 54–63.

Kohn, M.L. and Schooler, C. (1978) 'The reciprocal effects of the substantive complexity of work and intellectual flexibility: a longitudinal study', *American Journal of Sociology*, 84(1): 24–52.

Kornhauser, A. (1965) *Mental Health of the Industrial Worker*. New York: John Wiley.

Kramer, R.M. and Tyler, T.R. (eds) (1996) *Trust in Organizations: Frontiers of Theory and Research*. Thousand Oaks, Calif.: Sage.

Kraut, R.E. and Lewis, S.H. (1975) 'Alternate models of family influence on student political ideology', *Journal of Personality and Social Psychology*, 31(5): 791–800.

Ladd, J. (1970) 'Morality and the ideal of rationality in formal organizations', *Monist*, 54: 488–516.

Landau, M. (1961) 'On the use of metaphor in political analysis', *Social Research*, 28(3): 331–53.

Langlois, C.C. and Schlegelmilch, B. (1990) 'Do corporate codes of ethics reflect national character? Evidence from Europe and the United States', *Journal of International Business Studies*, 22: 519–39.

Lansley, S. (1994) *After the Gold Rush – The Trouble with Affluence: Consumer Capitalism and the Way Forward*. London: Henley Centre for Forecasting/Century Books.

Larmer, R.A. (1992) 'Whistleblowing and employee loyalty', *Journal of Business Ethics*, 11(2): 125–8.

Larmore, C.E. (1987) *Patterns of Moral Complexity*. Cambridge: Cambridge University Press.

Lavoie, D. and Culbert, S.A. (1978) 'Stages of organization and development', *Human Relations*, 31(5): 417–38.

Law Commission (1996) *Legislating the Criminal Code: Involuntary Manslaughter* (Law Commission Report 237). London. HMSO. HC 171 1995–6.

Lawler, E.E. (1973) *Motivation in Work Organizations*. Monterey, Calif.: Brooks/Cole.

Lawrence, P.R. and Lorsch, J.W. (1967) *Organization and Environment: Managing Differentiation and Integration*. Boston, Mass.: Harvard Graduate School of Business Administration.

Lawrence, P.R. and Lorsch, J.W. (1969) *Developing Organizations: Diagnosis and Action*. Reading, Mass.: Addison-Wesley.

Leary, J. and Leary, M. (1988) 'Transforming your career', in M. Pedler, J. Burgoyne and T. Boydell (eds), *Applying Self-Development in Organizations*. Hemel Hempstead: Prentice-Hall. pp. 149–66.

L'Etang, J. (1992) 'A Kantian approach to codes of ethics', *Journal of Business Ethics*, 11(10): 737–44.

L'Etang, J. (1995) 'Ethical corporate social responsibility: a framework for managers', *Journal of Business Ethics*, 14(2): 125–32.

Lewin, K. (1951) *Field Theory in Social Science*. New York: Harper & Row.

Likert, R. (1961) *New Patterns of Management*. New York: McGraw-Hill.

Likert, R. (1967) *The Human Organization*. New York: McGraw-Hill.

Luhmann, N. (1988) 'Familiarity, confidence, trust: problems and alternatives', in D. Gambetta (ed.), *Trust: Making and Breaking Cooperative Relations*. Oxford: Blackwell. pp. 94–107.

Luijk, H. van (1994) 'Analyzing moral cases in European business', in B. Harvey, H. van Luijk and H. Steinmann (eds), *European Casebook on Business Ethics*. Hemel Hempstead: Prentice-Hall. pp. 3–12.

McCrystal, C. (1996) 'It's time to go home, Britain', *The Observer*, 23 June: 15.

McDonald, G.M. and Donleavy, G.D. (1995) 'Objections to the teaching of business ethics', *Journal of Business Ethics*, 14(10): 839–53.

McGregor, D. (1987) *The Human Side of Enterprise*. Harmondsworth: Penguin Books. (1st edn, 1960. McGraw-Hill).

MacIntyre, A. (1985) *After Virtue: A Study in Moral Theory*. 2nd edn. London: Duckworth. (1st edn, 1981).

Mackie, J. (1977) *Ethics: Inventing Right and Wrong*. Harmondsworth: Penguin Books.

MacKinney, A.C., Wernimont, P.F. and Galitz, W.O. (1962) 'Has specialization reduced job satisfaction?', *Personnel*, 39(1): 8–17.

Maclagan, P.W. (1979) 'Values and orientations to work: a study of police recruits', MSc dissertation, University of Strathclyde.

Maclagan, P.W. (1983) 'The concept of responsibility: some implications for organizational behaviour and development', *Journal of Management Studies*, 20(4): 411–23.

Maclagan, P.W. (1990a) 'Moral behaviour in organizations: the contribution of management education and development', *British Journal of Management*, 1(1): 17–26.

Maclagan, P.W. (1990b) 'Ethics and interpersonal trust in corporate management', in G. Enderle, B. Almond and A. Argandoña (eds), *People in Corporations: Ethical Responsibilities and Corporate Effectiveness*. Dordrecht: Kluwer. pp. 63–8.

Maclagan, P.W. (1991a) 'From moral ideals to moral action: lessons for management development', *Management Education and Development*, 22(1): 3–14.

Maclagan, P.W. (1991b) 'Having and being in organisations', *Management Education and Development*, 22(3): 234–41.

Maclagan, P.W. (1996) 'The organizational context for moral development: questions of power and access', *Journal of Business Ethics*, 15(6): 645–54.

Maclagan, P.W. and Evans-de Souza, C. (1995) 'Nepotism, politics and ethics in the purchase of organizational consultancy services – two European cases', in H. von Weltzien Høivik and A. Føllesdal (eds), *Ethics and Consultancy: European Perspectives*. Dordrecht: Kluwer. pp. 83–92.

Maclagan, P.W. and Snell, R.S. (1992) 'Some implications for management development of research into managers' moral dilemmas', *British Journal of Management*, 3(3): 157–68.

McMahon, C. (1995) 'The ontological and moral status of organizations', *Business Ethics Quarterly*, 5(3): 541–54.

Mahoney, J. (1990) *Teaching Business Ethics in the UK, Europe and the USA*. London: Athlone Press.

Mahoney, J. (1993) 'Women in business – a select bibliography', *Business Ethics: A European Review*, 2(1): 30–6.

Mahoney, J. (1994) 'Stakeholder responsibilities: turning the ethical tables', *Business Ethics: A European Review*, 3(4): 212–18.

Maier, N.R.F. (1967) 'Assets and liabilities in group problem solving', *Psychological Review*, 74: 239–49.

Mangham, I. (1986) *Power and Performance in Organizations*. Oxford: Blackwell.

Manley, W.W. (1992) *Handbook of Good Business Practice*. London: Routledge.

March, J. and Olsen, J.P. (1976) *Ambiguity and Choice in Organizations*. Bergen: Universitetsforlaget.

March, J. and Simon, H.A. (1958) *Organizations*. New York: Wiley.

Marshall, J. (1995) 'Gender and management: a critical review of research', *British Journal of Management*, 6 (Special Issue): S53–S62.

Maslow, A. (1943) 'A theory of human motivation', *Psychological Review*, 50: 370–96.

Melé, D. (1990) 'Human development and the images of the organisation', in G. Enderle, B. Almond and A. Argandoña (eds), *People in Corporations: Ethical Responsibilities and Corporate Effectiveness*. Dordrecht: Kluwer. pp. 93–104.

Merton, R.K. (1952) 'Bureaucratic structure and personality', in R.K. Merton, A.P. Gray, B. Hockey and H.C. Selvin (eds), *Reader in Bureaucracy*. New York: The Free Press. pp. 361–71.

Meyers, D.T. (1987) 'The socialized individual and individual autonomy: an intersection between philosophy and psychology', in E.F. Kittay and D.T. Meyers (eds), *Women and Moral Theory*. Totowa, NJ: Rowman & Littlefield. pp. 139–53.

Meyerson, D. and Martin, J. (1987) 'Cultural change: an integration of three different views', *Journal of Management Studies*, 24(6): 623–47.

Michalos, A. (1990) 'The impact of trust on business, international security, and the quality of life', *Journal of Business Ethics*, 9(8): 619–38.

Midgley, M. (1972) 'Is "moral" a dirty word?', *Philosophy*, 47: 206–28.

Milgram, S. (1974) *Obedience to Authority*. London: Tavistock.

Mills, A.J. and Murgatroyd, S.J. (1991) *Organizational Rules: A Framework for Understanding Organizational Action*. Milton Keynes: Open University Press.

Mills, C.W. (1959) *The Sociological Imagination*. New York: Oxford University Press.

Mintzberg, H. (1973) *The Nature of Managerial Work*. New York: Harper & Row.

Mintzberg, H. (1976) 'Planning on the left side and managing on the right', *Harvard Business Review*, 54 (July–August): 49–58.

Mintzberg, H. (1985) 'The organization as political arena', *Journal of Management Studies*, 22(2): 133–54.

Modgil, S. and Modgil, C. (eds) (1986) *Lawrence Kohlberg: Consensus and Controversy*. Lewes: The Falmer Press.

Mohr, L. (1973) 'The concept of organizational goal', *American Political Science Review*, 67(2): 470–81.

Monks, R.A.G. and Minow, N. (1995) *Corporate Governance*. Cambridge, Mass.: Blackwell.

Moore, G. (1995) 'Corporate community involvement in the UK – investment or atonement?', *Business Ethics: A European Review*, 4(3): 171–8.

Moore, J.M. (1993) 'International reflections on individual autonomy and corporate effectiveness', *Business Ethics Quarterly*, 3(2): 197–203.

Morgan, G. (1986) *Images of Organization*. Beverly Hills, Calif.: Sage.

Morse, N.C. and Weiss, R.S. (1955) 'The function and meaning of work and the job', *American Sociological Review*, 20(2): 191–8.

Moscovici, S. and Doise, W. (1994) *Conflict and Consensus: A General Theory of Collective Decisions*. Tr. W.D. Halls. London: Sage.

Mulgan, G. (1995) 'Trust me, they owe it to us', *The Times Higher Education Supplement*, 17 November: 14.

Munro, I.M.F. (1996) 'Moral regulation in business: an investigation into corporate codes of ethics', PhD thesis, University of Hull.

Murphy, P.E. (1988) 'Implementing business ethics', *Journal of Business Ethics*, 7(12): 907–15.

Murphy, P.E. (1995) 'Corporate ethics statements: current status and future prospects', *Journal of Business Ethics*, 14(9): 727–40.

Nadler, D.A. (1977) *Feedback and Organization Development: Using Data-Based Methods*. Reading, Mass.: Addison-Wesley.

Nagel, E. (1961) *The Structure of Science: Problems in the Logic of Scientific Explanation*. London: Routledge & Kegan Paul.

Nagel, T. (1970) *The Possibility of Altruism*. Princeton, NJ: Princeton University Press.

Nash, L. (1990) *Good Intentions Aside: A Manager's Guide to Resolving Ethical Problems*. Boston, Mass.: Harvard Business School Press.

Near, J.P. and Miceli, M.P. (1985) 'Organizational dissidence: the case of whistle-blowing', *Journal of Business Ethics*, 4(1): 1–16.

Newell, S. (1995) *The Healthy Organization*. London: Routledge.

Nichols, T. and Beynon, H. (1977) *Living with Capitalism*. London: Routledge & Kegan Paul.

Nicholson-Lord, D. (1995) 'The end of consumerism', *Earth Matters* (London: Friends of the Earth), 28: 8–11.

Niebuhr, R. (1932) *Moral Man and Immoral Society*. New York: Charles Scribner's Sons.

Nielsen, R.P. (1987) 'What can managers do about unethical management?', *Journal of Business Ethics*, 6(4): 309–20.

Nielsen, R.P. (1990) 'Dialogic leadership as ethics action (praxis) method', *Journal of Business Ethics*, 9(10): 765–83.

Nielsen, R.P. (1991) '"I am We" consciousness and dialog as organizational ethics method', *Journal of Business Ethics*, 10(9): 649–63.

Nielsen, R.P. (1993) 'Varieties of postmodernism as moments in ethics action-learning', *Business Ethics Quarterly*, 3(3): 251–69.

Nolan, Lord (1995) *1st Report of the Committee on Standards in Public Life* (2 volumes). London: HMSO (Cmnd 2850).

Nord, W.R., Brief, A.P., Atieh, J.M. and Doherty, E.M. (1990) 'Work values and the conduct of organizational behavior', in B.M. Staw and L.L. Cummings (eds), *Work in Organizations*. Greenwich, Conn.: JAI Press. pp. 255–96.

Oakley, J. (1992) *Morality and the Emotions*. London: Routledge.

Ostapski, S.A. and Isaacs, C.N. (1992) 'Corporate moral responsibility and the moral audit: challenges for Refuse Relief Inc.', *Journal of Business Ethics*, 11(3): 231–9.

Ostapski, S.A. and Pressley, D.G. (1992) 'Moral audit for Diabco Corporation', *Journal of Business Ethics*, 11(1): 71–80.

O'Sullivan, J. (1995) 'Ethics man takes on the fat cats', *The Independent*, 27 May: 15.

O'Sullivan, J. (1996a) 'Keep young and employable', *The Independent*, 9 February: 15.

O'Sullivan, J. (1996b) 'Who loves the firm today?', *The Independent* (Section Two), 8 August: 2–3.

Pamental, G.L. (1989) 'The course in business ethics: can it work?', *Journal of Business Ethics*, 8(7): 547–51.

Parkin, F. (1972) *Class Inequality and Political Order*. Paladin edn. St Albans: Granada Publishing. (1st edn, 1971. MacGibbon & Kee).

Parsons, T. (1951) *The Social System*. New York: The Free Press.

Passmore, J. (1974) *Man's Responsibility for Nature*. London: Duckworth.

Pastin, M. (1986) *The Hard Problems of Management: Gaining the Ethics Edge*. San Francisco: Jossey-Bass.

Pateman, C. (1970) *Participation and Democratic Theory*. Cambridge: Cambridge University Press.

Pearson, G. (1995) *Integrity in Organizations: An Alternative Business Ethic*. London: McGraw-Hill.

Peck, E. (1995) 'The performance of an NHS Trust Board: actors' accounts, minutes and observation', *British Journal of Management*, 6(2): 135–56.

Pedler, M. (1978) 'Negotiating skills training, part 4: learning to negotiate', *Journal of European Industrial Training*, 2: 20–5.

Pelz, D. (1978) 'Some expanded perspectives on the use of social science in public policy', in M. Yinger and S. Cutler (eds), *Major Social Issues: A Multidisciplinary View*. New York: The Free Press. pp. 346–57.

Pemberton, C. (1995) 'Organizational culture and equalities work', in J. Shaw and D. Perrons (eds), *Making Gender Work: Managing Equal Opportunities*. Buckingham: Open University Press. pp. 108–23.

Perrow, C. (1970) *Organizational Analysis: A Sociological View*. London: Tavistock.

Perrow, C. (1979) *Complex Organizations: A Critical Essay*. 2nd edn. Glenview, Ill.: Scott, Foresman. (1st edn, 1972).

Peters, R.S. (1960) *The Concept of Motivation*. 2nd edn. London: Routledge & Kegan Paul. (1st edn, 1958).

Peters, R.S. (1973) *Reason and Compassion*. London: Routledge & Kegan Paul.

Peters, T.J. and Austin, N. (1985) *A Passion for Excellence*. New York: Random House.

Peters, T.J. and Waterman, R.H. (1982) *In Search of Excellence: Lessons From America's Best-Run Companies*. New York: Harper & Row.

Petrovich, O. (1986) 'Moral autonomy and the theory of Kohlberg', in S. Modgil and C. Modgil (eds), *Lawrence Kohlberg: Consensus and Controversy*. Lewes: The Falmer Press. pp. 85–106.

Pettigrew, A.M. (1973) *The Politics of Organizational Decision-Making*. London: Tavistock.

Pettigrew, A.M. (1985) *The Awakening Giant: Continuity and Change in Imperial Chemical Industries*. Oxford: Blackwell.

Pfeffer, J. (1981) *Power in Organizations*. Marshfield, Mass.: Pitman.

Pfeiffer, R.S. (1990) 'The central distinction in the theory of corporate moral personhood', *Journal of Business Ethics*, 9(6): 473–80.

Pfeiffer, R.S. (1992) 'Owing loyalty to one's employer', *Journal of Business Ethics*, 11(7): 535–43.

Phillips, M.J. (1995) 'Corporate moral responsibility: when it might matter', *Business Ethics Quarterly*, 5(3): 555–76.

Piaget, J. (1932) *The Moral Judgement of the Child*. Tr. M. Gabain. London: Routledge & Kegan Paul.

Power, F.C., Higgins, A. and Kohlberg, L. (1989) *Lawrence Kohlberg's Approach to Moral Education*. New York: Columbia University Press.

Proctor, S., McArdle, L., Hassard, J. and Rowlinson, M. (1993) 'Performance related pay in practice: a critical perspective', *British Journal of Management*, 4(3): 153–60.

Raphael, D.D. (1985) *Adam Smith*. Oxford: Oxford University Press.

Raphael, D.D. (1994) *Moral Philosophy*. 2nd edn. Oxford: Oxford University Press. (1st edn, 1981).

Rasmussen, D.M. (1993) 'Business ethics and postmodernism: a response', *Business Ethics Quarterly*, 3(3): 271–7.

Raven, J. (1984) *Competence in Modern Society*. London: H.K. Lewis.

Rawls, J. (1972) *A Theory of Justice*. Oxford: Clarendon Press.

Reed, C. and McKie, R. (1996) 'Boots suppressed its own survey on cheaper drugs', *The Observer*, 28 April: 1.

Reed, M. and Anthony, P.D. (1992) 'Professionalizing management and managing professionalization: British management in the 1980s', *Journal of Management Studies*, 29(5): 591–613.

Reich, C. (1970) *The Greening of America*. New York: Random House.

Reidenbach, R.E. and Robin, D.P. (1991) 'A conceptual model of corporate moral development', *Journal of Business Ethics*, 10(4): 273–84.

Rescher, N. (1969) *Introduction to Value Theory*. Englewood Cliffs, NJ: Prentice-Hall.

Rest, J. (1986) *Moral Development: Advances in Research and Theory*. New York: Praeger.

Rhenman, E. (1968) *Industrial Democracy and Industrial Management*. London: Tavistock.

Rice, A.K. (1958) *Productivity and Social Organization: The Ahmedabad Experiment*. London: Tavistock.

Ridgway, V. (1956) 'Dysfunctional consequences of performance measurements', *Administrative Science Quarterly*, 1: 240–7.

Rodgers, P. (1996) 'The Greenbury effect – is it pushing pay higher?', *The Independent*, 26 April: 21.

Roethlisberger F. and Dixon, W.J. (1939) *Management and the Worker*. Cambridge, Mass.: Harvard University Press.

Rorty, R. (1989) *Contingency, Irony and Solidarity*. Cambridge: Cambridge University Press.

Ross, W.D. (1930) *The Right and the Good*. London: Oxford University Press.

Rossouw, G.J. (1994) 'Rational interaction for moral sensitivity: a postmodern approach to moral decision-making in business', *Journal of Business Ethics*, 13(1): 11–20.

Roszak, T. (1969) *The Making of a Counter Culture*. New York: Doubleday.

Roszak, T. (1981) *Person/Planet: The Creative Disintegration of Industrial Society*. Paladin edn. London: Granada. (1st edn, 1978).

Rothschild, J. and Miethe, T.D. (1994) 'Whistleblowing as resistance in modern organizations: the politics of revealing organizational deception and abuse', in J.M. Jermier, D. Knights and W.R. Nord (eds), *Resistance and Power in Organizations*. London: Routledge. pp. 252–73.

Rowan, J. (1976) 'Ethical issues in organizational change', in P. Warr (ed.), *Personal Goals and Work Design*. London: John Wiley. pp. 107–25.

Rowe, M.P. (1990) 'Barriers to equality: the power of subtle discrimination to maintain unequal opportunity', *Employee Responsibilities and Rights Journal*, 3(2): 153–63.

Rusbult, C. and Lowery, D. (1985) 'When bureaucrats get the blues: responses to dissatisfaction among federal employees', *Journal of Applied Social Psychology*, 15(1): 80–103.

Russell, B. (1935) *In Praise of Idleness and Other Essays*. London: Allen & Unwin.

Ryle, G. (1949) *The Concept of Mind*. London: Hutchinson.

Salancik, G.R. and Pfeffer, J. (1974) 'The bases and use of power in organizational decision making: the case of a university', *Administrative Science Quarterly*, 19: 453–73.

Sampson, A. (1995) *Company Man: The Rise and Fall of Corporate Life*. London: HarperCollins.

Scanlon, T.M. (1975) 'Rawls' theory of justice', in N. Daniels (ed.), *Reading Rawls: Critical Studies of 'A Theory of Justice'*. Oxford: Blackwell. pp. 169–205.

Scarff, W. (1996) 'Blowing the whistle on bad practice at work', *Professional Manager*, (London: The Institute of Management Foundation), 5(3): 7.

Scase, R. and Goffee, R. (1989) *Reluctant Managers: Their Work and Lifestyles*. London: Unwin Hyman.

Schein, E.H. (1966) 'The problem of moral education for the business manager', *Industrial Management Review*, 8: 3–14.

Schein, E.H. (1968) 'Organizational socialization and the profession of management', *Industrial Management Review*, 9: 1–15.

Schein, E.H. (1980) *Organizational Psychology*. 3rd edn. Englewood Cliffs, NJ: Prentice-Hall. (1st edn, 1965).

Schein, E.H. (1985) *Organizational Culture and Leadership*. San Francisco: Jossey-Bass.

Schein, E.H. (1987) *Process Consultation, Vol.II: Lessons for Managers and Consultants*. Reading, Mass.: Addison-Wesley.

Schein, E.H. (1988) *Process Consultation, Vol.I: Its Role in Organization Development*. 2nd edn. Reading, Mass.: Addison-Wesley. (1st edn, 1969).

Schwartz, A. (1982) 'Meaningful work', *Ethics*, 92(4): 634–46.

Schwenk, C.R. (1984) 'Devil's advocacy in managerial decision-making', *Journal of Management Studies*, 21(2): 153–68.

Selznick, P. (1948) 'Foundations of the theory of organizations', *American Sociological Review*, 13(1): 25–35.

Selznick, P. (1949) *TVA and the Grass Roots*, Berkeley: University of California Press.

Selznick, P. (1957) *Leadership in Administration*, Evanston, Ill.: Row, Peterson.

Shaw, J. and Perrons, D. (eds) (1995) *Making Gender Work: Managing Equal Opportunities*. Buckingham: Open University Press.

Sher, G. (1975) 'Justifying reverse discrimination in employment', *Philosophy and Public Affairs*, 4(2): 159–70.

Shotter, J. (1993) *Conversational Realities: Constructing Life through Language*. London: Sage.

Shrivastava, P., Mitroff, I.I., Miller, D. and Miglani, A. (1988) 'Understanding industrial crises', *Journal of Management Studies*, 25(4): 285–303.

Siegel, H. (1986) 'On using psychology to justify judgments of moral adequacy', in S. Modgil and C. Modgil (eds), *Lawrence Kohlberg: Consensus and Controversy*. Lewes: The Falmer Press. pp. 65–78.

Silver, M. (ed.) (1991) *Competent to Manage: Approaches to Management Training and Development*. London: Routledge.

Silverman, D. (1970) *The Theory of Organisations*. London: Heinemann.

Simon, H.A. (1957) *Administrative Behavior*. 2nd edn. New York: The Free Press. (1st edn, 1947).

Simon, R.L. (1988) 'Comparable pay for comparable work?', in T.L. Beauchamp and N.E. Bowie (eds), *Ethical Theory and Business*. 3rd edn. Englewood Cliffs, NJ: Prentice-Hall. pp. 363–74.

Sims, R.R. (1992) 'Linking groupthink to unethical behavior in organizations', *Journal of Business Ethics*, 11(9): 651–62.

Sinclair, A. (1993) 'Approaches to organizational culture and ethics', *Journal of Business Ethics*, 12(1): 63–73.

Singer, P. (1993) *Practical Ethics*. 2nd edn. Cambridge: Cambridge University Press. (1st edn, 1979).

Smircich, L. (1983) 'Concepts of culture and organizational analysis', *Administrative Science Quarterly*, 28: 339–58.

Smith, A. (1904) *An Inquiry into the Nature and Causes of the Wealth of Nations*, ed. E. Cannan. London: Methuen. (1st edn, 1776).

Smith, A. (1976) *The Theory of Moral Sentiments*, ed. D.D. Raphael and A.L. Macfie. Oxford: Clarendon Press. (1st edn, 1759).

Smith, N.C. (1990) *Morality and the Market*. London: Routledge.

Snell, R.S. (1993) *Developing Skills for Ethical Management*. London: Chapman & Hall.

Snell, R.S. and Maclagan, P.W. (1992) 'Towards a diagnostic instrument to facilitate managers' moral development', in Conference Proceedings, *Business Ethics – Contributing to Business Success*. Sheffield Business School, April 23–4.

Soler, C. (1990) 'Management as the symbolization of ethical values', in G. Enderle, B. Almond and A. Argandoña (eds), *People in Corporations: Ethical Responsibilities and Corporate Effectiveness*. Dordrecht: Kluwer. pp. 197–205.

Solomon, R.C. (1993a) *The Passions*. 2nd edn. Indianapolis, Ind.: Hackett. (1st edn, 1976. Doubleday).

Solomon, R.C. (1993b) 'Business ethics', in P. Singer (ed.), *A Companion to Ethics*. Oxford: Blackwell. pp. 354–65.

Sparkes, R. (1995) *The Ethical Investor*. London: HarperCollins.

Sridhar, B.S. and Camburn, A. (1993) 'Stages of moral development of corporations', *Journal of Business Ethics*, 12(9): 727–39.

Srivastva, S. and Cooperrider, D.L. (1986) 'The emergence of the egalitarian organization', *Human Relations*, 39(8): 683–724.

Staw, B.M. (1980) 'Rationality and justification in organizational life', in B.M. Staw and L.L. Cummings (eds), *Research in Organizational Behavior*, Vol.2. Greenwich, Conn.: JAI Press. pp. 45–80.

Steinbeck, J. (1951) *The Grapes of Wrath*. Harmondsworth: Penguin Books. (1st edn, 1939. Heinemann).

Stewart, R. (1967) *Managers and their Jobs*. London: Macmillan.

Stewart, R. (1991) *Managing Today and Tomorrow*. Basingstoke: Macmillan.

Stock, F. (1995) 'We can't bank on trust alone', *The Independent*, 1 March: 19.

Sutton, B. (1993) 'Introduction: the legitimate corporation', in B. Sutton (ed.), *The Legitimate Corporation*. Oxford: Blackwell. pp. 1–13.

Sutton, B. (ed.) (1993) *The Legitimate Corporation*. Oxford: Blackwell.

Swanson, D. (1992) 'A critical evaluation of Etzioni's economic theory: implications for the field of business ethics', *Journal of Business Ethics*, 11(7): 545–53.

Széll, G. (ed.) (1992) *Concise Encyclopaedia of Participation and Co-Management*. Berlin: De Gruyter.

Tannenbaum, R. and Davis, S. (1983) 'Values, man and organization', in W. French, C.H. Bell and R. Zawacki (eds), *Organization Development: Theory, Practice and Research*. 2nd edn. Plano: Texas: Business Publications. pp. 47–59. (Article first published 1969, in *Industrial Management Review*, 10[2]).

Tannenbaum, R. and Schmidt, W. (1973) 'How to choose a leadership pattern', *Harvard Business Review*, 51 (May–June): 162–80.

Tawney, R.H. (1938) *Religion and the Rise of Capitalism*. Pelican edn. Harmondsworth: Penguin Books. (1st edn, 1926. John Murray).

Tawney, R.H. (1961) *The Acquisitive Society*. Fontana edn. Glasgow: Collins. (1st edn, 1921. G. Bell & Sons).

Taylor, F.W. (1911) *The Principles of Scientific Management*. New York: Harper.

Thomas, A.B. (1993) *Controversies in Management*. London: Routledge.

Thompson, M. (1993) *Pay and Performance: The Employee Experience*. Brighton: University of Sussex, Institute of Manpower Studies.

Toffler, B.L. (1986) *Tough Choices: Managers Talk Ethics*. New York: John Wiley.

Toft, B. and Reynolds, S. (1994) *Learning from Disasters*. Oxford: Butterworth-Heinemann.

Torbert, W.R. (1987) *Managing the Corporate Dream: Restructuring for Long-Term Success*. Homewood, Ill.: Dow Jones–Irwin.

Treviño, L.K. (1986) 'Ethical decision making in organizations: a person-situation interactionist model', *Academy of Management Review*, 11(3): 601–17.

Treviño, L.K. and McCabe, D. (1994) 'Meta-learning about business ethics: building honorable business school communities', *Journal of Business Ethics*, 13(6): 405–16.

Treviño, L.K. and Nelson, K. (1995) *Managing Business Ethics*. New York: John Wiley.

Trist, E.L. (1983) 'Referent organizations and the development of inter-organizational domains', *Human Relations*, 36(3): 269–84.

Trist, E.L. and Bamforth, K.W. (1951) 'Some social and psychological consequences of the longwall method of coal-getting', *Human Relations*, 4(1): 3–38.

Trist, E.L., Higgin, G.W., Murray, H. and Pollock, A.B. (1963) *Organizational Choice*. London: Tavistock.

Trusted, J. (1987) *Moral Principles and Social Values*. London: Routledge & Kegan Paul.

Turner, B.A. (1994) 'Causes of disaster: sloppy management', *British Journal of Management*, 5(3): 215–19.

Vallance, E. (1995) *Business Ethics at Work*. Cambridge: Cambridge University Press.

Vandivier, K. (1972) 'Why should my conscience bother me?', in R.L. Heilbroner (ed.), *In the Name of Profit*, New York, Doubleday pp. 3–31.

Vanek, J. (ed.) (1975) *Self-Management: Economic Liberation of Man*. Harmondsworth: Penguin Books.

Velasquez, M. (1983) 'Why corporations are not morally responsible for anything they do', *Business and Professional Ethics Journal*, 2(3): 1–17.

Vickers, Sir Geoffrey (1968) *Value Systems and Social Processes*. London: Tavistock.

Vickers, Sir Geoffrey (1970) *Freedom in a Rocking Boat: Changing Values in an Unstable Society*. London: Allen Lane.

Vickers, Sir Geoffrey (1980) *Responsibility: Its Sources and Limits*. Seaside, Calif.: Intersystems Publications.

Victor, B. and Cullen, J.B. (1988) 'The organizational bases of ethical work climates', *Administrative Science Quarterly*, 33: 101–25.

Vitell, S.J., Nwachukwu, S.L. and Barnes, J.H. (1993) 'The effects of culture on ethical decision-making: an application of Hofstede's typology', *Journal of Business Ethics*, 12(10): 753–60.

Vogel, D. (1978) *Lobbying the Corporation: Citizen Challenges to Business Authority*. New York: Basic Books.

Vroom, V. (1964) *Work and Motivation*. New York: John Wiley.

Vroom, V. and Yetton, P.W. (1973) *Leadership and Decision-Making*. Pittsburgh, Pa.: University of Pittsburgh Press.

Wallach, M.A., Kogan, N. and Bem, D. (1962) 'Group influence on individual risk-taking', *Journal of Abnormal and Social Psychology*, 65: 75–86.

Wallach, M.A., Kogan, N. and Bem, D. (1964) 'Diffusion of responsibility and level of risk-taking in groups', *Journal of Abnormal and Social Psychology*, 68: 263–74.

Walton, C.C. (1988) *The Moral Manager*. New York: Harper & Row.

Warren, R. (1993) 'Codes of ethics: bricks without straw', *Business Ethics: A European Review*, 2(4): 185–91.

Warren, R. (1996) 'Business as a community of purpose', *Business Ethics: A European Review*, 5(2): 87–96.

Waters, J. and Bird, F. (1987) 'The moral dimension of organizational culture', *Journal of Business Ethics*, 6(1): 15–22.

Waters, J., Bird, F. and Chant, P.D. (1986) 'Everyday moral issues experienced by managers', *Journal of Business Ethics*, 5(5): 373–84.

Watson, T.J. (1994) *In Search of Management: Culture, Chaos and Control in Managerial Work*. London: Routledge.

Waxman, M. (1990) 'Institutionalized strategies for dealing with sexual harassment', *Employee Responsibilities and Rights Journal*, 3(1): 73–5.

Weaver, G.R. (1995) 'Does ethics code design matter? Effects of ethics code rationales and sanctions on recipients' justice perceptions and content recall', *Journal of Business Ethics*, 14(5): 367–85.

Weber, J. (1991) 'Applying Kohlberg to enhance the assessment of managers' moral reasoning', *Business Ethics Quarterly*, 1(3): 293–318.

Weber, J. (1993) 'Institutionalizing ethics into business organizations: a model and research agenda', *Business Ethics Quarterly*, 3(4): 419–36.

Weber, M. (1930) *The Protestant Ethic and the Spirit of Capitalism*. Tr. T. Parsons. London: Unwin. (First published 1904–5, in *Archiv für Sozialwissenschaft und Sozialpolitik*, Vols xx and xxi).

Weber, M. (1947) *The Theory of Social and Economic Organization*. Tr. A.R. Henderson and T. Parsons. New York: Oxford University Press. (1st edn, 1921).

Webley, S. (1992) *Business Ethics and Company Codes*. London: Institute of Business Ethics.

Webley, S. (1996) 'The Interfaith Declaration. Constructing a code of ethics for international business', *Business Ethics: A European Review*, 5(1): 52–7.

Weick, K.E. (1969) *The Social Psychology of Organizing*. Reading, Mass.: Addison-Wesley.

Weinreich-Haste, H. (1986) 'Kohlberg's contribution to political psychology: a positive view', in S. Modgil and C. Modgil (eds), *Lawrence Kohlberg: Consensus and Controversy*. Lewes: The Falmer Press. pp. 337–61.

Werhane, P. (1985) *Persons, Rights and Corporations*. Englewood Cliffs, NJ: Prentice-Hall.

Werhane, P. (1989) 'Corporate and individual moral responsibility: a reply to Jan Garrett', *Journal of Business Ethics*, 8(10): 821–2.

Westen, P. (1985) 'The concept of equal opportunity', *Ethics*, 95(4): 837–50.

Whitely, W. (1981) 'Sources of influence on managers' value dimension structure, value dimension integrity, and decisions', in G. Dlugos and K. Weiermair (eds), *Management under Differing Value Systems: Political, Social and Economical Perspectives in a Changing World*. Berlin: De Gruyter. pp. 481–535.

Whyte, W.H. (1956) *The Organization Man*. New York: Simon & Schuster.

Williams, B. (1962) 'The idea of equality', in P. Laslett and W.G. Runciman (eds), *Philosophy, Politics and Society* (Second Series). Oxford: Blackwell. pp. 110–31.

Winfield, M. (1990) *Minding Your Own Business: Self-Regulation and Whistleblowing in British Companies*. London: Social Audit.

Woodward, J. (1965) *Industrial Organization: Theory and Practice*. Oxford: Oxford University Press.

Woolf, M. (1995) 'Loaded and lethal', *The Observer*, 22 October: 19.

Zabid, A.R.M. and Alsagoff, S.K. (1993) 'Perceived ethical values of Malaysian managers', *Journal of Business Ethics*, 12(4): 331–7.

Index